Practical Steps to the Research Process for Middle School

Information Literacy Series

The Thoughtful Researcher: Teaching the Research Process to Middle School Students. By Virginia Rankin

Practical Steps to the Research Process for High School. By Deborah B. Stanley

Practical Steps to the Research Process for Middle School. By Deborah B. Stanley

Fostering Information Literacy: Connecting National Standards, Goals 2000, and the SCANS Report. By Helen M. Thompson and Susan A. Henley

Turning Kids on to Research: The Power of Motivation. By Ruth V. Small and Marilyn P. Arnone

Pathways to Knowledge™ and Inquiry Learning. By Marjorie L. Pappas and Ann E. Tepe

Practical Steps to the Research Process for Middle School

Deborah B. Stanley

2000
Libraries Unlimited
A Division of Greenwood Publishing Group, Inc.
Greenwood Village, Colorado

"If you embrace change, you can control it!
If you only respond to change, you have lost your voice."
Theresa Saunders, Ed.D.,
Hoover High School, Glendale, CA, 1997–1998.

Libraries Unlimited
A Division of Greenwood Publishing Group, Inc.
7730 East Belleview Ave., Suite A200
Greenwood Village, CO 80111
1-800-237-6124
www.lu.com

Library of Congress Cataloging-in-Publication Data

Stanley, Deborah B.
Practical steps to the research process for middle school / Deborah B. Stanley.
p. cm. -- (Information literacy series)
Includes bibliographical references (p.) and index.
ISBN 1-56308-763-4
1. Library orientation for middle school students--United States. I. Title. II. Series

Z711.2 .S73 2000
027.62'6--dc21

00-059353

Contents

Figures

Acknowledgments

A special thanks to my husband for his continued support and encouragement during my long hours of computer work.

Many thanks to the collaborating teachers at Gaspar de Portola Middle School in San Diego, California, from 1996 to 1997, and especially to my incredible library technician, Mrs. Carol Tocco, for making library teaching possible. Many thanks also to the teachers at Central Middle School in Riverside, California, beginning in 1998, for making the Research Process come alive!

Special credit goes to Norma Dick and Barbara Jeffus, Fresno Pacific College, from 1990 to 1994, for their incredible insight and training in collaborative instruction. They taught me how to creatively embrace change and manage information.

I owe a particular debt of gratitude to C. A. Nash, instructor in Los Angeles City College District, who updated my knowledge of citations following my staff development presentation for the Los Angeles Unified Library Media Teachers in February 2000. I dedicate those important changes in this manuscript to her timely words of wisdom. I, myself, am a work in progress.

Introduction

A Perspective

The makers of electronic games seem to understand what curriculum creators often miss. Kids are attracted to games not because they are easy, but because they are fun! Likewise, kids are turned off to school not because it's hard, but because it's boring.[1]

This book is about information management; specifically, it is a practical guide for teaching research. Let's face it, research is boring to many students, especially when compared to the engaging ease of electronic plagiarism. But is it the job of educators to make the curriculum fun, as much as it is their responsibility to make it interesting? Although "fun" has its place in any venue, "interesting" can include making educational tasks relevant and meaningful. This is important to secondary students who come to feel, like adults, that they don't want to perform tasks they perceive to be a waste of their time.

It is definitely not the job of educators to make the curriculum "easy" to appease boredom, but it is their responsibility to make tasks "doable" and yet challenging. This is accomplished by assessing and addressing a student's (dis)abilities and making educational tasks one step more difficult to promote growth. The goal for every student is success in learning, which is self-defeated by instruction and curriculum that a student may perceive to be frustratingly unclear, even impossible.

The Research Process advocates strategies that make information management both interesting and doable. How can this be accomplished? If good students as well as learning-challenged students are resorting to plagiarism, maybe it's not just because research is boring. Maybe it's because it isn't being clearly taught. This book is about both classroom teachers and library media teachers addressing the very real issue of actually teaching students practical steps for making research interesting and doable. Let's see how this seeming impossibility can happen.

A Unique Approach

This guide to the Research Process is a unique, four-day diary of scripted research lessons. It is based on a generic concept of research and addresses the ever-increasing need for methods to manage information in a practical way. As a working library media teacher, I have had the opportunity to teach research strategies at all grade levels: elementary, middle school, and high school. This book is the result of successful adaptations of the Research Process at all grade levels, and it presupposes the following:

- Past and present research theories are the "what." This guide is the "how" (*Figure I-1*). It goes beyond *what* research is to *how* to actually teach it. In simple, practical ways, this book gives back to library media teachers the concepts of research found in their original training classes, and it equips classroom teachers with strategies to integrate information literacy standards.

- The lessons and strategies are all based on authentic teaching experiences. Nothing is hypothetical or simply trial tested; all the units are the result of ongoing interactions with teachers and students. Therefore, this is a "working" document. I constantly find more interesting or effective ways to present this material and therefore assume the reader will apply these lessons creatively. The purpose is empowerment, not insistence on doing things one way.
- The underlying assumption of all lessons and strategies presented is collaboration. As I often tell my classes when I begin a unit, "I will probably learn as much from you and your teacher as you will learn from these lessons." Because you already own it, you are strongly encouraged to use, adapt, or completely reinvent this material. I do not claim sole ownership of any of these lesson strategies because everything was done in collaboration. We are all here to help each other, with the ultimate goal being student success in managing information and in becoming a productive citizen in the global community. The goal is information literacy!

Guide Book Clarification

Literacy

Content

There are four general sections to this book. Only Section 2 is the actual Research Process.

Technology Proficiency

- Section 1: Planning and Preparation
- Section 2: The Research Process
- Section 3: Application and Accountability
- Section 4: Enrichment and Extension

Information Literacy

Section 2 (chapters 4 through 9) contains the scripted student lessons adapted to fit into three or four days of instruction at the middle-school level. An important feature is that direct instruction to clarify research steps and strategies is alternated with hands-on activities, as best fits the needs of any particular group of students. Section 3 presents directions and examples of hands-on activities and accountability which, in fact, apply to all previous research steps. Chapters 10 and 11 are set aside to emphasize their overall application.

Content-Area Standard

As it states, Section 4 goes beyond necessary skills to stretch the creativity of both students and teachers. This section is very time dependent.

Design

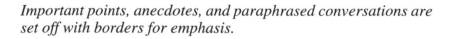

ELL/Special Modifications

Important points, anecdotes, and paraphrased conversations are set off with borders for emphasis.

The sidebar icons represent some of the major trends in educational reform. The point of this book is to demonstrate that the Research Process, when meaningfully integrated into the general school curriculum, can be a "magic bullet" for addressing and applying these educational trends. The icons appear throughout the book to support and demonstrate this powerful claim.

Lifelong Skills

Education can greatly benefit from instruction in the Research Process. Therefore, schools need great library media teachers at all levels who function as both instructional partners (peers) and educational innovators (leaders) in the push toward information literacy. Whether you agree with this diary of strategies or not, try it, adapt it, and at least come away saying, "I know a much better way to do this." Then do it!

Problem Solving

Notes

1. Paraphrased from a special advertising section by Seymour Papert, "The Face of Innovation, Capturing a Revolution in Progress," *Smithsonian* 29, no. 8 (November 1998).

Fig. I-1. Managing a World of Information

What General Research Is	How the Research Process Works
Topic Selection (Thesis Statement)	How do I choose a topic? How do I focus with subtopics?
Evaluate/Select/Cite (Primary vs. Secondary Print and Nonprint)	How do I manage so many kinds of sources? How do I correctly cite sources?
Locate Information in Sources	How do I read for comprehension?
Notetake/Cite Sources in Notes	How do I take notes? How do I give credit for information?
Outline Information	How do I organize my notes?
Rough Draft and Final Draft	How do I use my notes to write?
Final Citations List	How do I organize my citations?
Enrichment, Publishing, Presenting	How do I integrate technology to enrich, publish, or present my project?
Points/Grade Rubric/Authentic Assessment	How can research be tracked and evaluated effectively?

Section 1

Planning and Preparation

Chapter 1
What Is the Research Process?

Chapter 2
Collaborative Planning

Chapter 3
Lesson Preparations

Chapter 1

What Is the Research Process?

"This is working wonders for these kids. We need to tell all the teachers about this."

—Teacher aide

Fig. 1-1. Research Process

Topic *A good topic is "doable," but slightly challenging to your assessed abilities.*

A. Locate a topic in textbooks, library sources, or the teacher's topic list.
B. Check in the library media center for at least three formats of supporting information.
C. Cross-check in an encyclopedia to narrow or broaden a topic.

Subtopics *Ask yourself: What do I want to know about my topic?*

A. General subtopics may be brainstormed. Examples:
   Person: early life, education, work (be specific), later life.
   Place: origin, history, leaders, geography, economy.
   Thing: who, what, when, where, why/how.
B. Specific subtopics must be located in, for example, an encyclopedia's subheads.
C. The number of subtopics is based on the number of days of research.

Sources *A good source is any kind of supporting information that you can read.*

A. Format (the form information comes in) Examples include:
   Print: books, encyclopedias, magazines, newspapers.
   Nonprint: videos, laser disks, CD-ROMs, computer software, Internet.
B. Use at least three formats of information. Using one source is not research!
C. Credit sources using MLA-style citations.

Read/Think/Select *Good research promotes comprehension and evaluation.*

A. Read an entire "chunk" (a paragraph or a page) with your pencil down.
B. Think about what was read. What was important?
C. Select only a few key facts from each "chunk" to match your subtopics.

Notetake *A good note creates information ownership. This is learning!*

A. One note per card, titled with subtopic. Use as many cards as needed.
B. Record important keywords, facts, or a list, up to about 20 words (use your judgment).
C. No small words like *a*, *the*, *an*, *is*, *was*. Instead use commas and dashes.
D. No copying of sentences (without quotation marks and footnotes).

Sort and Number Notes *Good organization of notes makes writing easier.*

A. Sort notes by subtopic section, about five notes per paragraph (use your judgment).
B. Read notes in one section at a time and put in an order that makes sense.
C. Number notes consecutively through all sections without starting over at number 1.

Extension

Write/Publish/Present
Final citations list
Technology integration

Evaluation Student tracking

Another Theory?

There are many popular theories and methods of information management. It is important that the Research Process (*Figure 1-1*) is not offered as a broad generalization but is a specific process that embodies practical steps exclusively for student research by identifying strategies taught at each step. The purpose of the Research Process is:

Information Literacy

To reflect generic concepts of information management intuitively understood by teachers and students and interpret them into easily understandable, specific strategies.

To endorse current popular theories of research because they are also based on generic concepts of accessing, evaluating, and using information, known as information management.

To empower teachers and library media teachers with something they already know but perhaps have been hard pressed to apply for lack of simple, effective strategies.

Content-Area Standard

To distill the complex into something simple: Namely, to contextualize strategies for literacy (*Figure 1-2*) and technology (*Figure 1-3*) into content-area, standards-based units of study through collaborative lessons. These strategies for student-centered, inquiry-structured research are presented to students at simple and appropriate learning levels, engaging them in meaningful and challenging information management experiences. Less is more!

Lifelong Skills

To teach students to think! Each step of the Research Process involves specific strategies to manage information. Learning to navigate the ocean of information *is* information literacy. The more students perform the strategies, the more adept they become at logical thinking patterns that can be applied in later situations. This is lifelong learning.

Managing information is more than hardware or software instructions. It's like hitting a home run. It requires the learning and practicing of logical strategies to make something easy to do.

Fig. 1-2. Integrating Literacy

LMT/Teacher	Student
The collaborative planning of content-area units of study between the LMT and classroom teacher successfully incorporates all aspects of literacy: • Reading • Writing • Listening • Speaking	Readability of sources of information is essential so "basic concepts" are accessible for learning to take place. Levels to consider: • Primary language • Grade • Age • Interest • Special needs and/or (dis)abilities
Lesson 1: Part 1: Topic Part 2: Subtopics	Reads to determine if there is enough accessible, available information to select and support topic and subtopics.
Lesson 2: Sources	Reads in a variety of print and nonprint formats including: • Books • References • Magazines • Newspapers • Pamphlets • Maps • Charts, graphs • Computer software • Internet • Internet search tools • CD-ROMs • Videos
Lesson 3: Part 1: Read/Think/Select	Reads from the sources to access information. (Validates reading.) Reads for comprehension using special reading-for-research strategies. Reads to evaluate and relate information to topic and subtopics.
Part 2: Notetake	Reads to select and record notes: keywords, quotations, paraphrase, summarize.
Lesson 4: Sort/Number notes	Reads notes to sort, sequence, and number them.
Extension/Lesson 5: Write from notes Finalize citations Technology integration	Reads sequenced notes to write a rough draft. (Validates writing skills.) Reads the rough draft to revise, edit, and write a final draft. Reads the final draft for oral presentation. (Validates listening skills.) Reads entries to write the final citations for all sources.
Evaluation	

Fig. 1-3. Integrating Technology

Research Process Lessons	LMT/Teacher	Student
Technology is used to access, evaluate, and use information for the teaching and learning of each of the six research steps.	Instructional/Mentor Level: • Technology proficiency	Personal Level: • Technology proficiency
Lesson 1: Part 1: Topic Part 2: Subtopics	Creates interesting student handouts using: • Word processing • Desktop publishing • Graphics/Charts	Pre-searches topic/ subtopics using: • Internet • CD-ROMs • Computer software
Lesson 2: Sources	• Creates hardware and software pathfinders. • Creates signage. • Gives orientations: Internet CD-ROMs Computer software	Accesses/locates information: • Internet • Internet-based search tools • CD-ROMs • Computer software
Lesson 3: Part 1: Read/Think/Select		• Evaluates printouts from any of the above to process info.: read, comprehend, evaluate, select.
Part 2: Notetake		• Records keywords, facts, quotes.
Lesson 4: Sort/Number notes		• Uses notepad function of electronic encyclopedias.
Extension/Lesson 5: • Write from notes • Final citations • Technology integration	• Tracking sheets • Evaluation reports • Electronic portfolios • Lesson database • Distance learning • Technology fair • LMC/school web site	• Word processing • Desktop publishing • Multimedia presentations • Web site construction • Color scanner • Digital camera • Video camera
Evaluation		

Fig. 1-4. Approaches to Information Management

<table>
<tr><th>Bloom's Taxonomy</th><th>BIG 6™
Eisenberg/Berkowitz</th><th>5 A's ©
Ian Jukes</th><th>Research Process</th></tr>
<tr><td rowspan="4">Knowledge
↓</td><td rowspan="2">Task Definition
↓</td><td rowspan="2">Asking
↓</td><td>Topic</td></tr>
<tr><td>Subtopics</td></tr>
<tr><td>Information Seeking Strategies</td><td rowspan="2">Accessing
↓</td><td rowspan="2">Sources
↓</td></tr>
<tr><td>Location & Access</td></tr>
<tr><td>Comprehension</td><td rowspan="4">Use of Information
↓</td><td>Analyzing
↓</td><td>Read, Think, Select</td></tr>
<tr><td>Application</td><td rowspan="4">Applying
↓</td><td rowspan="2">Notetake</td></tr>
<tr><td rowspan="2">Analysis</td></tr>
<tr><td rowspan="3">Sort & Number Notes</td></tr>
<tr><td>Synthesis</td><td>Synthesize</td></tr>
<tr><td>Evaluation</td><td>Evaluate</td><td>Assessing</td></tr>
</table>

Do You See the Connections?

Were you lucky enough to have had a teacher back in elementary or middle school who actually taught students that research had steps? Did your teachers understand research enough themselves to explain how to locate information in a source, how to record facts on a million little note cards, and how to write real source citations? Even more important, did they not only teach those steps but also allow instructional time for students to perform them? Even if you didn't have a person like this in your past, you can still become that person.

Important Idea

Thank you, Mrs. Thornton, my sixth-grade social studies teacher. From middle school to high school, from college to graduate school, no one else ever actually taught me research! I could not have been the student I was then, or the teacher I am now, without you!

When you went through education training classes, or perhaps the certification for library media teacher/specialist, did an instructor have you develop a unit of study? In that unit, were you required to develop research strategies (information literacy) integrated into a content area, resulting in a meaningful student product that included technology integration? If so, you must have developed or included your own version of what you see in this book.

Technology Proficiency

My training began at a time when current theories reflected in *Figure 1-4* were not yet well known. We wrote our first practice units using intuitive concepts of research. In other words, we figured it out! Bloom's Taxonomy enjoyed great popularity in the 1980s as a wave of critical thinking instruction swept our educational environment. It figured strongly in classroom teaching at the time but was not directly tied into research training. It took Eisenberg and Berkowitz to fully utilize Bloom's work in their BIG 6™ approach to information management, and it was later reintroduced by Ian Jukes in the mid-1990s in his "5 A's" guide to research.

With certificate in hand, when confronted with the reality of managing a classroom or a school's busy library media center, did the demands of the job overshadow the inclination for you to apply research theories? Now, the power of information literacy puts us all back in the hot seat to revive those graduate school research unit strategies and use them, perhaps in new and different ways.

Information Literacy

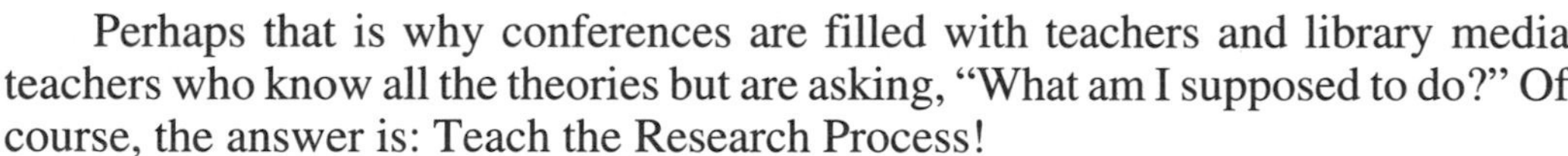

Perhaps that is why conferences are filled with teachers and library media teachers who know all the theories but are asking, "What am I supposed to do?" Of course, the answer is: Teach the Research Process!

How Do You Eat an Elephant?

This is the bottom line: If you're a library media teacher, do you teach? If not, what are the overwhelming issues (the "elephants") that are preventing collaborative planning and teaching from occurring?

Time

Juggling our many jobs is the daily plight of the library media teacher. We are pulled in so many different directions. For those of you who are alone in the library media center, without the support services of a clerk or technician, booking most of the periods of your day for direct instruction is out of the question. There is simply no way you can schedule collaborative planning and teaching time and still perform all the other routine management activities of a busy facility. Time is your overwhelming "elephant," and there's nothing that will give you more hours in your day. Teaching the Research Process to students will remain on your "Get Real" list until funding, or people, support you. Or, just maybe, there is something else that might assist you: a practical method of information management.

Money

Some library media teachers are running a facility that has not yet been automated for circulation, much less been wired for Internet or CD-ROM tower networking. For many others who have small budgets but large numbers of students who are "literacy challenged," updating your collection to meet curriculum standards precludes the purchase of expensive electronic sources. For you, the variety of information formats in the "Sources" step of the Research Process will remain on your wish list. Money for current resources, either print or electronic, is your "elephant." You may be trapped into time-consuming fund raising through grant writing, pleading for school improvement funds, appealing to the parent club, organizing library activities, etc. Who has time to teach?

Training

Technology Proficiency

Library media teachers (LMTs) just entering the field, and even those who have been around for a while, find they are expected to be media experts. But it takes years to learn the many hardware and software technologies, much less the Internet, that we must pull together to model for our colleagues. For many LMTs, technology training is the "elephant."

Library media teachers are expected to be jacks-of-all-trades, but often we are the masters of none. The reality—the good news—is that we don't have to master everything. We just need to have a wide variety of basic, transferable technology skills, as we saw in *Figure 1-3*.

"I'm going to get you started on this program (or piece of equipment), and then I want to see how quickly you can begin to teach me things about it." —LMT to students.

You

There are many LMTs who seem to have it all—full-time paid support personnel, a budget for books, funds for technology hardware and software, technology prowess that enables them to design web sites, a supportive administrator, great rapport with fellow faculty members, and enthusiasm for the job—yet collaborative teaching just isn't happening. Maybe the science teacher says, "I just need two days in the library media center for my classes to find resources for our project on ecosystems," or the language arts teacher asks, "My students know what they need, can we come for a few days to locate some biography materials?" You're so busy juggling other tasks that collaborative teaching has to wait until "next time."

For you, the "elephant" is . . . you. The school thinks you're wonderful, and you are! But the puzzle pieces are still floating in the air. You haven't found that simple system that lets the pieces fall, magically assembled, onto the board. With your own "spin," the Research Process presented here can be the library media or classroom teacher's solution to information management: breaking research down into digestible, doable bites.

How do you eat an elephant? One bite at a time.

Fig. 1-5. Sample Research Project Syllabus

Science Project Report

You have all semester to complete a science project. However, the research portion for the "Background Information" segment of the project board is due in the next two weeks.

The topic of the paper will be the same as the focus of your science project. You are expected to use at least five sources of information, and write at least a five-page paper.

Here is a list of the criteria and points for this research paper:

Research notes	15 points
Title page	5 points
Five-page typed paper	50 points
Visual image or chart	15 points
Citations	15 points

These criteria are very clear, but if you have any questions or need help, see me during my conference period or schedule an appointment before or after school.

The Missing Link

Content-Area Standard

When a content-area teacher assigns a research project, the focus is necessarily on that teacher's own curriculum. How many times have you heard a teacher say:

> *"Class, your big grade for the semester is the Science Fair project. Here is a detailed project guide* (Figure 1-5). *Pay attention to the number of points possible for each section. Are there any questions? This should be pretty clear. We have a few days of library time scheduled. I'm here to help, but this paper is due in two weeks."*

Quite unintentionally, and because they're not trained as library media teachers, teachers may confuse the parts of a research paper or project for the strategies needed to accomplish those parts (*Figure 1-5*). They carefully explain to students what is expected for the title page, the body of the report, the source citations, the illustrations, and the footnotes, but do not give instructions for choosing an appropriate topic, locating appropriate sources, reading the sources critically, selecting and recording genuine notes, and writing a report or creating a presentation from those notes. How to do each of these research steps is entirely left out, as illustrated in *Figure 1-6*. Do we really wonder why kids copy?

Fig. 1-6. Process vs. Product

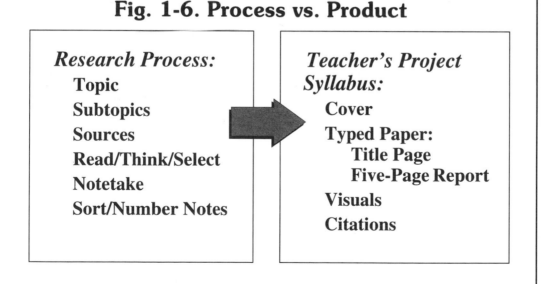

Research Process:

Topic
Subtopics
Sources
Read/Think/Select
Notetake
Sort/Number Notes

Teacher's Project Syllabus:

Cover
Typed Paper:
Title Page
Five-Page Report
Visuals
Citations

I believe the same "missing link" exists for students as it does for teachers. Without instruction, students cannot go off and magically perform genuine research on their own. They simply do not know what they have not been taught. This brings us back to the question: What is research for students?

Information Literacy

What It Is

The Research Process is a series of logical strategies to manage information: accessing, evaluating, and using.

What It Is Not

Logical does not mean self-taught. Each step of the Research Process makes perfect sense, once someone is shown how to do it!

The Total Package

Important Idea

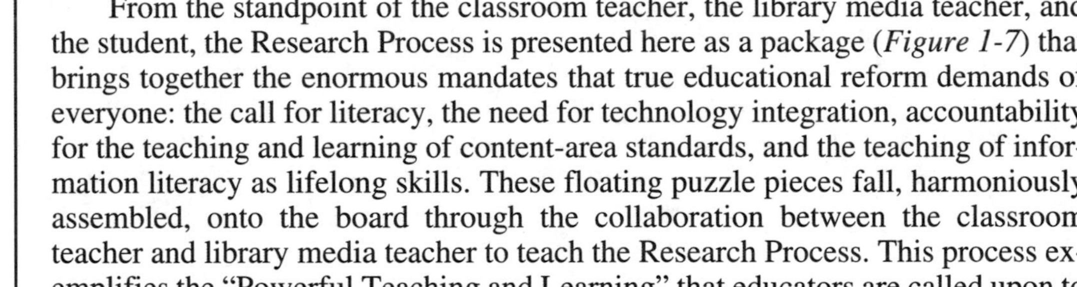

From the standpoint of the classroom teacher, the library media teacher, and the student, the Research Process is presented here as a package (*Figure 1-7*) that brings together the enormous mandates that true educational reform demands of everyone: the call for literacy, the need for technology integration, accountability for the teaching and learning of content-area standards, and the teaching of information literacy as lifelong skills. These floating puzzle pieces fall, harmoniously assembled, onto the board through the collaboration between the classroom teacher and library media teacher to teach the Research Process. This process exemplifies the "Powerful Teaching and Learning" that educators are called upon to model: hands-on, student-centered, discovery-based, and meaningful.

Fig. 1-7. Powerful Teaching and Learning

- Content-Area Standard
- ELL/Special Modifications
- Information Literacy
- Technology Proficiency
- Literacy
- Problem Solving
- Lifelong Skill

Lesson 1 **Topic** **Subtopics**	The source of appropriate topics is content-area standard units of study. Choice of topic and numbers of subtopics are modifications for all special students including gifted, resources specialist, special education, and English language learners (ELL).
Lesson 2 **Sources**	Accessing, evaluating, and crediting a variety of print and electronic sources is a key element of information literacy and reinforces student technology proficiencics.
Lesson 3 **Read/Think/Select** **Notetake**	Reading for comprehension is literacy. Thinking about facts for notetaking by evaluating information is problem solving.
Lesson 4 **Sort/Number Notes**	Sorting good from bad notes, then prioritizing and numbering notes for writing, is problem solving.
Extension/Lesson 5 **Write** **Final Citations** **Technology Integration**	Any time students learns any of the Research Process techniques to access, evaluate, and use information, they are learning lifelong skills for information management.
Evaluation	Tracking is authentic assessment.

Chapter 2

Collaborative Planning

"I don't have a lot of time to plan."

—Social science teacher

"That's okay. I'll catch you at lunch."

—LMT

Fig. 2-1. Teacher's Planning Calendar

(Subject)			
September 1 2 5 6 7 8 9 12 13 14 15 16 19 20 21 22 23 26 27 28 29 30	**Unit:** **Project:** **Technology:**	**February** 1 2 3 4 7 8 9 10 11 14 16 17 18 19 22 23 24 25 26 29	**Unit:** **Project:** **Technology:**
October 3 4 5 6 7 10 11 12 13 14 17 18 19 20 21 24 25 26 27 28 31	**Unit:** **Project:** **Technology:**	**March** 1 2 3 4 7 8 9 10 11 14 15 16 17 18 21 22 23 24 25 28 29 30 31	**Unit:** **Project:** **Technology:**
November 1 2 3 4 7 8 9 10 11 14 15 16 17 18 21 22 23 24 25 28 29 30	**Unit:** **Project:** **Technology:**	**April** 1 4 5 6 7 8 11 12 13 14 15 18 19 20 21 22 25 26 27 28 29	**Unit:** **Project:** **Technology:**
December 1 2 5 6 7 8 9 12 13 14 15 16 19 20 21 22 23 26 27 28 29 30	**Unit:** **Project:** **Technology:**	**May** 2 3 4 5 6 9 10 11 12 13 16 17 18 19 20 23 24 25 26 27 30 31	**Unit:** **Project:** **Technology:**
January 3 4 5 6 7 10 11 12 13 14 17 18 19 20 21 23 24 26 27 28 31	**Unit:** **Project:** **Technology:**	**June** 1 2 3 6 7 8 9 10 13 14 15 16 17	**Unit:** **Project:** **Technology:**

Making Time for Collaborative Planning

Undoubtedly, the first step in the Research Process is planning, but how many of you have found that this first hurdle is indeed a high one? Have you heard colleagues say any of the following:

"I don't have time to cover my own curriculum. Planning a unit with the library media teacher is one more layer I can't fit in."

"Can't I use the library the way I would like? Why do I have to plan with the library media teacher?"

"I'm just not the planning kind of person. I need spontaneity!"

"I just need library time. My students already know what they need to look for."

Sound familiar? You are not alone. For the LMT, an important first step toward initiating meaningful planning with teacher colleagues is to become accessible, eliminating barriers. How do you present yourself and your desire to teach information literacy lessons to teachers who may be resistant to change, or who simply say, "I don't have time"? *Figure 2-1* introduces planning from a yearlong perspective to address the need for making time for good research training.

The Microwave Oven Syndrome

Offer teachers something they don't know they can't live without!

Important Idea

- Call yourself a library media teacher instead of a librarian, so fellow teachers get the clear message that you are a certified faculty member. Call the library media center your "classroom."

Information Literacy

- Create a handout of information literacy standards (*Figure 14-1*) so fellow teachers understand that although you have your own curriculum, it is never taught in isolation. In fact, your curriculum will enhance their program through meaningful integration into content-area units of study.

Content-Area Standard

- Get to work on genuine lesson plans (*Figure 2-6*), not just instruction sheets, to accomplish a technology or library task. Create research forms in your computer, or adapt them from this book, so you can digitally tweak lessons to meet each teacher's needs.

Billboard Yourself

Information Literacy

Do your fellow teachers even know the library media program has its own standards and curriculum, called *information literacy*? You are your own best advertisement. Literally billboard yourself and the information management strategies you are preparing to teach. Choose one good colleague with whom to plan and teach that first set of lessons. Create a wall-sized mural documenting the sequence of lessons and activities. To do that, choose a color scheme and attractively matte and paste, in sequential order, each day's research or activity forms, supported by actual student work. Enliven the display with snapshots of students: pre-searching for topic and subtopic ideas, locating and accessing a variety of sources, reading for comprehension, taking notes, writing a rough draft, and adding technology enhancements to their finished product.

Important Idea

Sell Yourself

Whenever a teacher comes to schedule library time, take that person to the mural and walk him or her through each step of the Research Process. Teachers quickly realize this is something they haven't been covering with their students. "You do this?" they'll ask. You should also explain how you can adapt each step of the Research Process to exactly fit their content-area requirements, time constraints, or special needs students.

Support Teaching Styles

Just as a doctor needs a great bedside manner to be really effective, the LMT needs to "read" each teacher's personality and instructional style and adapt or offer services accordingly. Learn teachers' differences, then match the time and complexity of planning accordingly. The popular theme "Unity Through Diversity" may be the most positive approach to the unique role of the LMT in dealing with every teacher on a campus. In other words, channel the teachers' differences in teaching styles, and their willingness to collaborate, into creative and positive experiences for you both.

Adjust

Hitting everyone with the entire Research Process isn't always appropriate. The Spanish teacher may find that his first experience with you in the fall doesn't have to be a fully planned lesson at all, but just a quick, "Hey, I found a great new web site for cultural awareness your class might enjoy letting me demonstrate." Making yourself accessible to initiate planning with staff members is a simple way to get started. I guarantee better things will follow! The following sections offer other techniques to encourage LMT accessibility while balancing the demands on your time with the needs of your diverse clientele.

The Role of the LMC Master Calendar

Important Idea

Toss out the planning book! The key word here is "book." A book is a barrier. Would you go into another teacher's classroom and write something in *her* planning book? Do you go into your spouse's wallet or purse? There are some assumed boundaries we're all hesitant to cross. Instead, grab that desk mat calendar. You know, the one handed out free at the beginning of the year. Stick a couple of tacks into the most accessible bulletin board or wall space in the library media center. Find the spot that everyone must pass on the way to the faculty meeting. Presto! The next thing you know:

"Hey, can I just sign myself up so my classes can get on the computers?" asks the history teacher.

"Sure," replies the LMT. "Just use a pencil, in case your plans change later."

A wall calendar is a very friendly, inviting, and open means of scheduling. The buy-in is instant and tremendous because teachers feel they are scheduling for what's already theirs—the library. I found this simple device quite by accident a few years ago. I knew that, due to new job opportunities for my family, I would be resigning at the end of the school year. I also knew that the LMT position would not necessarily be funded the following year. Although I initiated a variety of strategies to enable a smooth transition to a teacher-run facility, the wall chart for self-scheduling became the overwhelming favorite (*Figure 2-3*). Suddenly, I had solved all those scheduling problems that had plagued me for years. The teachers took to it instantly, and I've used it every year since! Following are some simple calendar guidelines, born of experience and tested by time.

Color Coding

Red: Unchangeable district data such as school holidays.

Blue: Unchangeable school site data such as staff development days and situations where the school books the library media center for meetings or events.

Green: Unchangeable LMT obligations such as on- or off-site meetings and conferences.

Pencil: All teacher sign-ups. The ability to erase is essential for both the collaborative teacher and the LMT. *Figure 2-2* demonstrates that, to make things simple, the LMT can pencil into the calendar a quick lesson plan guide for a confirmed collaborative unit.

Aligning the Calendars

Using all other official calendars, fill in the red, blue, and green sections. Be sure to sufficiently block out the calendar days for district and site schedule interruptions so that teachers do not mistakenly schedule over them. The LMT's personal commitments might not interfere with some LMC activities. Therefore, I draw a green box around my meeting times, leaving the interior of the box available for teacher sign-ups. Once I began this system, I quite literally never had another scheduling foul-up, except when I over-committed myself!

Signing Up

Buy-in to the library media program will be a bountiful harvest resulting from sowing the seeds of ownership. Teacher self-sign-ups, shown in *Figure 2-3*, are the way my calendar usually looks. This system conveys to colleagues that it is truly everyone's library media center, providing a variety of services including those of a library media teacher. Using an LMT is a choice, not an obligation. It is remarkable how often teachers will begin to seek you out when they see the wonderful things you did with another class. "I want to do that, too!" is a sign of successful empowerment.

Although teachers sign up freely, I indeed try to catch everyone. Face-to-face dialog is an outreach opportunity I obsessively snag. While a teacher is signing up on the calendar and asking me about the coding directions, I may slip in, "By the way, let me know if I can assist you with anything when you bring your class in. Has your class had an Internet orientation yet?"

The teacher's subject area determines whether I offer research lessons. In middle school, sticking to science and/or history classes helps prevent student research lesson duplication. Although it is usually the language arts classes where you can still focus on literature, don't forget to pull fiction books to support other classes doing content-area research.

Fig. 2-2. The LMC Calendar

Monday	Tuesday	Wednesday	Thursday	Friday
31 Day 1: Riggs **Lesson:** Topic & Subtopics	1 Day 2: Riggs **Lesson:** Sources & MLA Citations	2 Assembly Day	3 Day 3: Riggs **Lesson:** Reading& Notetaking	4 Day 4: Riggs Research 10 notes
7 Day 5: Riggs Research 10 notes 20 total	8 LMT meeting Day 6: Riggs Research 10 notes 30 total	9 Day 7: Riggs **Lesson:** Sort & Number Notes	10 Day 8: Riggs **Lesson:** Write Introduction	11 Day 9: Riggs Writing (LMC or classroom)
14 Day 10: Riggs Writing (LMC or classroom)	15 Day 11: Riggs Writing (LMC or classroom)	16 Day 12: Riggs Typing & Technology Integration	17 Day 13: Riggs Typing & Technology Integration	18 Day 14: Riggs Typing & Technology Integration
21	22	23	24	25

Busy Calendar Day

Periods ↘ ↙ Date

Period			Date
1	Riggs 8 (R) Renais	Villa 8 (I) Span	3
2	Riggs 7 (R) Renais		
3	Riggs 7 (R) Renais	Villa 7/8 (C) ELL	
4	*LMT Lunch*	Villa 8 (I) Span	
5	Riggs 8 (R) Renais	Villa 8 (I) Span	
6	Riggs 8 (R) Renais	Villa 7/8 (C) ELL	

Posting the Directions

Because a typical LMC often bustles with a variety of activities, coming up with simple ways to convey complex information, illustrated in *Figure 2-3*, is essential. When you also remember that the ultimate goal is to remove barriers for teachers, then the quick codes you see on a busy day (*Figure 2-2*) become even more important. Following are just a few benefits of these simple directions:

- They minimally affect teachers' busy schedules.
- They reduce or eliminate conflicts resulting from an overbooked facility.
- They translate the idea of research into a concrete time frame.
- They call attention to time needed for technology integration.

Pencils Only

"And no erasing of anyone's name but your own!" you remind teachers with a wink. If your LMC calendar often seems like Grand Central Station, pencil is the surest way to keep the trains from colliding.

On Friday, Mrs. X signs up her five classes for two full days of Internet research, then stops back in on Monday, all in a flurry, and wants to change to next week because the science experiments haven't been completed yet. "Just erase," I say. "Mr. Z came in a moment ago and will be glad to take your place." Isn't a happy staff wonderful! You may not be able to meet everyone's needs all the time, but with a pencil, you can come pretty close.

Let's Do Lunch

Creating accessible planning time between classroom teachers and the LMT can often make or break a program, yet optimal planning time with teachers rarely seems to exist. Solution: Let them pick the time and the place. If that doesn't work, simply catch them at lunch! Rather than feeling interrupted, teachers are usually just as glad not to have to make another meeting time.

The trick is speed and simplicity. Model efficient planning, and teachers will come back again and again. This is accomplished by devising a simple template, such as *Figure 2-4*, in your computer, but never ask a teacher to fill it in! Remember those barriers we're trying to eliminate? You don't even need to carry it with you when you finally catch that elusive teacher. You already know what to ask because remembering what's on the template equips you with the basic questions.

While sitting at lunch, reach into the middle of the table, grab a napkin, and jot down the lesson information from your conversation. Type it into the computer yourself when you get back to your desk (see *Figure 2-5*). Don't forget to provide the teachers with calendars, long-range (*Figure 2-1*) or lesson-specific (*Figure 2-6*), which can be "fine tuned" later and aligned with their lesson plan books. This is not more work for you when you weigh this small effort against the template's big advantages. The template:

- provides "at a glance" basic lesson or unit information;
- clearly defines separate roles and responsibilities for both the teacher and the LMT, to ensure true collaboration;
- provides a generic database adaptable to every teacher's needs;
- allows the LMT quick turnaround time from inputting data to giving back to the teacher a "working" lesson plan;
- provides a quick way to alter and improve lessons following a final debriefing at the conclusion of the project; and
- provides a repository of polished lessons for site review or accreditation, grant writing, and networking with other library media teachers.

Fig. 2-3. Simple Wall Calendar Directions

Calendar

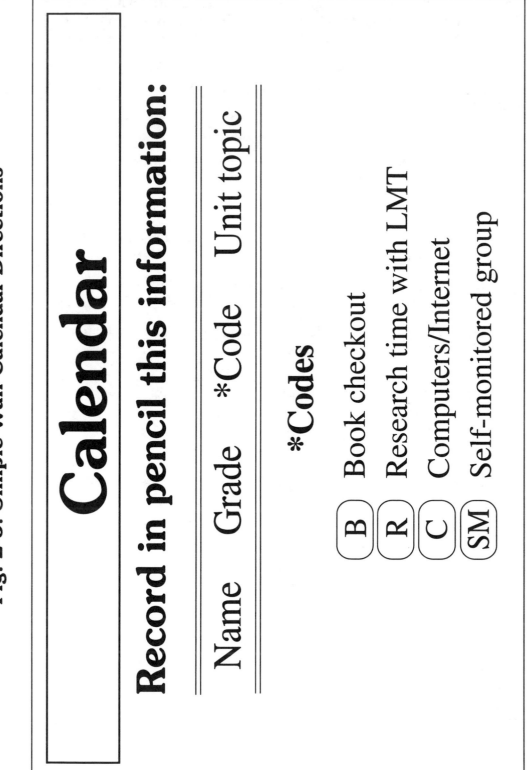

Record in pencil this information:

Name	Grade	*Code	Unit topic

***Codes**

- B — Book checkout
- R — Research time with LMT
- C — Computers/Internet
- SM — Self-monitored group

Fig. 2-4. Lesson Plan Template

UNIT/LESSON TOPIC: ________________

Teacher: ________________

Project: ________________

Grade: ______ **#Students:** ______ **Periods:** ______ **#Days:** ______

LMT's Information Skills	Teacher's Content Skills/Goals
1. Topic: ________ 2. Subtopics: ________ ________ ________ 3. Number of sources: ________ Number of formats: ________ 4. Number of notes: ________ Note modification: ________ 5. Reading "chunk": ________ 6. Sort/number notes: ________ **EXTENSION** ________	1. Content-area standards: ________ ________ 2. Reading: ________ 3. Writing: ________ 4. Geography: ________ 5. Technology: ________ 6. ________ 7. ________ 8. ________
LMT Preparation	**Teacher Preparation**
_____ Collaboratively plans unit/lesson with teacher. _____ Provides lesson plan and materials. _____ Prepares student handouts. _____ Previews/locates resources. _____ Collaboratively guides students through Research Process, teaching lessons with information literacy. _____ Provides as-needed technology instruction and assistance. _____ Other:	_____ Meets with LMT to plan unit. _____ Prepares unit requirements. _____ Assists with suggesting or locating topics and sources. _____ Pre-teaches unit concepts. _____ Helps track students' progress through the Research Process. _____ Monitors on-task behavior and student discipline. _____ Other:

Fig. 2-5. Sample Completed Lesson Plan

UNIT/LESSON TOPIC: Renaissance period in art (adapted to the ELL classes)
Teacher: Edward Villa and Steve Riggs
Project: Report of information with oral presentation
Grade: 7th/8th **#Students:** 30-34 per class **Periods:** 1, 3, 4, 5, 6 **#Days:** 10

LMT's Information Skills	Teacher's Content Skills/Goals
1. **Topic:** Choice of artist 2. **Subtopics:** 3 (2 for ELL/SpEd. and 4 for G.A.T.E.) **General:** life, art, Renaissance **Specific:** pre-search (by permission) 3. **Sources:** 3 formats. Choose from: • Books • References • CD-ROM • Internet 4. **Read:** a "chunk" is a page 5. **Number of notes:** 10 per subtopic, 30 total. (ELL/G.A.T.E. adaptations) **Note modification:** ELL, as needed 6. **Sort and number notes:** in class **EXTENSION: Write:** three-page report **Technology:** electronic card catalog, CD-ROM/Internet search skills	1. **Standards:** • Social science: Renaissance • Visual arts: perspective • Information literacy (see left) 2. **Reading:** a variety of formats of information 3. **Writing:** Report of Information 4. **Final report:** • Typed • Attractive cover • 3 pages (ELL/G.A.T.E. adaptations) • Final annotated citations • Visual image inserted electronically 4. **Technology:** • Word processing • Image insertion
LMT Preparation	**Teacher Preparation**
_____ Collaboratively plans unit/lesson with teacher. _____ Provides lesson plan and materials. _____ Prepares student handouts. _____ Pre-searches topic list and sources. _____ Collaboratively guides students through Research Process, teaching lessons with information literacy. _____ Provides as-needed technology instruction and assistance. _____ Tracking: Assists teacher with daily student accountability.	_____ Meets with LMT to plan unit. _____ Pre-teaches unit concepts. _____ Prepares unit syllabus. _____ Assists with suggesting or locating topics and source. _____ Assists students with technology. _____ Assists LMT with daily student accountability for each step of the Research Process. _____ Monitors on-task behavior and student discipline.

Fig. 2-6. Sample Completed Lesson Plan Calendar

Calendar for Renaissance Unit

WEEK ONE

Day 1: Lesson 1. Topic and subtopics.
Hand out student packet: Orientation on the Research Process.
Lesson/discussion on topic. Lesson/discussion on subtopics. Time is given for students to pre-search sources and confirm topic and gather subtopics.
Record on Research Checklist. **Tracking Sheet**

Day 2: Lesson 2. Sources.
MLA citations lesson. Using overheads, LMT fills out a sample citation form for a book, encyclopedia, Internet web site. Time is given for students to write a citation for their topic's actual encyclodedia volume. **Tracking Sheet**

Day 3: Assembly day. No research.

Day 4: Lesson 3. Reading and notetaking.
Using overheads with many student samples, LMT explains the concepts and strategies for notetaking including: strategies for reading for research, evaluating, selecting, and recording notes. Time is given for students to prepare their actual note cards according to instructions. **Tracking Sheet**

Day 5: Research. Source directions. Ten notes due using first source. **Tracking Sheet**
Each day, students move automatically to next source as 10 notes are completed.

WEEK TWO

Day 6: Research. Ten more notes due for a total of 20. **Tracking Sheet**

Day 7: Research. Ten more notes due for a total of 30. **Tracking Sheet**

Day 8: Lesson 4. Sort and number note cards.
Using overheads, LMT demonstrates how to sort, prioritize, and number note cards. Time is given for students to sort their cards. **Tracking Sheet**

Day 9: Lesson 5. Using a student writing sample, LMT gives instructions for writing an introduction and demonstrates good writing using note cards.
Tracking Sheet

Day 10: Writing in LMC or in classroom.

WEEK THREE (optional)

Day 11: Writing in LMC or in classroom.

Day 12: Writing in LMC or in classroom/typing/technology enrichment.

Day 13: Typing/technology enrichment.

Day 14: Typing/technology enrichment.

Day 15: Typing/technology enrichment. Monday: Project DUE!

EVALUATION: See the Tracking Sheet for students' completion of each step of the Research Process, to observe class's general process, and to meet needs of individual students.

Integrated Collaboration

"Don't add one more thing into my curriculum!" teachers say to each other in the lunch room. Sometimes that is a valid reason for not planning a unit with the LMT. It falls to the LMT to convey the nature of the job, namely, that it is built entirely upon collaboration! Collaboration in this case means integration. Integration means "teaching better, not teaching more." Teaching information literacy standards embedded in a teacher's content-area unit of study really does mean a better way of teaching more information in the same amount of time as in the past. It's smarter teaching! Smart, integrated teaching can be accomplished by teaming instead of just partnering. The usual teacher/LMT unit is based on planning between two people. A truly integrated unit is one in which the departments of the school support each other as well as the library media center. For example, while planning the Renaissance unit featured in this book, the art teacher was struggling with two classes of English Language Learner (ELL) students. It wasn't the art that was the problem, it was the adaptation of research and writing for special needs students involved with a report. He didn't feel comfortable grading papers with so many language arts anomalies. An integrated unit solved all our curriculum needs:

ELL/Special Modifications

"What I really think we should do," says the art teacher, "is get together with the ELL/Spanish teacher as well as the history teacher, and all do this together in one library research unit."

"What a great idea," I chime in. "You could accomplish your art history goals, I can teach the students all of the steps for research, and the ELL teacher will have a written report to meet his language arts needs! At the same time, the students will be reinforcing ideas and information for their unit in history."

Purposeful Planning

It is during the planning stage for Research Process instruction that the library media teacher has perhaps the greatest chance to influence the school's instructional program.

- Push toward educational reform by modeling collaboration.
- Teach information literacy through sequential strategies.
- Align print and electronic resources with curriculum standards.
- Promote literacy for purpose and for pleasure.
- Support staff and student technology proficiencies through technology integration into research lessons.

All other areas of the curriculum have their own standards, but information literacy standards are meaningfully taught only through the content of the other subject areas. What drives what? Do the information literacy standards drive the need for literacy and technology integration, or does the mandate for schools to teach literacy and technology drive the need for a library media teacher who can effectively spearhead information literacy instruction? If the answer is "yes" to one or the other, or both, the underlying mandate is for the LMT to be an active teaching partner. The library media teacher assumes the vital role of "change agent" and should, at the very minimum, strive to fulfill the three parts of the title:

Content-Area Standard

Library: *Plan to meaningfully integrate a variety of print sources into units of study. All students should have access to reading materials that are age, grade, subject, language, and interest appropriate.*

Technology Proficiency

Media: *Plan to meaningfully integrate technology into units of study. A wide variety of technology hardware, software, and networking services are never taught in isolation, as in the old days of "library skills," but are embedded in teachers' units of study through all steps of the Research Process* (Figure 1-3). *Be innovative as well as resourceful.*

Information Literacy

Teacher: *Collaboratively plan to teach information literacy through the Research Process. The LMT does more than point to the location of information and give instructions for accessing print and electronic sources. Be an innovative partner in teaching information literacy.*

Chapter 3

Lesson Preparations

"Thanks for the packet of research forms. Is it okay if I use them for my students when the library is booked?"

—Collaborating teacher

Fig. 3-1. Research Process: Three Lessons

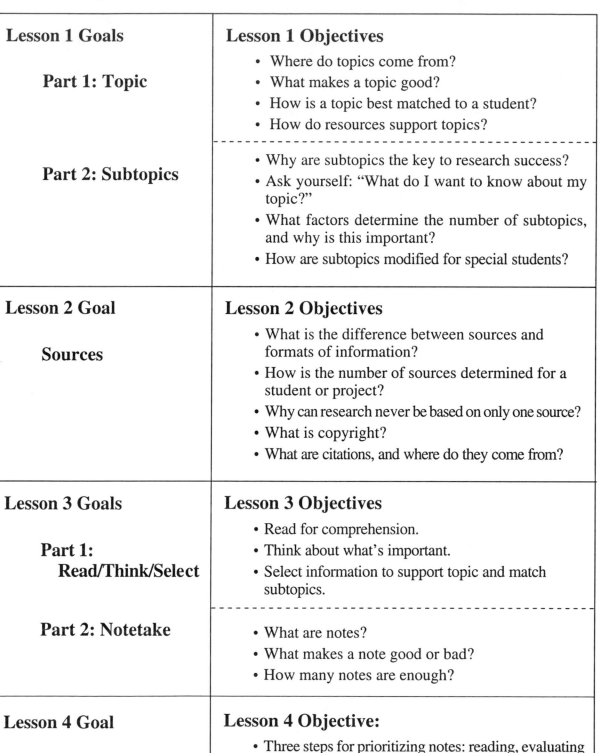

Lesson 1 Goals	**Lesson 1 Objectives**
Part 1: Topic	• Where do topics come from? • What makes a topic good? • How is a topic best matched to a student? • How do resources support topics?
Part 2: Subtopics	• Why are subtopics the key to research success? • Ask yourself: "What do I want to know about my topic?" • What factors determine the number of subtopics, and why is this important? • How are subtopics modified for special students?
Lesson 2 Goal **Sources**	**Lesson 2 Objectives** • What is the difference between sources and formats of information? • How is the number of sources determined for a student or project? • Why can research never be based on only one source? • What is copyright? • What are citations, and where do they come from?
Lesson 3 Goals	**Lesson 3 Objectives**
Part 1: Read/Think/Select	• Read for comprehension. • Think about what's important. • Select information to support topic and match subtopics.
Part 2: Notetake	• What are notes? • What makes a note good or bad? • How many notes are enough?
Lesson 4 Goal **Sort and Number Notes**	**Lesson 4 Objective:** • Three steps for prioritizing notes: reading, evaluating (selecting/sequencing), numbering.

Research Instruction

How Many Lessons?

Information Literacy

Content-Area Standard

The library media teacher and classroom teacher approach collaboration with essential mandates in place: each has his or her own set of standards. An important difference is that classroom teachers can independently accomplish their content-area standards in the classroom, unit by unit, under their own time frame. The library media teacher, on the other hand, cannot teach information literacy standards (*Figure 14-1*) in isolation. The Venn diagrams in *Figure 3-2* attempt to illustrate that when no collaborative teaching occurs, classroom curriculum standards are still taught but information literacy standards are almost completely neglected. "Almost" takes into account what were formerly called "library skills." Do you still present library skills in isolated instances? For example, Dewey decimal access to sources may be demonstrated in year-beginning student orientations, but don't expect great results until the exercise is meaningfully integrated into a teacher's unit of study. Instead of being shown Dewey decimal, the student must have a genuine need, for example, to find three different sources of information about magnetism for a science project. Perhaps "library skills" are part of information literacy, but not always vice versa. Information literacy goes far beyond access to the evaluation and use of information, including critical thinking and creative expression embedded in purposeful activities.

How many lessons does it take to teach information literacy (see *Figure 3-1*)? If there are six steps in the Research Process, are there six lessons? Wouldn't it be nice if time permitted such thoroughness? But we all know that if you asked even your best friend to team up for six lessons, and that didn't include time for students to complete their own individual hands-on research, collaborative teaching would die at conception. Therefore, flexibility becomes the number one criterion for planning research lessons. Flexibility is based on skills and time.

Skills

Which specific information objectives (*Figure 3-1*) are most important to the collaborating teacher's unit needs? Remember to allow a day for LMT instruction of the research strategy and time for students' hands-on application.

Time

Is there teaching time available on the LMC calendar? How much time is available in the collaborating teacher's unit agenda? One day, two days, two weeks? Adjust accordingly (*Figure 3-2*). Whatever choice the classroom teacher makes, do it! Happy teachers come back for more.

Fig. 3-2. Time for Research Lessons Can Be Flexible

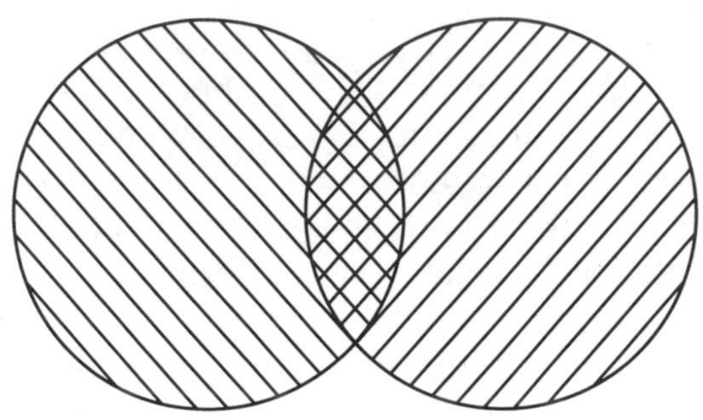

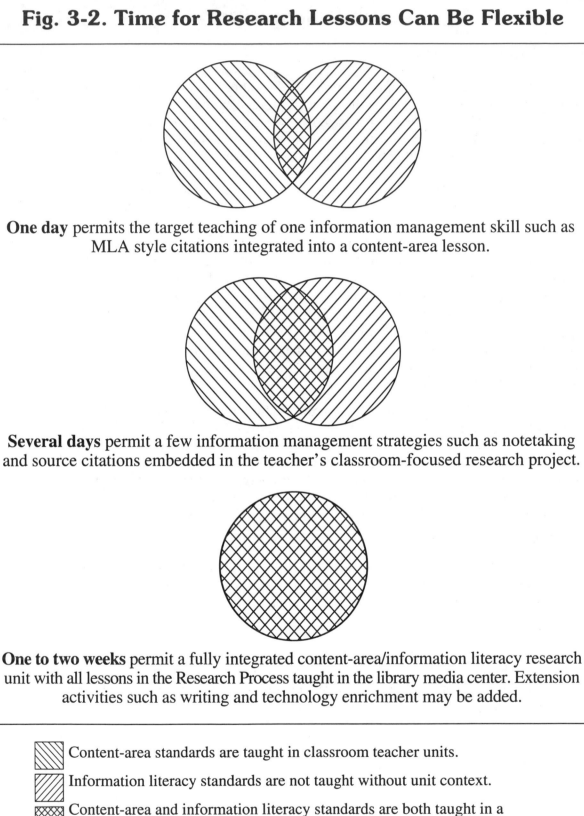

One day permits the target teaching of one information management skill such as MLA style citations integrated into a content-area lesson.

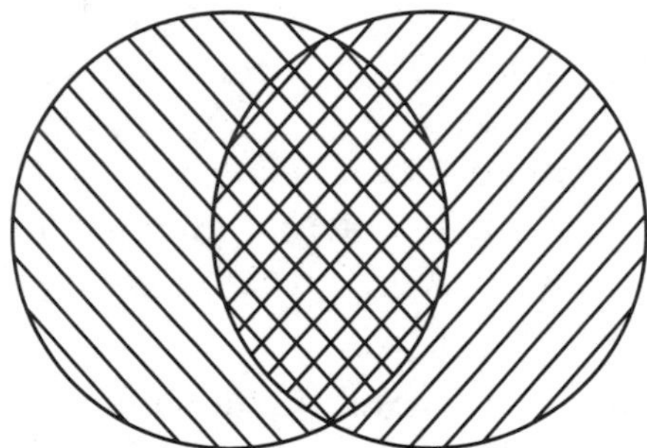

Several days permit a few information management strategies such as notetaking and source citations embedded in the teacher's classroom-focused research project.

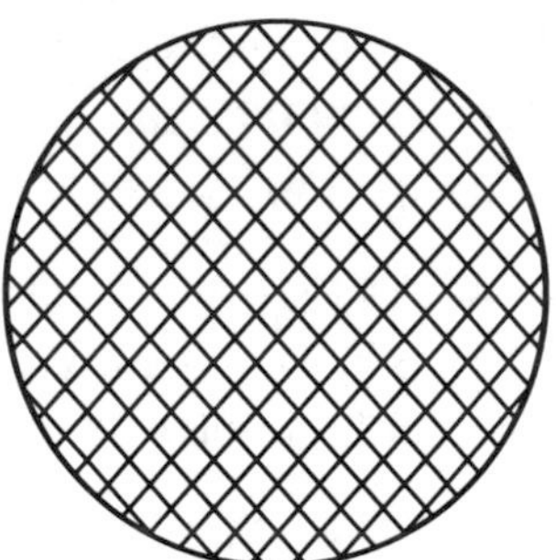

One to two weeks permit a fully integrated content-area/information literacy research unit with all lessons in the Research Process taught in the library media center. Extension activities such as writing and technology enrichment may be added.

Content-area standards are taught in classroom teacher units.

Information literacy standards are not taught without unit context.

Content-area and information literacy standards are both taught in a meaningfully integrated way.

Preparing the Setting

Facility

Because research instruction falls primarily on the shoulders of the library media teacher, the logical setting for instruction is the library media center. It is important to set a tone for students that allows this facility, as an active teaching classroom, to redefine the school's "hub of information." Ideally, schools that have newer or remodeled library facilities have a classroom immediately adjacent to the LMC solely for instructional purposes.

Signage

Lacking an adjacent classroom, signage can be used effectively to simply block off an instructional section of the main room. That way, other classes and students can freely come and go in other areas. The obvious drawback is distraction and noise. This can be particularly troublesome for research classes with less-mature students, who are easily distracted under the best of circumstances. The solution lies in good collaborative planning. First, any teacher sharing the LMC has signed up on the calendar, so there are no surprises. Second, arrange for good crowd control with both the collaborating and the independent teachers. Strict behavior rules are in effect as in any classroom.

Pre-teaching preparations include creating table signs that say, "Reserved for Research" (*Figure 3-3*). Print them out from the computer on bright neon paper, laminate two signs back to back, and slip them over a bookend placed in the middle of each table. That way it's easy to say to the incoming class, "Please take a seat at the tables reserved for you." The signs can be quickly removed if the next period is not being used for instruction.

Classroom Alternatives

There are times when the entire library media center may be better utilized by classes or groups of students working independently, particularly if technology stations are in demand. Therefore, in some cases it may be just as effective for the library media teacher to go into the collaborating teacher's classroom for pre-research instruction, including a discussion of topic and subtopics and an overhead transparency demonstration for citing sources of information. For example, some ELL and special education classes have students who cannot handle instruction in a room the size of the library media center. They can hear, see, or concentrate better in their smaller, familiar environment. When hands-on research actually begins and students need to be shown print and electronic source locations to begin reading and notetaking, the class returns to the LMC.

ELL/Special Modifications

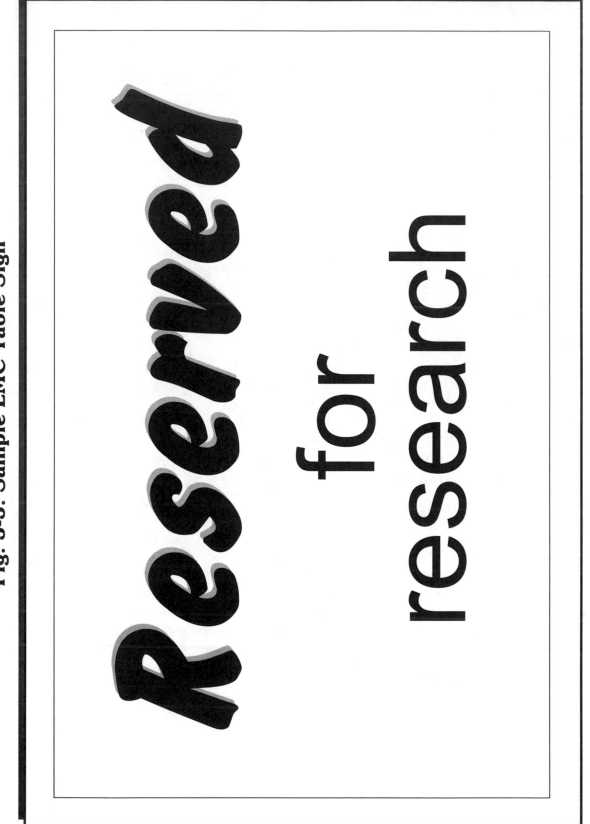

Fig. 3-3. Sample LMC Table Sign

Reserved

for
research

Locating Sources

Quality of Sources

What is the condition of the school's library media center collection? Do students have trouble finding the information they need? Do some teachers actually avoid using the facility because over the years they have learned they must send their classes to the public library for a better selection of materials? Preparing for collaborative research instruction is an ideal opportunity for the LMT to appeal for funding for collection improvement. Although the lessons of the Research Process remain essentially the same for each collaborative unit, students' topics should be based on different content-area standards that form the basis for teachers' units of study. Because the LMC collection should be updated in direct response to the resource needs of collaborative units, the library media teacher should logically become a site leader in aligning curriculum with standards.

Content-Area Standard

Variety of Sources

The Research Process reflects the need of all students to access, read, comprehend, evaluate, and use a variety of formats of information. *Sources* refers to anything used for information, whereas *formats* distinguishes among the kinds of sources such as a book, reference, CD-ROM, or the Internet. Lesson 2 on sources is based on the concept that doing research requires using more than one format of information. For students, different information management strategies are involved with each format. Therefore, in the Research Process, the three required formats provide a baseline for the minimum amount of information access training needed for middle school students to acquire the contextualized skills to access, evaluate, and use information successfully.

Information Literacy

Do not let lack of appropriate sources restrict or deter collaborative planning and teaching. Most LMCs, no matter how deprived, can provide a bare minimum of three formats of information, always including both print and electronic sources. For example, Lesson 1 revolves around the concept that a good topic depends on the availability of information matched to the ability of the student to read and comprehend. For a variety of reasons, some students absolutely require on-campus topics, while other students are able to access and use public libraries. Therefore, to be able to provide adequate topic selection, the LMC collection needs a baseline variety of well-chosen formats of information for the students who absolutely need them, not necessarily an enormous quantity to meet the needs of every single student. It is easy to see why an active, instructionally involved LMC is often a better-equipped or more well-rounded facility. This becomes a mandate for educational reform: Put library media teachers in every school who can determine standards-based, site-specific resources and deliver information literacy-based instruction.

Important Idea

Fig. 3-4. Sample LMC Planning Map: Gaspar de Portola Middle School, SDUSD

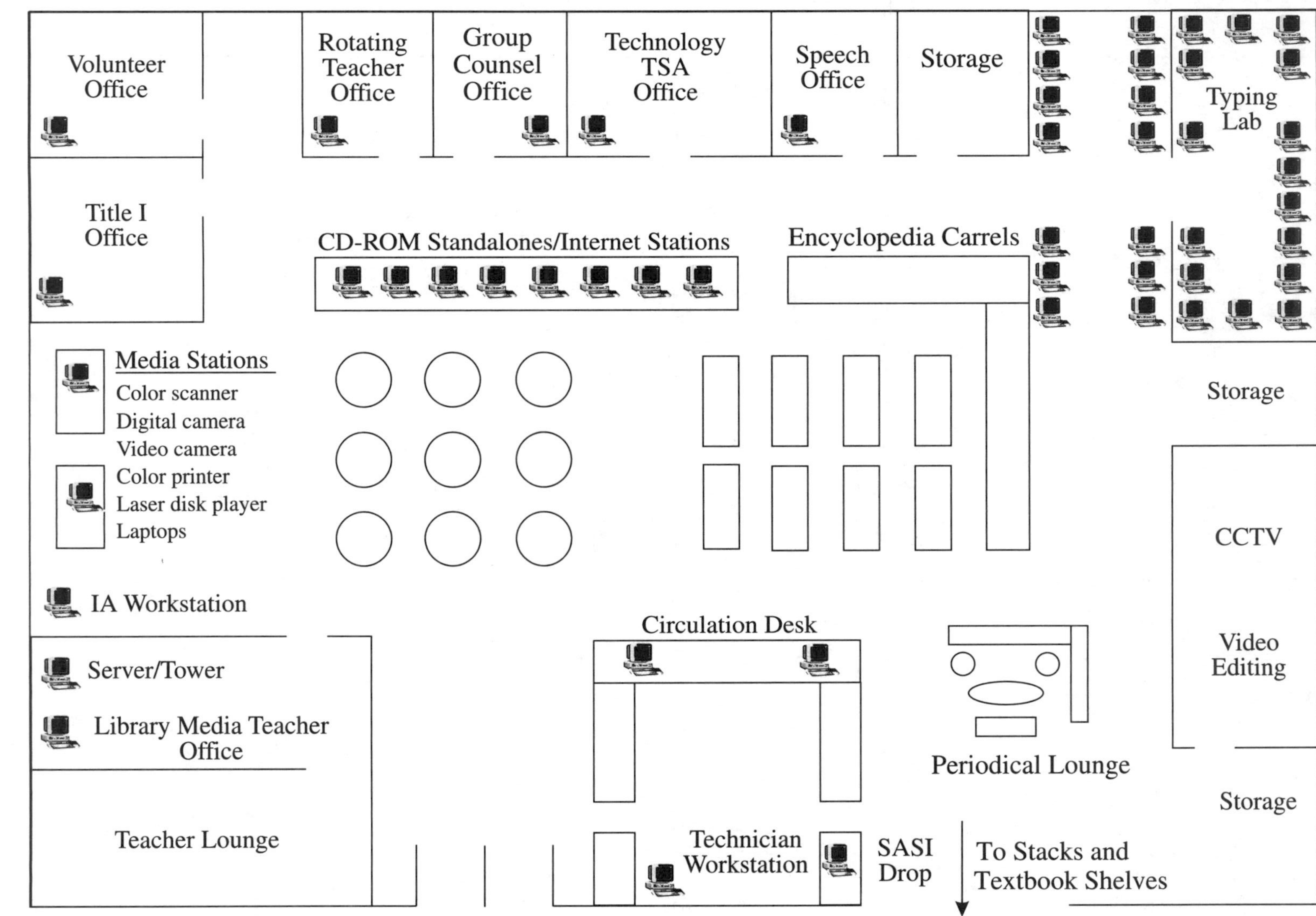

Preparing Equipment/Technology

The power of library media collaborative teaching, which services the needs of the entire faculty and student body of the school site, legitimizes the need to have a technologically advanced library media center because:

1. Preparing for the variety of formats so essential in Lesson 2, "Looking at Sources," requires the LMC to have a technology plan in place with specific yearly hardware and software goals based on information literacy needs.
2. It is advantageous for the library media teacher to prepare a computer map of the facility (*Figure 3-4*) that is always available for technology reconfiguration as changes in funding arise.
3. The wall calendar of scheduled technology-integrated research lessons and activities (*Figure 3-5*) vividly demonstrates to the administration that the LMC is truly in demand as a technology and information hub of the school.

Fig. 3-5. LMC Calendar Reflects Technology Integration

Periods → | Date: 3

Period		
1	Riggs 7 (R) Renais	Villa 8 (C) Span
2	Riggs 8 (R) Renais	
3	Riggs 7 (R) Renais	Villa 7/8 (C) ELL
4		Villa 8 (C) Span
5	Riggs 7 (R) Renais	Villa 8 (C) Span
6	Riggs 8 (R) Renais	Villa 7/8 (C) ELL

Consider the Lesson

Considering the technology needs of students, equipment preparation may include the long-term selection of hardware that accommodates the baseline software and networkable information sources. When students begin hands-on research, basic technology information access should include electronic standalone sources such as software and CD-ROMs, as well as networkable sources such as online search tools and the Internet. The LMT should caution students to make the best use of their limited time by first using those sources of information that are available to them only at school.

When it comes to flexibility in providing research instruction, setup and room switching are made easy by the old reliable pull-down screen and overhead projector. Indeed, this book has been formatted with templates for overhead transparencies in the four Research Process lessons, as well as in extension lessons activities. Conversion of these lessons and templates into a multimedia presentation would be a wonderful challenge to the research instructor. Role modeling innovative technology integration is a good reason for the library media teacher to request ongoing funding to update library media center computers and peripheral devices such as a color scanner, digital camera, and computer projection system.

Preparing for the Unit and Lessons

Unit Concepts

Content-Area Standard

Preparations to begin teaching the unit are defined in the planning stage through a division of tasks between the classroom teacher and the library media teacher. First, the classroom teacher introduces the students to the content-area concepts identified on the lesson planning sheet (*Figure* 2-5). Students need to have a definite purpose in mind when they arrive in the library media center. Second, the library media teacher teaches the information literacy concepts and strategies contextualized to individual topics to meaningfully accomplish the classroom teacher's goals for the project's research, construction, and completion.

Unit Time

Information Literacy

Generally speaking, through collaborative lessons, classroom teachers gain a much better understanding of adequate hands-on research time. Often, teachers are not familiar with the steps of research and the time it takes students to successfully learn and apply strategies for selecting topics and subtopics, locating and evaluating sources, reading critically, selecting and recording notes, correctly constructing source citations, writing rough and final drafts, and typing and preparing a presentation. Inadvertently, a teacher's brief research timetable may have caused students to resort to some measure of plagiarism. Collaborative teaching of the Research Process changes all that! For the first time teachers may understand that successfully learning how to accomplish the steps of research is just as important as the research product. This is what information literacy is all about: a focus on process as well as product so that students emerge from an information management experience equipped with lifelong skills.

Specifically, the teacher determines the extent of a collaborative project. It could be merely a one-period target or supplementary lesson, or it could constitute an entire unit. A definite factor in motivating classroom teachers to spend more time in collaborative projects is the library media teacher's willingness to make time concessions. Even the quick-paced several days of research lessons may be too much for a teacher's time constraints. Adjust accordingly, as shown in *Figure 3-2*. Teaching a research step out of sequence does not mean it is out of context. The teacher beginning science fair projects may have time only for a notetaking lesson so that students can gather information for writing the background report.

Important Idea

Compressing Research Process instructional time into a few days can be challenging to middle-school students. For this age group, it is extremely important to interweave activities with lessons. This is the critical factor for each library media or classroom teacher: Adjust the content of the research instruction lessons presented in this book with hands-on activities so that students are accomplishing real-time parts of their project. For example, on the day that MLA-style citations are demonstrated on the overhead, try to allow students time to fill in the forms for at least one of their actual sources. On the day when note card preparation is demonstrated, have students begin to prepare their actual cards, which may be finished for homework, so that they come to class the next day prepared to begin hands-on research. Above all, don't be afraid to "mess up" in your timing. You may spend years learning good pacing and still find that each lesson must be tweaked for a new group of students.

Unit Materials

Teacher materials: The collaborating teacher prepares classroom content-area materials and specific project requirements for the unit and gives copies to the library media teacher. Based on that teacher's unit needs, the LMT prepares specific information literacy materials to be used in the research lessons. As discussed in previous sections, preparations can include a wide range of teacher-specific materials, from facility signage and hardware/software pathfinders to lesson-specific handouts in the student research packet. This book reflects years of creating materials for collaborative research units that can be used as is or modified as needed.

Lifelong Skill

LMT materials: Let's face it, the teaching and learning of research strategies is not often dynamically, earth-shatteringly interesting to students! So how does a library media teacher accomplish the seemingly impossible? The key to creating effective information management lesson materials is relevance. Without it, learning how to write a correct source citation or how to construct a good note is, frankly, tedious and boring. If students don't see meaning and purpose relevant to their immediate project, they'll simply tune out. Few will perceive the research strategies in these lessons as lifelong skills until that connection is made personally meaningful. For the instructor, a measure of personality interjection—yes, even hype—may be called for! There are two important items for creating relevance. The first is humor. Many thanks are extended to the talented humorists who have granted copyright permission for the reproduction of their insightful cartoons in this book. At strategic points, they introduce, in a poignant way, what

would ordinarily be very dry and boring research concepts. The second extraordinarily important resource is the generous use of student samples. Seeing the good, and especially the bad, examples of fellow students' work provides invaluable, relevant information that dramatically raises the class's level of understanding.

A disclaimer: Separate the content of the lessons in this book from the style of presentation portrayed. Remember, besides presenting the steps of research, this is a diary of one person's successful instructional strategies. Readers must adapt the content to their own personal style of delivery. Be prepared! Despite an instructor's best efforts, there will be restlessness on the part of less-mature students. It is my experience that if you have had past success with your teaching style, attribute the small percent of student problems to information overload, not necessarily to boredom. Adjust lessons accordingly. The instructor's ability to ad lib anecdotes from personal experiences, with added touches of patience and perseverance, will be rewarded! By the first day of hands-on research, even the students who seemingly weren't paying attention will bustle off with true purpose. Others will begin to ask you incredibly intelligent questions about sources and notes. It's a miracle!

Student Handouts

Important Idea

Based on the concept that less is more, the research packet for middle-school students, presented on the following pages, represents years of research instruction distilled into only a few lesson-specific handouts. An important beginning point is that although the Research Process sheet (*Figure 3-6*) may be the backbone for all lessons, it may never actually be given out to middle-school students. "Just do it" is the motivating factor for teaching less-experienced, younger, or second-language students at the sixth-, seventh-, or even the eighth-grade levels. At the research teacher's discretion, more experienced or more mature students might find the Research Sheet an appropriate guide to independent work.

Generally, on the first day of instruction in Lesson 1, give students the Research Checklist (*Figure 3-7*) to record their topic and subtopics and to look ahead at general research requirements. In Lesson 2 on sources, give them format-specific, color-coded citation forms (*Figure 3-8*) to learn to record an accurate, MLA-style source citation. For example, students usually receive one white form for a book, one green form for a reference/encyclopedia, one pink form for the Internet, and perhaps a blue form for a CD-ROM. *Figure 3-8* is a composite template for an overhead transparency used by the instructor to lead the MLA citations activity. To make the student handouts, these forms are regrouped by format, usually three per page, then photocopied on colored paper and cut apart. The only other materials that students receive are notecards or, in some cases, a note sheet

created for a particular class or unit of study (*Figure 8-8*). *Figures 3-9* and *3-10* form a back-to-back handout given to more experienced students at any grade level who are ready to work independently on citations, the goal of information literacy!

Although all of these guide sheets appear later in this book in their appropriate chapters, these handouts are included here so that they may be clearly seen as the entire student packet for this series of lessons. A research packet for teachers is much more inclusive, containing overhead transparency templates, as well as student handouts.

Of special note is that, at the middle-school level, I often create a set of class folders, one for each period of instruction, and store them throughout the unit in a handy-dandy, portable plastic organizer bin. Saving student packets of work at the end of each class period eliminates the typical "I left my work at home" excuse. Simply allow a few minutes at the end of each class for students to gather and staple their handouts and note sheets, then collect them. For more responsible students, hole-punch the handouts and a zipping storage bag for loose note cards for easy clipping into their looseleaf binders.

Fig. 3-6. Research Process

Topic *A good topic is "doable," but slightly challenging to your assessed abilities.*

A. Locate a topic in textbooks, library sources, or the teacher's topic list.
B. Check in the library media center for at least three formats of supporting information.
C. Cross-check in an encyclopedia to narrow or broaden a topic.

Subtopics *Ask yourself: What do I want to know about my topic?*

A. General subtopics may be brainstormed. Examples:
  Person: early life, education, work (be specific), later life.
  Place: origin, history, leaders, geography, economy.
  Thing: who, what, when, where, why/how.
B. Specific subtopics must be located in, for example, an encyclopedia's subheads.
C. The number of subtopics is based on the number of days of research.

Sources *A good source is any kind of supporting information that you can read.*

A. Format (the form information comes in) Examples include:
  Print: books, encyclopedias, magazines, newspapers.
  Nonprint: videos, laser disks, CD-ROMs, computer software, Internet.
B. Use at least three formats of information. Using one source is not research!
C. Credit sources using MLA-style citations.

Read/Think/Select *Good research promotes comprehension and evaluation.*

A. Read an entire "chunk" (a paragraph or a page) with your pencil down.
B. Think about what was read. What was important?
C. Select only a few key facts from each "chunk" to match your subtopics.

Notetake *A good note creates information ownership. This is learning!*

A. One note per card, titled with subtopic. Use as many cards as needed.
B. Record important keywords, facts, or a list, up to about 20 words (use your judgment).
C. No small words like *a*, *the*, *an*, *is*, *was*. Instead use commas and dashes.
D. No copying of sentences (without quotation marks and footnotes).

Sort and Number Notes *Good organization of notes makes writing easier.*

A. Sort notes by subtopic section, about five notes per paragraph (use your judgment).
B. Read notes in one section at a time and put in an order that makes sense.
C. Number notes consecutively through all sections without starting over at number 1.

Extension

  Write/Publish/Present
  Final citations list
  Technology integration

Evaluation Student tracking

Fig. 3-7. Research Checklist

LMT/Teacher Tracking: **Date Due:/Points:**

Topic ______________________________

Subtopics

○ ______________________________

○ ______________________________

○ ______________________________

○ ______________________________

○ ______________________________

Sources

A. At least 3 formats. Circle choices:
Book, reference, CD-ROM, Internet, other: ______________

B. Total number of sources: ______________

Read/Think/Select

A. A "chunk" is ______________

Notetake

A. At least ___ notes for each subtopic.

B. Total number of notes: ______________

Sort and number notes

Write rough draft from notes

Teacher Grading: Title Page
Typed Report
Final Citation List
Image/Chart

Fig. 3-8. Citations Activity

Name____________________ **Teacher** ______________________________

Alphabetical order ______

(Reference) Encyclopedia: MLA Style Citation

Author *if available* (last name, first and middle names) ________________(period).

Article title ("quotation marks") _________________________________ (period).

Title of encyclopedia (<u>underlined</u>) ____________________________(period).

Year____________ followed by edition (abbreviated, *ed*) ____________ (period).

Example: Barnes, Isaac Jacob. "Camels." <u>The World Book Encyclopedia</u>. 1996 ed.

- -

Alphabetical order ______

CD-ROM Encyclopedia: MLA Style Citation

Author *if available* (last name, first and middle names) ________________(period).

Article title ("quotation marks") _________________________________ (period).

CD-ROM title (<u>underlined</u>) ___________________________________(period).

Edition (abbreviated, *ed*)______ (period). Write the words: CD-ROM _____ (period).

Year__________ followed by edition (abbreviated, *ed*) _____________ (period).

Example: Adams, Ernest D. "Spanish Armada." <u>The World Book Multimedia Encyclopedia</u>. Deluxe ed. CD-ROM. 2000 ed.

- -

Alphabetical order ______

Internet Web Site: MLA Style Citation

Title of web site ("quotation marks") _____________________________(period).

Date of access: Day Month (abbreviated, period.) Year _______________ (no period)

URL (<web site address in brackets>) ______________________________(period).

Example: "Presidential Campaign." 5 Oct. 2000 <http://www.cnn.com>.

Fig. 3-9. Citations: MLA Examples

*All examples cited from the web site below except starred items.
14 Jul. 2000 <http://ollie.dcccd.edu/library/Module4/M4-V/examples.htm>.

BOOKS:

No author*

People of Long Ago. Milwaukee: Rourke Publishers, 1986.

One author*

Newberry, Louis. Hair Design. Los Angeles: Newberry Press, 1986.

Two authors

Zwerdling, Alex, and Richard Voorhees. Orwell and the Left. New Haven: Yale UP, 1974.

More than two authors*

Kingsley, Eric, et al. Ships. New York: Alfred A. Knopf, 1995.

Edited

Foster, Carol E., Mark A. Siegel, and Nancy R. Jacobs, eds. Women's Changing Role. The Information Series on Current Topics. Wylie: Information Plus, 1990.

By a corporation*

Dallas County Community College District. Richland College. Institutional Self-Study. Dallas: Richland College, 1993.

SPECIAL BOOKS:

Anthology or multi-volume set

"Fromm, Erich 1900-1980." Contemporary Authors.Vol. 29. New Revision Series. Detroit: Gale, 1990. 55 vols. to date. 1981- .

Atlas

Atlas of the World. New York: Oxford UP, 1992. Munro, David, ed.

Dictionary

"Hard Rock." The American Heritage Dictionary of the English Language. 3rd ed. Boston: Houghton, 1993.

Poem, play, or short story from an anthology

Chekhov, Anton. The Cherry Orchard. Trans. Avraham Yarmolinsky. Norton Anthology of World Masterpieces. Ed. Maynard Mack. 4th ed. Vol. 2. New York: Norton, 1979. 1192-1230. 2 vols.

ENCYCLOPEDIAS:

In print, with author

Landry, Tom. "Football." World Book Encyclopedia. 1991 ed.

In print, no author

"Industrial Architecture." New Caxton Encyclopedia. London: Caxton, 1977. 20 vols.

Fig. 3-10. Bibliography: MLA Examples

CD-ROM:

Encyclopedia article

Kumbier, William A. “Science Fiction.” World Book 1997 Multimedia Encyclopedia. Deluxe ed. CD-ROM. 1997 ed.

Newspaper article

Birnbaum, Mary C. “Information-Age Infants: Technology Pushes the Frontiers of What Babies Know.” Dallas Morning News 23 Aug. 1994: 5C. NewsBank CD News. CD-ROM.

INTERNET:

Web site

“Hank Aaron.” 1996. Total Baseball. Tot@lSports. 6 May 1997 <http://www.totalbaseball.com>.

Encyclopedia article

Enfield, David B. “El Niño.” Britannica Online. Vers. 98.2. Apr. 1998. Encyclopedia Britannica. 1 Jul. 1998 <http://www.eb.com>.

Magazine article

Kluger, Jeffrey. “The Gentle Cosmic Rain.” Time. 9 June 1997. 11 Jun. 1997 <http://www.pathfinder.com/index.htm>.

Newspaper article

Johnson, George. “Don’t Worry: A Brain Still Can’t Be Cloned. ” New York Times. 2 Mar. 1997, forums sec. 11 Jun. 1997 <http://forums.nytimes.com/library/national/0302clone-review.html>.

E-mail

Jeser-Skaggs, Sharlee (sjs@dcccd.edu). “Keyword Quirks.” E-mail to Gary Duke (gd@dcccd.edu). 28 Feb. 1995.

MAGAZINES:

Article, with author

Idelson, Holly. “Gun Rights and Restrictions.” Congressional Quarterly Weekly Report. 24 Apr. 1993: 1021-27.

Article, no author

“Stolen Art Treasures Found in Texas.” Facts on File. 22 Jun. 1990: 459.

NEWSPAPERS:

Article, with author

Moreno, Sylvia. “Senate Endorses Gun Bill after Brief Filibuster.” Dallas Morning News. 18 May 1993: 1A+.

Article, no author*

“Aiding the Arts.” The Milwaukee Sentinel. 15 Jan. 1997: 3B

MISCELLANEOUS

Film and video

The Wrong Stuff: American Architecture. Videocassette. Dir. Tom Bettag. Carousel Films, 1983.

Interview

Face to face: Pei, I. M. Personal interview. 27 Jul. 1983.

Telephone: Poussaint, Alvin F. Telephone interview. 10 Dec. 1980.

Pamphlet

Treat like a book.

Section 2

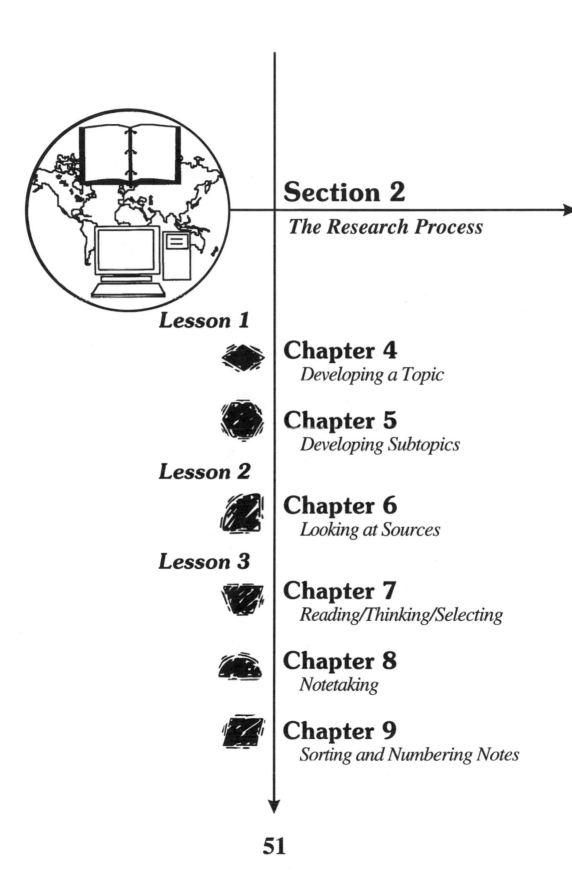

The Research Process

Lesson 1

Chapter 4

Developing a Topic

Chapter 5

Developing Subtopics

Lesson 2

Chapter 6

Looking at Sources

Lesson 3

Chapter 7

Reading/Thinking/Selecting

Chapter 8

Notetaking

Chapter 9

Sorting and Numbering Notes

Chapter 4

Developing a Topic: Lesson 1, Part 1

Instructor Information

Student Lesson

"We're switching topics to match the books that are in the library."

—New special education teacher

Fig. 4-1. Research Process: Topic

Topic *A good topic is "doable," but slightly challenging to your assessed abilities.*

A. Locate a topic in textbooks, library sources, or the teacher's topic list.
B. Check in the library media center for at least three formats of supporting information.
C. Cross-check in an encyclopedia to narrow or broaden a topic.

Subtopics *Ask yourself: What do I want to know about my topic?*

A. General subtopics may be brainstormed. Examples:
  Person: early life, education, work (be specific), later life.
  Place: origin, history, leaders, geography, economy.
  Thing: who, what, when, where, why/how.
B. Specific subtopics must be located in, for example, an encyclopedia's subheads.
C. The number of subtopics is based on the number of days of research.

Sources *A good source is any kind of supporting information that you can read.*

A. Format (the form information comes in) Examples include:
  Print: books, encyclopedias, magazines, newspapers.
  Nonprint: videos, laser disks, CD-ROMs, computer software, Internet.
B. Use at least three formats of information. Using one source is not research!
C. Credit sources using MLA-style citations.

Read/Think/Select *Good research promotes comprehension and evaluation.*

A. Read an entire "chunk" (a paragraph or a page) with your pencil down.
B. Think about what was read. What was important?
C. Select only a few key facts from each "chunk" to match your subtopics.

Notetake *A good note creates information ownership. This is learning!*

A. One note per card, titled with subtopic. Use as many cards as needed.
B. Record important keywords, facts, or a list, up to about 20 words (use your judgment).
C. No small words like *a, the, an, is, was*. Instead use commas and dashes.
D. No copying of sentences (without quotation marks and footnotes).

Sort and Number Notes *Good organization of notes makes writing easier.*

A. Sort notes by subtopic section, about five notes per paragraph (use your judgment).
B. Read notes in one section at a time and put in an order that makes sense.
C. Number notes consecutively through all sections without starting over at number 1.

Extension
  Write/Publish/Present
  Final citations list
  Technology integration

Evaluation Student tracking

Chapter Concepts

Where Do Topics Come From?

Topic selection is a critical factor in student success. Topics come from a standards-based unit of study. They can range from a whole-class topic for novice researchers, to group or partner choices, to individual topics for experienced learners. In any case, there must be direction and guidelines. A list provided by the teacher is the most obvious source of topics, but other sources range from no-choice student assignments to guided choices in specific content-area materials such as texts or pre-searched library sources. Independent topic selection is a research goal for producing lifelong learning skills. Once an independent topic is located in one source, the student learns to triangulate in the library media center to confirm the topic in at least two other sources.

What Makes a Topic Good?

The one-word answer is: Information. Is information about the student's topic available on campus or off, and is the student physically able to retrieve it? Is topic information appropriate to the student's age, grade level, interest level, language, and learning ability? Is it appropriately challenging? Will it provide a valuable learning experience for the unit?

Does the Topic Match the Student?

This is perhaps the most important point of this chapter. By seeking both availability and readability of information, by evaluating information to broaden or narrow, enabling easy access or challenge to the student, the ultimate goal of a topic is genuine learning. The real question students learn to ask themselves is: "Is the topic good for me?"

What Is the Role of the Instructor in Matching Topics to Students?

One of the important services a library media teacher can offer is to take the collaborative teacher's pre-existing topic list and align the choices with the availability of library media center sources of information, including both print and electronic sources. The goal of any project is student success. High achievers sometimes can be referred to off-site libraries. Average achievers should have topic information available at the school site. Low achievers should have topics pre-selected from school site resources appropriate to their learning level.

Instructor Information

Finding Topics

"You have two days to find your topic." Have you heard teachers give that assignment to their students? Are students given further guidance? Collaborating with a library media teacher for topic development to begin a unit will be the first big relief for overburdened teachers. During collaborative planning, the LMT and classroom teacher(s) discuss where students' topics will come from. An assessment of prior research experience is weighed against the type of project to be accomplished. It is advisable, for example, not to start students out on their first research project for middle school with science fair topics. Those are necessarily completely independent and not always easy to locate, confirm, or match to a student's ability level. A teacher with 150 students may have 150 headaches!

Important Idea

Start those new seventh-graders out with a very guided project where topics can be chosen from the teacher's list (*Figure 4-2*) and perhaps accomplished in groups or partners. Better yet, pre-search this list to confirm that topics are appropriate. For middle scholars, this often means topics are found right in the school's library media center. This is so important, it could be the single factor that determines the entire success of a student's project.

Matching the Topic with the Student

ELL/Special Modifications

Personal success is always the key to a good topic, and that success arises from information that the student can access, evaluate, and use. Assigning students topics that are not physically and readily accessible is dooming those children to failure before they have even started. This cannot be emphasized enough. A second-language student may need that fourth-grade level Leonardo da Vinci book sitting on the "Quick Picks" shelf, so that becomes the topic. An average learner may have a mom who'll help her with her reading and take her anywhere:

> *Teacher, I can take a harder topic because my mom volunteers at the public library and she said she'd find some books for me.*

On the other hand, ask gifted students if they can get to the public library before assigning them topics that don't have enough challenging sources right in the school library media center.

Fig. 4-2. Teacher's Original Topic List

Topic List for Renaissance Unit Artists

Choose from the following list of artists. You have one week to make your selection and sign up. No duplication of topics.

Bellini, Giovanni
Boccaccio, Giovanni
Bosch, Hieronymus
Botticelli, Sandro
Brueghel, Pieter, the Elder
Brunelleschi, Filippo
Caravaggio
Carpaccio, Vittore
Cellini, Benvenuto
Cervantes, Miguel de
Crivelli, Carlo
da Vinci, Leonardo
Donatello
Dürer, Albrecht
El Greco
Fiorentino, Rosso
Fra Angelico
Francesca, Piero della
Ghiberti, Lorenzo
Ghirlandaio, Domenico
Giorgione
Giotto di Bondone
Giovanni da Bologna
Grünewald, Matthias
Holbein, Hans, the Younger
Lippi, Fra Filippo
Mantegna, Andrea
Masaccio
Masolino
Messina, Antonello da
Michelangelo
Perugino, Pietro
Palladio, Andrea
Parmigianino, Francesco
Pollaiuolo, Antonio Del
Pontormo, Jacopo da
Raphael
Tintoretto, Jacobo
Titian
Uccello, Paolo
van Eyck, Jan
Veneziano, Domenico

The Instructor's Role in Topic Selection

Content-Area Standard

How can an instructor guide the selection of appropriate topics for about 150 students ranging from gifted to average to learning- and language-challenged? Whew! For example, a teacher came to the LMT with a list of Renaissance artists (*Figure 4-2*) from which the students were supposed to pick. Good start. At least the students weren't just told to "Come up with a topic." If one purpose of an articulated curriculum unit is to introduce students to new people and ideas, how can they possibly know what to pick? In this case, the library media teacher responded to the teacher:

> *"I'm so glad to see that you have a list for the students to choose from. We have a few weeks before the unit begins, do you mind if I take this list and look up every single artist in our own library? That way we can see if we should add or perhaps subtract some of these names. I'll arrange the list for you according to how much information is readily available here at school, so that you can more easily match the topics to your students."*

ELL/Special Modifications

The teacher was ecstatic! He was worried about topics for the ELL students, but he hadn't really considered that the other students would have difficulty with a topic as well. More important, he was far too busy with his daily teaching schedule to tackle this part of the unit. This little seed planted by the LMT began to grow. When the teacher mentioned to another teacher in the lunch room that day what the LMT was doing to help him prepare for his unit, that person showed up in the library media center soon afterward to plan a unit as well!

The results of the pre-searched topic list for the Renaissance unit appear in *Figure 4-3*. This made it much easier for the teacher to say to each student, "Sometime this week while you are finishing your art project, please select a topic from list A (or B, or C)." Without advertising students' ability levels, we knew that list A contained well-known artists with ample, readable information in a wide variety of sources, good for language- and learning-challenged students. List B had very adequate information in many sources for average students. List C was for advanced students who needed the extra challenge of digging for and thinking about information.

Fig. 4-3. LMT's Confirmed Topic List

Period ___ Topic List for Renaissance Artists

Directions:
1. Ask your teacher which list to pick from.
2. Put your initials beside the artist you pick.
3. Only two students per artist.
4. Try to pick someone you've never heard of!

A List

___ ___ Botticelli, Sandro
___ ___ da Vinci, Leonardo
___ ___ Donatello
___ ___ Michelangelo
___ ___ Raphael
___ ___ Titian

B List

___ ___ Alberti, Leon Battista
___ ___ Bellini, Giovanni
___ ___ Brueghel, Pieter, the Elder
___ ___ Caravaggio
___ ___ Correggio
___ ___ Dürer, Albrecht
___ ___ El Greco
___ ___ Fra Angelico
___ ___ Giorgione
___ ___ Giotto di Bondone
___ ___ Grünewald, Matthias
___ ___ Holbein, Hans, the Younger
___ ___ Mantegna, Andrea
___ ___ Masaccio
___ ___ Perugino, Pietro
___ ___ Tintoretto, Jacopo
___ ___ Uccello, Paolo
___ ___ van Eyck, Jan
___ ___ Venaziano, Domenico
___ ___ Verocchio, Andrea

C List

___ ___ Bosch, Hieronymus
___ ___ Brunelleschi, Filippo
___ ___ Carpaccio, Vittore
___ ___ Cellini, Benvenuto
___ ___ Cosimo, Piero di
___ ___ Crivelli, Carlo
___ ___ della Francesca, Piero
___ ___ della Robbia, Luca
___ ___ Francesca, Piero della
___ ___ Ghirlandaio, Domenico
___ ___ Lippi, Fra Filippo
___ ___ Masolino
___ ___ Messina, Antonella da
___ ___ Palladio, Andrea
___ ___ Pontormo, Jacopa da
___ ___ Veronese, Paolo

Empowering Topic Independence

Lifelong Skill

The Renaissance unit presented in this book does not encompass all of the variables the library media teacher and collaborating teacher may need to consider when selecting topics for a research unit. How to narrow or broaden a topic, for example, is not included in the student lesson script. This is an advanced research skill that is more effectively taught and learned when students require independent topic selection for special projects such as Science Fair or History Day. It's also important for eighth-graders preparing for high school.

A brief explanation of this process, shown in *Figure 4-4,* can easily be folded into the general topic lesson. To illustrate this example, the LMT can create overhead transparencies from encyclopedia pages about Italian art and the *Pieta* to show students exactly how they can narrow a large topic or broaden a small topic. In this way, students are taught to find, independently, a more perfect match between what they are interested in doing and what is practical, between unobtainable and obtainable information.

"But I really want to do that topic," a frustrated student will say after hunting everywhere for information.

"Why would you give yourself a test you couldn't take?" the LMT replies. "Let's just expand this topic and make it a subtopic of a bigger idea that's easier to find. What good is a topic that's not doable?"

Preparing for the First Day's Lesson

Middle school library media centers may not be physically large enough to accommodate more than one class at a time. However, if another class is scheduled to share the LMC during a collaborative research unit, prearrange teaching conditions with both teachers. First, it is important that the independent, self-monitoring teachers keep their classes quiet and on task, without the library media teacher's assistance. This is when good signage and pathfinders, discussed in Chapter 3, come into play. Second, whether sharing the LMC or not, the collaborative teaching partner must understand the importance of time, housekeeping, discipline, and making meaning.

Time

Getting to the library media center on time is not just courteous, it's essential. Whenever possible, arrange to have the class report directly to the LMC instead of their classroom.

Housekeeping

Arrange with the teacher to have classroom management activities such as attendance or collecting homework taken care of while students are being seated in the LMC. At the same time, pass out handouts for that day's research lesson.

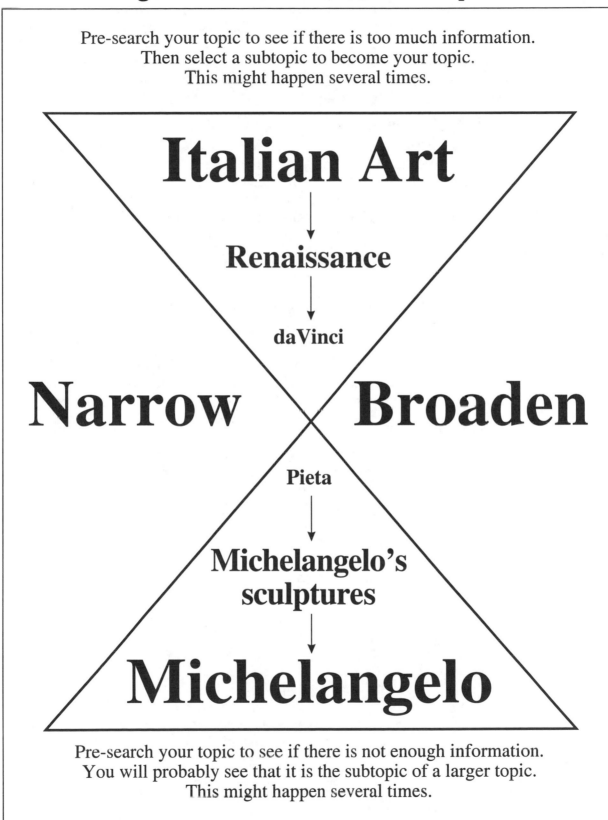

Fig. 4-4. Narrow or Broaden a Topic

Pre-search your topic to see if there is too much information.
Then select a subtopic to become your topic.
This might happen several times.

Italian Art

↓

Renaissance

↓

daVinci

Narrow

Broaden

Pieta

↓

Michelangelo's sculptures

↓

Michelangelo

Pre-search your topic to see if there is not enough information.
You will probably see that it is the subtopic of a larger topic.
This might happen several times.

Discipline

Important Idea

Introduce yourself to the students as the library media *teacher*. Remind them that the library media center is a classroom and that schoolwide rules apply. Funny looks on some students' faces will emphasize how critically important these lessons are for establishing the role of the LMT as an instructional faculty member. Remember to arrange special seating of students the teacher knows will be distracting. Tactfully remind the teacher not to leave the room.

Making Meaning

Lifelong Skill

The self-absorption of middle-schoolers is a cliché, but the fact is, they truly do not have a concept of "lifelong skills" that high schoolers begin to comprehend. It is simply lack of experience. Therefore, it is not always important to explain the Research Process sheet (*Figure 4-1*). I might put it on the overhead projector briefly during the first lesson of a new unit, but only to point out that research has steps.

In the following student lesson, an analogy is drawn between research steps and the steps required to get ready for school every morning. It is pointed out that if one of those steps is skipped, like putting on clothes (or makeup), forget it! Students won't be ready to face their friends. For students, relevance is built through direct association with an obvious task that is completed only through a series of steps. Without needing to understand the "big picture," namely, that information literacy prepares them for a complicated technological world, in an effective lesson kids can come away at least with the idea that research is easily accomplished if it is broken down into meaningful, bite-sized pieces.

One collaborating teacher commented, "I hate to teach research because I never really learned a good system myself." After only the first day's lesson from this series, another teacher commented, "Why wasn't I shown this in school? It's like riding a bicycle. The students will never forget it!"

Student Lesson

Getting Started

Timing: A few minutes.

Content-Area Standard

LMT: Welcome to the library media center. We're here to begin a unit for your art (or ELL) teacher, but it also ties in to what you're doing with your history teacher. Who can tell me what your class is studying?

Student: The Renaissance.

LMT: Yes, very good. I think you will really enjoy this unit because you will get to see and learn about many interesting people as well as see beautiful works of art. We're going to learn about art history through research, so let's look at the steps we'll be following in the next week or so. (Put *Figure 4-1* transparency on the overhead projector.) On this transparency, I mainly want you to clearly see that research has steps. (Take a moment at this point to quickly name each one.) Tackling a big research project without any guidance can be kind of like stuffing a whole pizza in your mouth. (Students look at each other and smile.) It's so overwhelming it gets gross. But if you cut the pizza into slices, then take bites, it's terrific! That's like the steps of research.

Student: Are you trying to tell us doing research will be terrific?

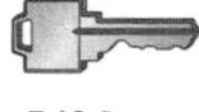
Lifelong Skill

LMT: Hmmm. . . . I may not go that far. I'll actually let you be the judge of that in about a week or so. I can make a promise that what we are about to do will make your school life a whole lot less painful. So, we are going to begin a research project and make each step into a bite-sized piece so that, hopefully, it will be very tasty. Maybe even make sense! Our goal is that at some point you will be doing these steps automatically, on your own. Whether you think so now or not, learning this is actually getting you ready for high school, even college.

At each research step, I may briefly call your attention back to this Research Process sheet. But for now, let's get started with the Research Checklist (*Figure 3-7*). This sheet is for *you* to guide yourself through the project we are starting today. Be sure to write your name, your teacher, and the class period at the top.

Making Meaning

Optional section, depending on time.

LMT: To give you an idea of what we're about to begin, let me ask you a funny question: What did you have to do to get to school today? Seriously, someone raise your hand and name one thing you had to do to be sitting right here, at this moment, in class. I'm going to write the important things you say here on this blank overhead transparency.

Student: Wake up! Not you, teacher. I mean me.

LMT: Looking around the room, I'm not so sure that's quite happened yet! But yes, that's a great start. (Begin the list in *Figure 4-5*.) Someone else?

Student: Catch the bus.

LMT: Are you still in your pajamas? Think of things in the order you do them. You've just gotten up. What's next?

Student: Shower.

Student: Get dressed.

Student: The girls slop makeup all over and fix their hair. That must take about an hour!

LMT: Okay, okay. You're doing fine. Anything else?

Student: Eat breakfast.

LMT: Whew! Brain food. I'm glad you said that. Fine, let me add that to our list and we'll stop there. Up here we have about six important things you had to do to get to school today:

Fig. 4-5. "Ready for School" Steps

Wake up

Shower

Get dressed

Do hair and makeup

Eat breakfast

Catch the bus

Problem Solving

LMT: Some days you spend more time on some steps than others, right? But if you leave any of these things out completely, you will not be in very good shape when you get to school. That is just like research. Look back at the Research Process sheet (*Figure 4-1*) We are here to learn about the steps it takes to accomplish a research project. Sometimes, when you come to the library media center with another teacher, we'll spend less time on some of the steps. But if we were to leave any one of them out completely, a research project could not be accomplished. So let's begin to break research down into such manageable bites that you'll say, "I can do this!" Remember:

How do you eat that giant pizza? One bite at a time.

Making Sense out of Topic Searching

Content-Area Standard

LMT: If you look at the top blank line on the Research Checklist sheet (*Figure 4-6* transparency), our first job today is for each of you to choose a topic. Before coming today you selected an artist from the Renaissance. I know some of you are saying to yourself, "I thought this class was about art, like drawing and painting. What am I doing here in the library?" Did you ever think that you will be a better artist if you understand what the art is about? Could you draw a house, for example, if you had never seen a house?

In the Renaissance, the art was much more complicated than a house. For the first time in history, Renaissance artists really tackled the problem of how to make that house look like it is going back into space. What's that called?

Student: A zone . . . ummm I mean, a dimension.

Problem Solving

LMT: Yes, good! The idea here is to take something flat, something two-dimensional, and make it appear three-dimensional. Let me show you. I'll change a square into a cube. (Draw a square on a clear transparency on the overhead and add lines to make it a cube.) We won't go into the art lesson today, but like the Renaissance artists, we have some problems your topic needs to solve. For example, what was the Renaissance, why was it so important, and who was involved in it? In school, how do you go about solving problems?

Student: With a calculator in math.

LMT: Yes, but here in the library media center?

Student: With books?

Information Literacy

LMT: And much more! Have you ever heard of the Information Age? (A few heads nod.) We're going to solve these problems with information, and that means it can come from many different kinds of places, as you'll see in the next few days. Before we begin to check our topics, someone quickly remind us, what is a topic?

Student: What my project is going to be about. That's obvious!

LMT: I'm really glad you said that. At each step of the Research Process, I hope you will say:

But that's obvious!

Lifelong Skills

LMT: When you can say that, it means that a step makes sense to you, and if it makes sense, you will be able to do it later on your own. That is our goal: to learn how to do research completely on your own, so you will be well prepared to handle the flood of information you will encounter in high school. Meanwhile, I know you signed up for a Renaissance artist last week during class.

Student: I know. I never even heard of this guy before!

LMT: So how do you know if it's a good topic for you? Any ideas?

Student: If I like his art work?

LMT: That's a good thought. But what if the art kind of all looks alike to you? What else is important for research, right here in the LMC?

Student: I guess if there's enough information.

Important Idea

LMT: Now you've got it! The key to whether a topic is good is information! Remember I just said you'll need a variety of sources? That means today you need to look for your topic in at least two, and hopefully three, places to confirm if there's enough information. You could have a topic idea you love, but what good will it be if you look around and there's absolutely no information? Here's another way to make my point. How many of you like to take tests?

Student: Oh, you've got to be kidding!

LMT: Exactly! No one does. Especially a really hard test. Well, giving yourself a topic that has no information is like giving yourself a test that's too hard to take! Why would you do that? But any topic will be good, whether you've heard of it or not, if there is enough information about it that you can actually read and understand. So let's take about 20 minutes now for an activity where you will each hunt up as many as three sources here in the library where you can find information about the artist you picked.

Student Activity

Timing: 20 minutes.

Literacy

LMT: Let me tell you how to begin today's activity. Do you see this cart of books? (Make eye contact to spot-check for direction following.) To save us some time, I have pulled out all of the library media center's books, and even some references, about the Renaissance. We're going to take about 20 minutes, and here is what I want you to accomplish in that time:

Fig. 4-6. Research Checklist: Topic

LMT/Teacher Tracking: **Date Due:/Points:**

	Date Due	Points
Topic *Michelangelo*	*10/31*	*5*
Subtopics ○ ________ ○ ________ ○ ________ ○ ________ ○ ________		
Sources A. At least 3 formats. Circle choices: Book, reference, CD-ROM, Internet, other: ________ B. Total number of sources: ________		
Read/Think/Select A. A "chunk" is ________		
Notetake A. At least ___ notes for each subtopic. B. Total number of notes: ________		
Sort and number notes		
Write rough draft from notes		
Teacher Grading: Title Page		
Typed Report		
Final Citation List		
Image/Chart		

Using the table of contents and the index of a book (hold up a book and point out those sections), search until you find your artist. I call this "pre-search" because it comes before research! The Research Process sheet said a great place to get good topic ideas is out of a textbook, but because art doesn't have a text, we'll use library books. See, that's a strategy: Use textbooks or library books to get topic ideas or to make sure your topic works.

The next place I want you to look is in an encyclopedia. Find the volume for the last name of your artist and look him or her up. An easier way is to use the index for the whole set. If you find your topic in this second place, that means it's getting better. Why? More information!

Technology Proficiency

Finally, if you still have time, quickly sit down at a computer and look up your artist in one of the CD-ROM electronic encyclopedias. Don't print anything out today. Just quickly check to see if the person is there. Do you see what strategy you are using? The more places you find your artist, the more information there is for your report.

When I call "time," return to your seat. If you have located your topic in at least two places, and preferably three, then write it on the topic line of the Research Checklist sheet. You have successfully confirmed your topic!

ELL/Special Modifications

For those of you who have difficulty, come see me. Your teacher and I will assist you in deciding on a topic that will work for you. That is what today is all about. It's perfectly okay to switch your topic depending on how much information you find, and whether you can read it!

Finally, before you go running off, someone remind us, how are you going to know if your topic is any good? I'll give you a hint, it has to do with a direction I just gave you. Will it be good just because you've heard of the artist before, like Michelangelo or Donatello?

Student: Yeah, I always thought Donatello was a turtle!

Student: Whether or not I can find anything about it.

LMT: Good!

Accountability

LMT: Let's get started. Meet me back in your seats in 20 minutes. If your topic works, write it on the topic line at the top of your Research Checklist. I'm going to be checking you off on a tracking sheet each day to be sure every one of you completes every step. And by the way, bring your encyclopedia back with you to your seat. You'll see why in a few minutes.

Chapter 5

Developing Subtopics: Lesson 1, Part 2

Instructor Information

Student Lesson

"Can I add another subtopic? Please? I know I'll have time after school to get some more notes."

—Seventh-grader

Fig. 5-1. Research Process: Subtopics

Topic *A good topic is "doable," but slightly challenging to your assessed abilities.*

A. Locate a topic in textbooks, library sources, or the teacher's topic list.
B. Check in the library media center for at least three formats of supporting information.
C. Cross-check in an encyclopedia to narrow or broaden a topic.

Subtopics *Ask yourself: What do I want to know about my topic?*

A. General subtopics may be brainstormed. Examples:
   Person: early life, education, work (be specific), later life.
   Place: origin, history, leaders, geography, economy.
   Thing: who, what, when, where, why/how.
B. Specific subtopics must be located in, for example, an encyclopedia's subheads.
C. The number of subtopics is based on the number of days of research.

Sources *A good source is any kind of supporting information that you can read.*

A. Format (the form information comes in) Examples include:
   Print: books, encyclopedias, magazines, newspapers.
   Nonprint: videos, laser disks, CD-ROMs, computer software, Internet.
B. Use at least three formats of information. Using one source is not research!
C. Credit sources using MLA-style citations.

Read/Think/Select *Good research promotes comprehension and evaluation.*

A. Read an entire "chunk" (a paragraph or a page) with your pencil down.
B. Think about what was read. What was important?
C. Select only a few key facts from each "chunk" to match your subtopics.

Notetake *A good note creates information ownership. This is learning!*

A. One note per card, titled with subtopic. Use as many cards as needed.
B. Record important keywords, facts, or a list, up to about 20 words (use your judgment).
C. No small words like *a*, *the*, *an*, *is*, *was*. Instead use commas and dashes.
D. No copying of sentences (without quotation marks and footnotes).

Sort and Number Notes *Good organization of notes makes writing easier.*

A. Sort notes by subtopic section, about five notes per paragraph (use your judgment).
B. Read notes in one section at a time and put in an order that makes sense.
C. Number notes consecutively through all sections without starting over at number 1.

Extension

Write/Publish/Present
Final citations list
Technology integration

Evaluation Student tracking

Chapter Concepts

Why Subtopics Are Essential

"If you don't have subtopics, you have no idea what you're doing!" is the statement you'll see in the student lesson script. This concept cannot be too strongly stressed. Subtopics are the frame, the filter, the guide, the evaluative criteria for the information search. They tell the student what to look for in every source and, just as important, what to skip.

What Do You Want to Know?

"What do you want to know about your topic?" is the essential question that directs students to "pre-search" subtopics before they can "re-search" for supporting information. Pre-searching is a cursory, evaluative step that is mandatory to determine if there is enough available, readable information to warrant the more in-depth research needed for reading, evaluating, and notetaking about a topic.

Developing Subtopics

General subtopics can be brainstormed. Specific ones must be located in sources. For example, they may arise from bold subheadings in encyclopedias or from chapter titles in the table of contents of books about the topic. Time for hands-on research is a critical factor for the LMT and collaborating teacher in setting the number of subtopics that can be accomplished successfully by average students. The form subtopics takes is based on practical usage.

Matching Subtopics to Student Needs

The number of subtopics is a key factor in matching the topic to the student. Advanced students have more subtopics; special needs students have fewer. In this way, the literacy and learning needs of all students are met in a simple and highly appropriate way. The success of every student as measured by improved achievement is real.

Instructor Information

Why Subtopics Are Essential

Teachers have always understood subtopics in the context of an outline. They condense, elucidate, and clarify main ideas. But they have always come from the text or context. An outline is usually thought of as "after the fact." Therefore, subtopics may not have been seen as a technique to outline for information not yet gathered. Identifying subtopics as a strategy for gathering information seems to be the "missing link" of general research. In the Research Process, subtopics become the guide to gathering, as well as analyzing, information. This point cannot be emphasized enough!

Important Idea

What Do You Want to Know?

The absolutely essential question in any research endeavor is: What do you want to know about your topic? The answer lies, first, in successfully identifying subtopics and, second, in matching information to them. If one reason students plagiarize is that they are overwhelmed with information that is of no greater or lesser value, then with subtopics as identifying tools, pertinent information in any kind of source is much more easily identified and, later, sorted.

Developing Subtopics

Problem: How can students develop subtopics for unknown information?

Solution: They are not expected to! At least not without specific strategies.

General

For less-experienced students, general subtopics are "created" through group discussion. For example, in the following lesson script, student discussion "yields" three general subtopics. Actually, these subtopics were pre-decided by the teacher and LMT during collaborative planning.

Specific

For experienced researchers, specific subtopics are located in a "pre-search" for topic-supporting information. Students must be given the time to locate subtopic ideas, and they must be taught specific strategies such as checking the subheadings in encyclopedias and the chapter titles in a nonfiction book's table of contents. The presence of subtopics in a variety of sources signals the existence of plenty of supporting information.

How many subtopics are enough, or too much? The three subtopics in the Renaissance unit modeled in this book were determined mainly by time: The teacher's schedule allowed for only three days of hands-on research. Other contributing factors included the learning (dis)abilities of the students, their prior research experience, and the availability of a variety of readable sources.

What form do subtopics take? As recorded on the Research Checklist (*Figure 5-2*), they are the keyword(s) taken from the essential questions the student wants the research to answer. Or vice versa: They become the roots for flexible guide questions to locate information. This hints at the nature of research: It is problem solving.

Subtopics should answer the following questions:

- What sources do I **access** to locate topic information?
- How do I **evaluate** information to select notes?
- How do I **use** notes to write?

Matching Subtopics to Student Needs

ELL/Special Modifications

Whether general or specific, subtopics become the outline of the entire research project, the "dry bones" that are "fleshed out" with knowing what to read and notetake and what information to skip. With subtopics, suddenly the project is not nearly as threatening, which is especially helpful to learning-challenged students. This key strategy of information management enables students to see clearly what they're supposed to do. The increase in efficient, on-task use of hands-on research time in the library media center is a remarkable sight to see!

Determining Sources

Literacy

Technology Proficiency

It is remiss not to point out a chicken-or-the-egg situation. Subtopics can be used to check sources for supporting information, but sources can themselves be a key for developing subtopics. In a quick check of a variety of sources, including books, references, CD-ROMs, and the Internet, the LMT can confirm whether general or specific subtopics are more appropriate to a unit. General subtopics were used for the Renaissance unit in this book mostly because all students had an artist as a topic, but also because the number and variety of sources was limited. Students had to share the few Renaissance books from the tiny school library collection, and their subtopics would have all been the same anyway.

If the students had been better readers, or more mature and experienced with research, we could have initially created an entirely different type of project where students would have had greater topic and subtopic independence. This is the beauty of collaborative planning: complete control of the nature of the project to enhance, even guarantee, student success.

Determining Appropriate Topics

Teachers have enough to do! Wouldn't they be happy if students themselves had a strategy for locating appropriate unit (standards-based) topics? "Appropriate" means topics that have enough readable and available information in a variety of sources on campus. "Enough" information means the topic can be broken down into information-rich subtopics. Subtopics determine whether there is enough appropriate information to pursue a topic meaningfully.

I'll never forget the year I gave "Space Medicine" as the topic for a health term paper to a sixth-grader! Did I bother to go to our little school library to see if that topic had supporting information? No one ever told me I should do that! Meanwhile, this poor student's exasperated parents spent many nights in the local college library trying, with great difficulty, to access information in periodicals and such. This child could barely read his sixth-grade text, much less manage college-level information. You can guess who really did that project.

This was a completely irresponsible act on my part as a teacher. I did not do my homework to properly prepare a topic list and then match information availability to student ability. But then, there were no library media teachers at that time!"

Narrowing or Broadening Topics

When subtopics are used to identify the availability of readable information, it is obvious when there is too much or too little. A beloved topic that has only a few paragraphs of supporting information should become the subtopic of a larger concept. The subtopic should become the topic when information is obviously too abundant. Students pre-search with subtopics to determine whether a topic should be narrowed or broadened. This is a critical thinking decision they learn to make more easily with guided practice.

Determining Availability of Topics

If choice of topic is a key factor in a student's success in research, then a topic without enough supporting information should not be made available to inexperienced researchers. To accomplish this, the LMT can use the subtopics selected during collaborative planning to pre-search the teacher's topic list. Without spending an inordinate amount of time, a quick search can reveal which topics do not have enough readable information in LMC sources. Toss those out and substitute substantiated ones, or group them by student ability. The LMT should point out that not all subtopics are found in every source, which is why many sources are used. When students are given time to pre-search for subtopics, the availability of information can produce interesting results. Some students gain confidence in their topic by discovering an abundance of information. Some students find very little subtopic information, become frustrated, and ask the teacher if they can change their topic. The point is: Allow that to happen! That's the power of subtopics as a frame for independent information management.

ELL/Special Modifications

The Research Checklist

Important Idea

The Research Checklist sheet (*Figure 5-2*) is a template created so that students have clear expectations about each step of the research project. It's not a "gotcha" for the teacher. This sheet empowers students!

A research project appears to be a teacher-invented, teacher-required, teacher-controlled, teacher-graded activity. The Research Checklist is an indicator that the whole purpose of these research lessons is to give control of information back to students. It is their choice of topic, their choice of subtopics, their choice of sources, their ability to read and comprehend, and their choice of facts that go into their creation of a great project.

The Research Checklist reflects the question posed to students in the subtopic lesson: "What do I want to know about my topic?" Although predetermined by the LMT and collaborating teachers in planning the Renaissance unit, students "decided" that they wanted to know about the artist's life and art and about the Renaissance in general. Further discussion directed them to circle *life*, *art*, and *Renaissance* as keywords pulled from the essential research questions.

The reason this was done is simplification. The LMT explained to the students that in the next few days, these subtopics would become the titles of their note cards and that it would be too tedious to record a long question over and over again. The idea being reinforced throughout all of the Research Process lessons is to make things "doable." Students are guided to create logical shortcuts that make information management simple and practical. The alternative is being overwhelmed, perhaps resulting in, unfortunately, plagiarism!

It is important for students to record their subtopics on the Research Checklist sheet during the lesson. The reason is definition of purpose: If you can say it, you can do it! It brings to a conscious level for the students their course of action. This works just as well for the instructors, who can readily monitor the checklist to see if each student is prepared to proceed to the next research step. "I must see your topic and subtopics recorded or you cannot go on" is the clear direction given by the LMT on this very first day.

Instructional Strategies

Relevance

A first strategy that is effective to make meaning for middle-schoolers is to tell a story they can relate to. *Figure 5-3* is a very generic story to tell, which, time permitting, introduces students to the concept of subtopics. I have told this same story in elementary, middle, and high schools. It always seems to work!

Important Idea

Fig. 5-2. Research Checklist: Subtopics

LMT/Teacher Tracking: **Date Due:/Points:**

Topic *Michelangelo* | 10/31 | 5

Subtopics | 10/31 | 5

○ *What was his personal (life) like?*

○ *What was his (art) like?*

○ *What was the (Renaissance) ?*

○ ____________

○ ____________

Sources

A. At least 3 formats. Circle choices:
Book, reference, CD-ROM, Internet, other: ____________

B. Total number of sources: ____________

Read/Think/Select

A. A "chunk" is ____________

Notetake

A. At least ___ notes for each subtopic.

B. Total number of notes: ____________

Sort and number notes

Write rough draft from notes

Teacher Grading: Title Page
Typed Report
Final Citation List
Image/Chart

Fig. 5-3. Subtopic Story

To best illustrate the importance of subtopics, I tell this dinosaur story.

Several years ago, when I was a library media teacher in an elementary school, a little boy came walking into the library media center and said, "I have to write a report about dinosaurs."

Do you have any idea how big that topic is? HUGE! Do you know how many kinds of dinosaurs there are? How many millions of years they lived on this planet?"

I didn't want to tell the little boy we could be here for the next 20 years, so I asked him, "But what do you want to know about dinosaurs?"

What I was really asking him to do was identify subtopics, so I said, "Maybe you'd like to know what a dinosaur looked like—its body."

"Yes!" he said, "I sure would!"

"Maybe you'd like to know what food it eats."

"Of course, I do need to know that," he said.

"How about where it lives—its habitat?"

"Oh man, yeah. My teacher said to include that too."

"Can you think of anything else you'd be interested to know about your dinosaur? What its babies were like, or its enemies?"

By this time a light bulb had gone off in the little boy's head. He realized that he had five things to look for about dinosaurs. When he opened a book he said, "Hey, here's something about its food!" And he took "food" notes. He opened an encyclopedia and said, "Wow, here's some information about where it lives." And he took "habitat" notes. He continued looking on a CD-ROM, and he took notes on "body," "enemies," and "babies."

The point is: If you do not select subtopics, you have no idea what you are doing in the library! You will be confused, frustrated, and likely end up copying a lot of stuff from books or printouts.

Once you have subtopics, you know how to manage information. By titling your notebook page notes or note cards with a subtopic, you instantly presort everything you find. Best of all, you know what you are looking for, and you know what to skip! This enables you to manage time as well as information.

Exaggeration

A second effective instructional tool, as indicated parenthetically in the student lesson script, is the use of verbal hyperbole and dramatic gestures to dramatically emphasize to students how important subtopics are as a strategy for managing information:

> *"For this project, or any research project you ever do for any teacher or any subject for the rest of your life, you cannot continue on in your research until you have recorded subtopics. Subtopics are the keywords to the essential questions about your topic that your research will answer, thereby equipping you with lifelong strategies for managing information."*

Extension Lesson for Advanced Students

Lifelong Skill

An optional instructional section has been added to cover projects where more advanced students have specific subtopics. The goal is greater independence in information management. In that lesson, a different set of directions is given to complete the Research Checklist:

Select: Subtopics are flexible! They determine what information to look for in a source but can also be subject to that information. "Whose paper is this?" I ask the class to empower them to control information by selecting, adding, changing, combining, or eliminating subtopics.

Record: Subtopics should be recorded in pencil to indicate, almost symbolically, that students have control over their information.

Quantity: The minimum number of subtopics is set by the teacher. With teacher approval, the student can choose to exceed that number, allowing for the additional time it takes to meet the notetaking requirements.

At the end of this first lesson, the LMT can have advanced students record on their checklists the total number of sources and notes that are expected for the entire project, because they often have the research skills to pace themselves or to work ahead. But like all students, they are still accountable for the smaller, daily goals. When given small steps that are readily accomplished, advanced students often exceed requirements. The result can be greater mastery not only of the LMT's information literacy goals but also of the content-area curriculum.

Due Dates

The teacher's project syllabus usually sets dates for students to complete the parts of a final product. This is always different from the due dates for the steps of research on the Research Checklist sheet, which is actually a tracking of the information management process. This concept of creating a definite, but reasonable, timetable for tracking each research step is critical to student success.

Looking Ahead at Accountability

Student accountability for developing those critical subtopics not only appears on the Research Checklist but is also a component of the tracking sheet developed by the LMT and collaborating teacher during the initial planning stage. A carefully tailored tool makes it easy to track each student for each step of research while yielding very accurate data to augment the teacher's grading criteria. In looking ahead at the student Research Tracking sheet in Chapter 12 (*Figure 12-1*), the number of subtopics can be exactly recorded: three for Jane (average), two for John (special education), and five for Susie (gifted). Some teachers prefer a simpler system of plus, check mark, or minus signs. Whatever the method, it's the tracking that's important. I know from experience that it is amazing how the quantity (and quality) of work increases when students are tracked in exact amounts. Still focusing on the product required for their own content area, some teachers choose not to track the Research Process at all. When this issue arises during collaborative planning, I often ask that teacher if I can track the research steps anyway simply as a way of keeping students on task. Once the teacher sees the difference tracking makes in student outcome, the LMT has often won another convert to focusing on the process of information management.

Student Lesson

Timing: 25 minutes.

Why Subtopics Are Essential

LMT: Put your Research Checklist sheet (*Figure 5-2*) back in front of you and look at the section called "Subtopics." Yesterday you confirmed your topic, so our job today is to fill in the blank spaces here. Would you believe me if I told you that locating your topic is not the most important thing in getting started on your research?

Student: But how can I start if I don't know what I'm doing?

LMT: I want you to begin to understand that no matter what your topic is, there are some simple ways, called strategies, to go about looking for information. The most important strategy is to develop subtopics that enable you to sift through the mountains of information, keeping the important facts and ideas and tossing out the rest. Once you learn strategies for finding and using subtopics, you can use them with the topic you have for this project and with every other topic any teacher asks you to do in high school and in college. In other words, these are called lifelong skills because once you learn them, you will be able to use them forever.

Lifelong Skill

What Do You Want to Know?

LMT: No matter what your topic is, you need to ask this question:

What do I want to know about my topic?

Student: But I don't know anything about a Renaissance artist! How can I even think of what I want to know?

LMT: I am really glad that you expressed that feeling of frustration. Isn't that what some of you feel whenever your teacher tells you to go off and do a big research project? I promise you that if you begin to understand and use subtopics, that feeling of being overwhelmed will start to go away. Let's see how this can happen. First, the answer to the question, "What do I want to know about my topic?" will be your subtopics. They are absolutely the keys to unlocking the doors of information. I will go so far as to say that if you don't have subtopics, you have absolutely no idea what you are doing! To give you an example, listen to this true story (read *Figure 5-3*).

Developing Subtopics

LMT: So let's figure out how to do research by thinking of some subtopics for our Renaissance artists. All of us have the same kind of topic—a person—so we'll do this by just jumping in and brainstorming some ideas: What do you want to know about your artist? Anyone have an idea?

Student: Where was he born?

LMT: Yes, that's a good place to start. Everyone needs to find that out. But think about this: For each subtopic you will need to find at least ten notes. If your suggestion has a one-word answer, that will be only one fact to record as a note later on. That's not enough. In trying to figure out what is a subtopic, we've just hinted at an answer: A subtopic is big enough to take lots of notes about. Does that make sense? Can anyone help us make "Where was he born?" into a bigger idea?

Student: You wouldn't say habitat, like for an animal.

LMT: No, but you're really thinking! Let's make it really big. Actually, don't you want to learn everything about his life, more than just where he was born? Can anyone help us form this into a research question that searching and reading will solve?

Student: What was the artist's whole life like?

LMT: Very good. "Whole life" would be his personal life, right? So let's record "What was his personal life like?" on the first line space on your Research Checklist sheet (*Figure 5-2*) under "Subtopics." (Write on an overhead transparency as students copy.)

A research question guides you to information, that's great. But what's not so great is it's too long to keep repeating later in your notetaking. We can simplify this question into a subtopic. This hints at the second thing a subtopic is—very simple. It's just a word or two, like a title. So let's circle just the word "life." (Circle "life" as seen in *Figure 5-2*.) Later, when you start taking notes, you will see that this is like giving yourself a shortcut code to make research less complicated. Does that make sense?

I am confident this first subtopic will work for everyone even though some of your artists have a lot of personal information.

Unfortunately, some of your artists were not as well known, even during the Renaissance. Remember that we said that a topic is good if it has lots of information?

Student: Yeah, but does that mean some of us are stuck with rotten topics?

LMT: That's actually a very appropriate question. The answer can again be found in your subtopics. Based on what we just said about topics, what do you think makes a good subtopic?

Student: I guess it would also be the amount of information about it.

Important Idea

LMT: Yes, exactly. So if we pick a very broad and general subtopic like the whole personal life of the artist, then all of you should be able to find enough information in the different kinds of sources we will be using. Because your research time is limited, turn the Research Checklist sheet over to the back and let's list some of the things the artist's personal life would include, so you'll have a very clear idea of what information this subtopic should include. What would you like to know about your artist's personal life? (Time permitting, you can solicit student ideas and record them on a blank overhead transparency; see *Figure 5-4*.)

ELL/Special Modifications

Literacy

LMT: Do you have to find all of these things? No! An artist like Michelangelo will have more information than you can handle, and that's where subtopic guidelines will help you know what to skip. On the other hand, very little is either known or written about an artist like Antonio del Pollaiuolo, and that's where subtopics will guide you to those important facts. Remember, the more sources you look in, the more information you will find! We'll be talking more about that tomorrow when we cover sources of information. Meanwhile, turn your checklist back over to the front and let's continue brainstorming another subtopic. Any ideas besides his life? Think BIG!

Fig. 5-4. What Was the Artist's Personal Life Like?

- Dates of birth and death
- City and country of birth and death
- Special training (apprenticeship during the Renaissance)
- Childhood or adult family
- Notable events in his or her life

Student: Ummm, what he was, like, famous for?

LMT: Great! The important research question you're talking about is what the artist's artwork was like to make him so famous. So on the second line space let's make that into a research question: "What was his artwork like?" Again, let's turn this question into a simple subtopic by circling just the word "work." (Model this on the Research Checklist overhead transparency, *Figure 5-2*.) Turn your checklist over to the back, and I'll give you some requirements your teacher and I decided you need to learn about your artist's work. (Record the following items on a transparency; see *Figure 5-5*.)

Fig. 5-5. What Was the Artist's Artwork Like?

- Write the name and date of three works of art by your artist.
- Using the seven "Elements of Art" learned in art class, described each of the three pieces.

LMT: I believe there is one more really big and really important thing about your artist that we have not covered yet. Any ideas? Why are you here?

Content-Area Standard

Student: Oh yeah, to learn about the Renaissance.

LMT: That's it! That's the last important thing that answers "What do you want to know about your artist?" Let's record a last research question about the Renaissance in the third line space. What can we say?

Student: Well, the simplest thing is "What was the Renaissance?"

LMT: Perfect. I'll write it here in the third line space under "Subtopics" on the overhead, and you copy it onto your paper. You can probably easily guess what to circle to make the subtopic. Yes, just the word "Renaissance." (Again, model circling the subtopic on the overhead transparency.) Once again, here are some guidelines for your research. (Add ideas on a transparency while students write; see *Figure 5-6*.)

Fig. 5-6. What Was the Renaissance?

- When did it happen?
- Where did it happen?
- Why was it important?
- What influence did your artist have on this time period and vice versa?

Using Subtopics to Evaluate Information

Optional, depending on time.

LMT: Let me ask you this question: Why do kids copy?

Student: It's easy. And quick!

Student: I put down everything that looks good to me.

LMT: Yes! That's an important point. Everything looks good to you, so you begin to copy. In other words, without subtopics, you have no way to pick and choose information. I'm convinced that another important reason that kids copy, besides the good ones you just mentioned, is that they're either overwhelmed or confused. Subtopics eliminate confusion by allowing you to identify exactly the information you have said is important about your topic. These days, with so much information available, the best news is that subtopics also tell you what is not important to your topic. When you encounter information that is not one of your subtopics, guess what you get to do?

Problem Solving

Student: Skip it!

LMT: Are things beginning to look a little less confusing? Do you see that subtopics are the critical way to begin managing information about each one of your topics?

Matching Subtopics to Students

This extension lesson is for advanced students who have independent topics.

LMT: By this time of year, most of you have been through the Research Process here in the library media center with different subject-area teachers. You are ready for independent research. Some of you have great topic ideas for the Renaissance already in mind from your classroom discussions. Some of you still have no idea. To save time, we are going to combine two steps. At the same time that you are confirming a good topic by locating it in several sources, both printed and electronic, you can be locating and recording good subtopics.

Lifelong Skills

Technology Proficiency

Let's review: There are two ways you can come up with subtopics. You can think of them yourself or get them from somewhere. It's that simple! The Research Process lists two kinds of subtopics, either general or specific. General subtopics can come out of your head by just thinking of them. For example, do you remember studying an animal back in elementary school? (Refer to the dinosaur story, *Figure 5-3*.) The teacher might have asked you, "What do you want to learn about an animal?" You and your classmates probably thought of easy, general ideas out of your heads such as "I want to learn about its body, its food, its habitat, or maybe its enemies." Then, when you read something about food, you simply wrote down a food note.

Now that you're older, the information is harder to read and understand, and topics are often unfamiliar. So if you want to use a general subtopic, I suggest using the very reliable who, what, when, where, why, how strategy that's on your Research Process sheet (*Figure 5-1*). You could search for information about *who* was involved with your Renaissance topic, *when* it happened, *where* it happened, and *why* or *how* it happened. This always works, and you don't have to take the time before research to hunt for subtopics. However, it may take a little longer during research to locate information because these general subtopics are not labeled as subheadings in sources. You have to read and evaluate information more carefully.

Perhaps a simpler approach for your individual topics is to locate specific subtopics in two or three sources. The information itself actually tells you what subtopics are good because you can clearly see there is enough supporting information. But this might take some time. It's called "pre-searching." Pre-search means to explore sources to locate subtopics already written there. Then you know exactly what sources to use and, best of all, it's easy to tell what to skip.

Literacy

You're experienced enough in research to pre-search your individual Renaissance topics. I recommend that you begin with an encyclopedia. For example, I have the "M" volume and I'll open it up to Michelangelo. (Demonstrate.) Did you know that for longer articles like this one, an encyclopedia is written with bold subheadings? Let me hold this up and walk around so you can see. Some of them would make great subtopics. (Turn pages and read some examples.)

Technology Proficiency

You will be required to have three subtopics for this project. But don't just take all of them straight from this source without comparing them to subtopics in other sources. For example, another place you'll want to look is a CD-ROM encyclopedia because it is also usually divided into subsections. Let's look at an overhead transparency from a CD-ROM encyclopedia. You can see this is also divided into bold subheadings. Some of them are similar to the printed encyclopedia, but some are much more specific than what you might really choose to use. (Show a transparency of a page from a CD-ROM encyclopedia.)

A third place to cross-check for subtopics is the table of contents of a book, such as this one about Michelangelo. As I read a few of the chapter headings, you can hear ideas for subtopics. Let's do a quick check for what you've learned. Someone raise your hand and tell me how you would know whether a chapter heading is a good subtopic.

Student: If you saw that same idea in the encyclopedia and in the CD-ROM.

LMT: And what is the advantage in knowing that same subtopic idea is in all three sources?

Student: Because then there is information about that subtopic in all those places that I can use for my research. So it's a great subtopic!

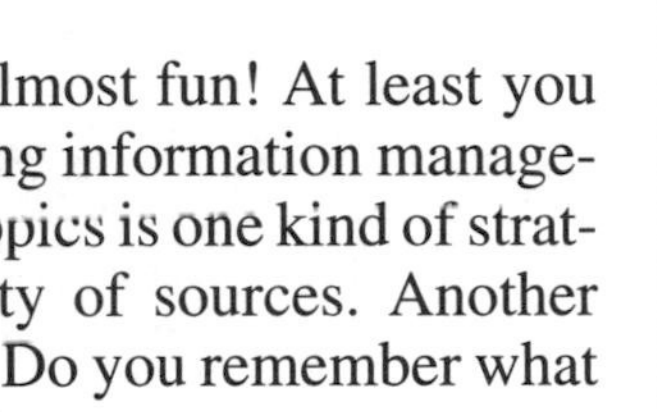

Lifelong Skills

LMT: Exactly! Doesn't that make sense? This is almost fun! At least you can see that research has clear steps for making information management easier. Knowing where to look for subtopics is one kind of strategy. You always need to check in a variety of sources. Another strategy is knowing how to select a subtopic. Do you remember what we said makes a topic or a subtopic "good"?

Student: The amount of information.

LMT: With that in mind, do you think you'd give yourself a subtopic that may not exist? But even after all you've learned, it happens! I'll give you an example.

A student came in here just yesterday. He said, "Teacher, I can only find three facts about how tobacco grows, and I need ten for each subtopic in my science report."

"Then why did you picks 'grows' as a subtopic?" I asked him. "Did you look through an encyclopedia for some bold subheadings for subtopic ideas?"

"No," he said. "I just thought of them at home."

"That's the same as giving yourself a test you can't possibly take," I replied. "Don't your teachers give you enough hard work? Why would you give yourself something that is impossible to do when you could find subtopics that have plenty of information in a few minutes here in the library?"

"Oh, yeah," he said. "Can I get the encyclopedia and find a different subtopic?"

"Whose project is this?" I asked.

LMT: What would have made that student's life a little easier?

Student: Yeah, yeah, spend a few minutes in the library.

LMT: Right! Do you begin to see the benefits of taking a little time to do pre-searching? It will really pay off later in saving time and making research easier.

The last thing we need to cover is the number of subtopics you are to select. If the choice of subtopics controls your information by telling you exactly what to look for and what to skip, then the number of subtopics lets you control how much information you can gather. Do you remember how many days your class spent on research the last time you were in here for a research project?

Student: My science fair class spent five days.

LMT: Okay. Do you remember how many subtopics we required you to have for that project?

Student: We needed five.

LMT: Get it? Does anyone see a comparison with this project?

Student: If we did five subtopics and had five days of research, does that mean that if we had three subtopics, we get three days of research?

The number of subtopics is an important strategy directly related to time spent on a unit. From experience, I encourage teachers to base the number of subtopics on how many days the class can come to the library to do research after the initial three days of lessons are finished. For five subtopics, five days of research is completely reasonable. Students who work quickly can increase the number of subtopics. Students who work slowly, or are absent, will decrease subtopics or work independently to catch up.

LMT: That's right. The number of days of research planned by your teacher determines the number of subtopics as well as the number of sources you'd reasonably have time to use.

Student: Will three days be enough?

Student: Can I do more than three subtopics?

LMT: Yes and yes! In three days you'll have plenty of time to do what's expected. You can always do more if you have time, but come see either me or your teacher for approval. We have our subtopics covered, so let's take the rest of the period to find them. Remember to record them on your checklist in pencil. Who knows why?

Student: Because we are allowed to change them during our research.

Accountability

LMT: I think we've done it! The last step each day is to assess what we've accomplished. At each research step, you can check yourself off on the Research Checklist sheet (*Figure 5-2*). In the box to the right of "Topic" put today's date and a big check mark beside it to show that you've all confirmed and recorded an artist for your topic. Next, put today's date and a big check mark in the box to the right of "Subtopics." You've all recorded three search questions and simplified them into subtopics.

Besides your own checklist, I will also be checking you off on a "Student Tracking" sheet so that I can track you every day of research and know exactly what you have, or have not, completed. (On the overhead, place a blank sample of a tracking sheet, *Figure 12-1*.)

Daily tracking tells me who has fallen behind or who needs extra help. It is just as important to me that you understand and complete each step of the research process as it is to have a wonderful final report. Tracking you also helps your teacher in grading the final project.

When you come in tomorrow we will go to the next step of research, the sources you will use to find information to match your subtopics. On your way to your seat tomorrow, please get an encyclopedia with the volume letter of your artist's last name. Sit together if you need to share. Can you remember to do that? Good. You did a great job today!

Chapter 6

Looking at Sources: Lesson 2

Instructor Information

Student Lesson

"I'll make you a Filamentality web site for easy access for your students to some great Internet sources for our collaborative unit."

—LMT

Fig. 6-1. Research Process: Sources

Topic *A good topic is "doable," but slightly challenging to your assessed abilities.*

A. Locate a topic in textbooks, library sources, or the teacher's topic list.
B. Check in the library media center for at least three formats of supporting information.
C. Cross-check in an encyclopedia to narrow or broaden a topic.

Subtopics *Ask yourself: What do I want to know about my topic?*

A. General subtopics may be brainstormed. Examples:
    Person: early life, education, work (be specific), later life.
    Place: origin, history, leaders, geography, economy.
    Thing: who, what, when, where, why/how.
B. Specific subtopics must be located in, for example, an encyclopedia's subheads.
C. The number of subtopics is based on the number of days of research.

Sources *A good source is any kind of supporting information that you can read.*

A. Format (the form information comes in) Examples include:
    Print: books, encyclopedias, magazines, newspapers.
    Nonprint: videos, laser disks, CD-ROMs, computer software, Internet.
B. Use at least three formats of information. Using one source is not research!
C. Credit sources using MLA-style citations.

Read/Think/Select *Good research promotes comprehension and evaluation.*

A. Read an entire "chunk" (a paragraph or a page) with your pencil down.
B. Think about what was read. What was important?
C. Select only a few key facts from each "chunk" to match your subtopics.

Notetake *A good note creates information ownership. This is learning!*

A. One note per card, titled with subtopic. Use as many cards as needed.
B. Record important keywords, facts, or a list, up to about 20 words (use your judgment).
C. No small words like *a*, *the*, *an*, *is*, *was*. Instead use commas and dashes.
D. No copying of sentences (without quotation marks and footnotes).

Sort and Number Notes *Good organization of notes makes writing easier.*

A. Sort notes by subtopic section, about five notes per paragraph (use your judgment).
B. Read notes in one section at a time and put in an order that makes sense.
C. Number notes consecutively through all sections without starting over at number 1.

Extension

Write/Publish/Present
Final citations list
Technology integration

Evaluation Student tracking

Chapter Concepts

Copyright and Citations

Copyright includes the legal conditions under which information can and cannot be used. Student understanding of the legal implications is critical to information management and use. Not just crediting sources, but crediting them correctly using MLA style, is emphasized in the "Sources" step of the Research Process. Appropriate to this lesson is the LMT role of urging teachers throughout the school, and even a district, to standardize a legitimate citation form for a wide variety of print and nonprint formats so that students do not become confused by different teachers requiring different citation styles.

Formats and Sources

A source is any kind of information accessed and used for ideas and information. Sources are generally referred to as either print or nonprint (electronic). Formats are the "kinds" of sources such as books, newspapers, CD-ROMs, or the Internet. Information literacy mandates that students use a variety of formats of information to prepare them with lifelong skills for information management.

Information Literacy

Source Requirements

A writing assignment from one source is called a summary, not research. The project goal is always clarified with the collaborative teacher. If a research project is the goal, then the assumption is accessing, evaluating, and using information from more than one source (format) of information.

This book proposes that the number of days of hands-on research should determine the number of sources required for research. For example, if a teacher's unit timetable can permit only three days for library research, then the number of required sources should be three. That is the number an average student can reasonably access, read, and process into a minimum of 10 notes per day. A minimum of three formats for middle-schoolers is also recommended.

Instructor Information

Copyright

The Problem

In the last few years, a distinct advantage of the deluge of information found on the Internet has been the push toward individual accountability for copyright infringement. Even radio and TV spots warn the general public against information "piracy." When it was only books, videos, or even records, library media teachers had an often lonely, uphill battle to keep students from "stealing" information. Now, the mouse-click availability of text and images appropriate to any unit of study gives all educators the opportunity to role model the legal use of information. They know

Important Idea

that the misuse of information can result in a hefty lawsuit, with the "deep pockets" of the school district and the taxpayers being the real losers. One easy way to solve this problem is to cite sources. In doing this, the following difficulties often arise:

- Teachers may not be using a correct or consistent citation style such as MLA.
- Grade-level teaching groups rarely meet to compare, much less standardize, citation requirements.
- Students at the same school site might have conflicting impressions of citation requirements because different teachers assign them differently.

The Solution

Although the widespread use of information networking mandates every teacher's personal responsibility for teaching and preserving copyright, a strategic role of the library media teacher still includes the dissemination of current copyright information. In focusing attention on information literacy as a school-wide goal, the issue of the use of copyrighted materials for students and teachers becomes paramount. It simply cannot be overemphasized.

Following are some strategies for dealing with copyright and bibliographic issues:

- Every year the library media teacher can volunteer a back-to-school orientation, perhaps at the first faculty meeting, on current copyright issues for all teachers, not just new teachers. Catch everyone before projects are assigned.
- The LMT can chair a committee to standardize a citation style at the school site or at the district level, to articulate middle school to high school to local college requirements.
- The LMT can model using the Internet as a source of current print and electronic copyright and citation guidelines, as seen in this book.

Citations

What Is MLA?

MLA stands for Modern Language Association. It is a "not-for-profit membership organization that promotes the study and teaching of language and literature."[1] The MLA has numerous branches and subgroups. It is well known for its style guide, *The MLA Handbook for Writers of Research Papers* (4th ed.), by Joseph Gibaldi.

Many MLA online guidelines compiled by various educational institutions can be accessed by typing into an Internet search engine the three letters "MLA" or by typing the full name. The variations seen in different online versions are the source of the disclaimer for the version that appears in this manual. The goal is MLA-based consistency and accuracy presented in a form that is easy for students to comprehend and use.

What Is APA?

"The American Psychological Association (APA), in Washington, D.C., is the largest scientific and professional organization representing psychology in the United States and is the world's largest association of psychologists. APA's membership includes more than 155,000 researchers, educators, clinicians, consultants, and students. Through its divisions in 50 subfields of psychology and affiliations with 59 state, territorial, and Canadian provincial associations, APA works to advance psychology as a science, as a profession, and as a means of promoting human welfare."[2]

In addition to the promotion of its publications directly related to psychology, the APA is known among educators for its style manuals for the writing of research and term papers, *Mastering APA Style: Instructors' Resource Guide,* by Harold Gelfand and Charles J. Walker, and *Publication Manual of the American Psychological Association.*

In the same manner as MLA guidelines, abbreviated style guidelines for these APA publications can be accessed on the Internet.

Formats and Sources

The Problem

Important Idea

Do teachers know the difference between sources of information and formats of information? Is this even important? Usually "no" and an emphatic "yes" are the answers to these two questions. Even you, the research instructor, may not have emphasized the difference to your students and fellow teachers, but I'll bet you've been teaching it all along! For example, you've probably been sending students to books, then to encyclopedias, then to the Internet.

Problem Solving

Information literacy requires students to access, evaluate, and use several formats, not just several sources, of information. Five sources for a project, for example, cannot mean five books, or five Internet web sites. There are different strategies for different formats requiring different thinking skills as well as different information management skills. Learning and using these strategies effectively is the goal of information literacy standards.

Of equal importance is clarifying to students, and sometimes to the collaborative teacher, that research cannot come from just one source. No matter how many words are changed, it is plagiarism for a research project to come from a single source. Restating an article or a source's information is a summary. This is a completely different type of legitimate writing activity that a teacher may assign.

The Solution

Through the Research Process, the library media teacher easily distinguishes between sources and formats (*Figure 6-1*). Students clearly understand that if five sources were recorded on their Research Checklist (*Figure 6-2*), then a combination of at least three formats—perhaps two books, one encyclopedia, and two Internet web sites. This distinction sheds a whole new light on information gathering:

- Students realize there is a greater variety of subtopic information available in the different print and nonprint formats. The result is a variety of reading opportunities, more reading comprehension, and therefore a more *literate* student.

- Students understand that different print and nonprint formats require different information-accessing strategies. The result is a more *information literate* student.

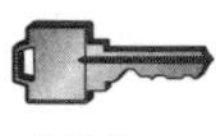

- Students pace themselves more effectively by having a clear understanding of where they need to look for information. The result is a more *time efficient* student.
- Students move with greater interest from books to CD-ROMs to the Internet. The result is a more *motivated* student.

Fig. 6-2. Research Checklist: Sources

LMT/Teacher Tracking: **Date Due:/Points:**

Topic *Michelangelo* | 10/31 | 5 |

Subtopics | 10/31 | 5 |

- ○ *What was his personal (life) like?*
- ○ *What was his (art) like?*
- ○ *What was the (Renaissance) ?*
- ○ ______
- ○ ______

Sources | 11/3-8 | 30 |

A. At least 3 formats. Circle choices:
(book), (reference), CD-ROM, (Internet), other: ______
B. Total number of sources: *3*

Read/Think/Select | | |

A. A "chunk" is ______

Notetake | | |

A. At least ___ notes for each subtopic.
B. Total number of notes: ______

Sort and number notes | | |

Write rough draft from notes | | |

Teacher Grading:

Title Page		
Typed Report		
Final Citation List		
Image/Chart		

Fig. 6-3. Copyright Cartoon

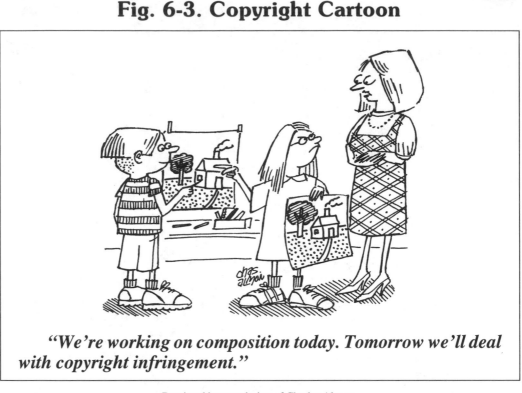

"We're working on composition today. Tomorrow we'll deal with copyright infringement."

Reprinted by permission of Charles Almon.

Student Lesson

Timing: 45 to 55 minutes.

What Is Copyright?

LMT: Hello, class. To begin today's lesson, look up at the cartoon on the overhead (*Figure 6-3*). This tells so much better than I can what we are here to talk about today. Do you see what the little girl and boy are doing? That little girl is mad! What is she so mad about? (Wait and give students time to look and think.)

Student: The little boy has the same picture. It looks like he copied.

LMT: Absolutely. There are times when you would be like the little girl. Wouldn't you be mad if you just solved the toughest problem in math class, for example, but the person behind you copied your answer, turned it in, and got credit for what should have been your best effort?

There are other times when you would be like the little boy. When? Let's say you have a paper due tomorrow and you haven't started it yet. So you come check a book out of the library, go home, and happily copy away until you have something ready to turn in. Like the smug little boy, you are simply quite pleased with yourself. A few of you may not see anything wrong with that. I am not here to condemn you, at least until I know that you have been taught how to fix this problem.

Now look at the teacher in the cartoon. (Read caption aloud.) Who knows what is a copyright?

Student: Copyright is something that lets you copy?

LMT: I'm actually glad you said that. I heard someone say one time, "It's not when you copy wrong, it's when you copy . . . *right!*" It's actually quite the opposite, however. Other ideas?

Student: It's like a legal thing. Someone owns the book?

LMT: Now you're on the right track. Think about how hard it is for you to write a long report. Now think about an author or artist who writes and creates all the time. Copyright is that person's legal protection for the work he or she has done. Look around you in this library media center. Every single item in here has a copyright. (Hold up a book.) Here on the back of the title page of this book appears a little circle "©" with a date.

After all their hard work of writing, then finally getting something published, this author, and all the others in this library, are granted legal protection. They own their work and need to get paid for it because that is probably how they feed their families and earn a living. All of you in here today don't look like anyone is neglecting you, right off hand. Your mom and dad bring home a paycheck, and you hit them up for a new outfit. Well, how do you think authors provide for their families?

LMT: But what does this mean for you directly? What does copyright mean for you as you begin this research project?

Student: We shouldn't copy?

LMT: Yes. I think you see my point that it is actually illegal for you to simply take information out of a book. An advertisement I just heard on the radio yesterday compared it to picking up a book or CD in a store, zipping it into your backpack, and trying to walk out of the store without anyone knowing. You are literally stealing from the author. When you have a big project to do for school, our job today is to see how you can avoid being like that little boy in the cartoon. There is a simple thing he could have done so that the little girl would not have been quite so mad at him. If the little boy in the cartoon had turned around and said, "I owe the whole idea for this wonderful work to my friend, Susie," I bet she wouldn't have been quite so upset.

Lifelong Skills

What I am saying is the point of this lesson: Give credit. How do you do that? You give credit to a source with something called a citation. We will have an activity today where I will not only show what a citation is, but I also will walk you through the steps of exactly how to put one together, so when you're in the library media center for this project and begin to use these sources, you will be legal and not have any authors mad at you. You will know how to give them credit.

Formats and Sources

LMT: Before we begin the citation activity, let's take a few minutes to clarify something important on your Research Checklist (*Figure 6-2*). What in the world are sources? Remember back in September during orientation when I asked you to look around the room and tell me all the places where you see information? Today, we've been calling all of these things "sources."

Let me compare all the sources of information in this room to all of the boxes of cereal on a grocery store's shelves. Sources are like cereal. We only need to look around us to see that the library media center is filled with sources just as some grocery store aisles are filled with cereal. But there are different kinds of cereal, called brands, such as Corn Pops and Wheat Toasties. Here in the LMC there are many different kinds of sources, and they are called formats. Maybe it's easier to remember that a format is a "form" of information.

LMT: Name some of the formats, or kinds of information, you see around you.

Student: Books.

Student: Encyclopedias.

Student: The computers.

Technology Proficiency

LMT: Yes, and there are different computer formats such as CD-ROMs, the Internet, and computer software. Each one of these kinds, or formats, is treated differently in a citation even though the information all comes from the computer. A few other formats you may use are magazines, newspapers, even maps and videos.

You live in a wonderful time when information comes in a wide variety of cereal boxes, all of the different formats we just named. We are here to make sure you taste all of them. That is why, when the Research Checklist says, "You must have three sources for your citation list," it is a bit misleading. Are you confused, or can someone explain what we're really asking? For example, can you use three books and then tell me you have all the sources you need for your report?

Student: No, because they're all the same format.

LMT: Excellent. You are really listening! Using only books is like eating only one brand, like Corn Pops, every day for breakfast and expecting to be satisfied. You're going to get mighty tired of them. Think of all the other kinds of cereal you are missing! You may have three good books, but think of all the facts about your topic that you're missing in other formats such as CD-ROMs or the Internet.

Student: But I have a computer at home and I've already found four great web sites on Leonardo da Vinci. Can't I use them?

LMT: Well class? Can she use them?

Student: No. She can only use one.

LMT: Actually, she can use all four web sites. Why? For this project, you may use as many of any one format as you like, as long as you use at least two other formats. You can have four boxes of Corn Pops as long as you have a box of Rice Krispies and a box of Wheaties. This student will need at least two other formats of information such as a book and perhaps an electronic or a printed encyclopedia. Then she can still use all four Internet sites.

Would it be okay for someone to use a book, an encyclopedia, and a magazine? That's three different formats?

Literacy

Student: Yes.

LMT: Actually, no! Confused? Who can tell me what those three items have in common that would not give you experience with a variety of formats? Aren't they all printed on paper?

Student: Oh yeah. None of those are computer.

LMT: Yes! They are all called print sources, but we also want you to use nonprint, or "electronic," sources, which also include videos and laser disks. You must learn and use different skills to locate the sources in print and electronic formats; this is called using "access" skills. These two kinds of formats also cause your brain to think differently about information; we call this using "evaluation" skills. To prepare you for high school, we want you to have experience with all these skills and strategies.

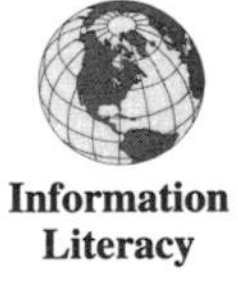
Information Literacy

Source Requirements

LMT: It's important for us to look at some other strategies for using sources correctly. Did you know it is plagiarism for you to use only one source for a report?

Student: But my teacher sometimes gives an assignment and tells us to use just one particular thing, like a newspaper article.

LMT: Good point! But there's a huge difference. That one article is fine if you are doing something called a "summary," perhaps for a current events assignment. A summary condenses and restates what happens in one article or one book, etc., and that's a legitimate kind of writing. But that is not the same as research, where you find snatches of information, called keyword facts, from many different places and recombine them using your own knowledge and creativity into a completely new piece of writing. See that giant word "RESEARCH" over there on the bulletin board? Doing research means going to many places to locate information.

Plagiarism can also refer to the way that you use a source. It is important to carefully select only keywords or facts, not whole sentences, to make the information yours instead of the author's. After all, you need to get the information from somewhere! We'll talk more about this in tomorrow's lesson on notetaking.

Student: I had a teacher who once told me that using one source for a report was fine as long as I really changed a lot of words.

LMT: I'm sorry, but that's just not research! It doesn't matter how many words you change, if your entire report comes from one place, why should I read yours? I'll just read the original!

Lifelong Skills

Let's review three important things to not plagiarize so that you use sources correctly. First, give credit with a citation. Second, use more than one source. Third, make the information your own by selecting keywords and facts, then putting everything from many sources back together in a new way. You'll see exactly how to do all this in our Research Process lessons. Today we'll learn the different kinds of citation entries for the three formats of sources required for this project.

So, if you come to the library media center on your own to do research, how would you know how many sources to use?

Student: As many as we have time for.

LMT: Actually, that's just about the right answer. Your teacher and I know from experience that it is very fair to have you use a different source for each day of hands-on research. We have scheduled you for three full days of uninterrupted research time, so using three sources is appropriate. Another question: How will you know which or what kind of sources to pick for your topic?

Student: The ones where I find information for my subtopics.

LMT: You were listening! Also, I always tell students to start with the easy formats first, such as encyclopedias, and then work your way toward the harder ones. Hard sources would be those that are more difficult for you to read and understand, or that don't match your subtopics in an obvious way, perhaps with chapter titles or subheadings.

Another bit of advice is to use your library time wisely. If you have the Internet at home, don't use it here. Start with the sources that are available to you only in this room. There may be some reference books, for example, that you will not be able to check out. Remember, research is *F-A-S-T*. Better not to be caught short.

Accountability

Information Literacy

LMT: Let's take just a moment to record project requirements on your Research Checklist (*Figure 6-2*). Look under "Sources," letter A. The sheet says you need a minimum of three formats. Does everyone understand that the word *sources* here means everything you use? But you must always use a minimum of three formats, or kinds, of sources. Makes it easy, huh? Just use three different things for information. Look at letter B and record the number three on the blank line to show that you understand the minimum requirement.

Is everyone clear about the difference in formats and sources? No one is going to ask me next week when it's too late why you can't use just three CD-ROM printouts?

Student: We get it, but can I use more than three?

LMT: Good question. Of course you can, but learn to judge your own time. Remember, we think you're smarter the more sources you use! This is usually a great way to get extra credit. Using more sources, and formats, than is required shows your teacher that you are motivated, that you are interested in your topic, and that you know how to credit your sources properly. This leads us into today's activity.

Student Activity: MLA-Style Citations

This activity is the focus of Lesson 2, so omit or condense any of the instructional sections to enable enough time for activity completion.

General Directions

LMT: To keep the little girl in the cartoon happy, and to keep your teacher happy too, you need to learn how to credit your sources with something called MLA citations. Where do citations come from?

Student: My teacher last year just said to put down a title, author, and the pages I used.

LMT: I'm glad you said that because I want to tell you that it is actually . . . wrong! You, your teacher, or even me as a library media teacher can't just make up what's on a citation. The instructions come from special organizations, such as the one called MLA. Anyone ever heard of that? (Pause.) It means Modern Language Association and only they,

and a few other organizations, have the official right to say what a citation is! That's important, because I didn't make up what we will learn today. It's just the way things need to be, both now and probably in high school and maybe college.

Let's begin our activity with a quick materials check. I'm glad that each of you followed directions so well at the beginning of the period today. Coming in the room, you went to the encyclopedia shelf and located the volume with the letter to match the last name of your artist. Some of you are seated together so that you can share a volume. Everyone take out a pencil so that you can erase mistakes. Remember what they say: We learn by our mistakes.

In the middle of your table are stacks of colored citation cards. We are going to practice filling these in as a whole class so that you will know exactly what to do during your own research for this project, or for any other research project you do during the school year. Make sure you have a green one for reference, a blue one for CD-ROM, and a pink one for the Internet. Each information format has its own color so that you can easily tell them apart. These forms are always available in plastic bins around the library media center at the place where that source of information is located. For example, the green reference forms are on the counter in the reference area near the encyclopedia shelves. The pink Internet forms and the blue CD-ROM forms are both by the printer because you will need a computer printout to complete them.

LMT: The color-coded forms also make it easy for both your teacher and I to track your progress. Since you will need three formats of information for this Renaissance project, I should be able to go around the room and quickly see what information sources you have, or haven't, used simply by seeing the colors on the table in front of you. Keep these citation forms out at all times. Don't lose them because you will need them later to write your final citations list, something we will demonstrate to you at the completion of research as part of the creation of your final project.

Print Encyclopedias

LMT fills in a transparency for Figure 6-4 *while students use the color-coded forms.*

Literacy

LMT: Put the green form in front of you. Write your name at the top in pencil. Let's begin this activity with your encyclopedia. This is also a good source to begin your research or when you are waiting for a computer. Who remembers why?

Student: Because we can't check them out.

LMT: Good. And because it is divided into subheadings that might match your subtopics. It gives you a jump-start on gathering information.

Fig. 6-4. Citations Activity

Name______________________ **Teacher** _________________________________

Alphabetical order _______

(Reference) Encyclopedia: MLA-Style Citation

Author *if available* (last name, first name, middle) ______________________ (period).

Article title ("quotation marks") ____________________________________ (period).

Title of encyclopedia (underlined) ___________________________________ (period).

Year______________ followed by edition (abbreviated, *ed*) _______________ (period).

Example: Barnes, Isaac Jacob. "Camels." The World Book Encyclopedia. 1996 ed.

- -

Alphabetical order _______

CD-ROM Encyclopedia: MLA-Style Citation

Author *if available* (last name, first name, middle) ________________________(period).

Article title ("quotation marks") __________________________________ (period).

CD-ROM title (underlined) ____ (period).

Edition (abbreviate, *ed*) _______ (period). Write the words: CD-ROM ______ (period).

Year____________ followed by edition (abbreviated, *ed*) _________________ (period).

Example: Adams, Ernest D. "Spanish Armada." The World Book Multimedia Encyclopedia. Deluxe ed. CD-ROM. 2000 ed.

- -

Alphabetical order _______

Internet Web Site: MLA-Style Citation

Title of web site ("quotation marks") ________________________________(period).

Date of access: Day Month (abbreviated, period) Year __________________ (no period)

URL (<web site address in brackets>) __________________________________(period).

Example: "Presidential Campaign." 5 Oct. 2000 <http://www.cnn.com>.

Looking at the form, notice that "Author" is the first item. The author is the most important part of a citation entry because that is from whom you would be stealing information if you did not give credit! Whenever an author's name is available, it will always be the first item in a citation and it will be used later to put the entry in alphabetical order. Many students skip over an author when using an encyclopedia because they don't think there is one. That's why we're using this particular encyclopedia. It is excellent at giving full name credit to each one of the thousands of authors who wrote the individual articles throughout all the volumes.

Open your volume and use the guide words at the top of the pages to locate your Renaissance artist. Here are sticky notes for you to write the artist's name and stick on the article to mark it. Once you've found it, this will save you time later. (LMT and teacher give students assistance.)

To locate the author, start at the beginning of the article and slide your finger down the columns to the end. Some of you may need to turn pages. Just above a section called either "Related Article" or "Study Aids" you should see in teeny, tiny letters a person's name; that is the author. Do not confuse the artist whom the article is about with the author who wrote the article. Is everyone finding those tiny little names? Your teacher will walk around and assist those of you in the back while I walk around the front area. (Instructors circulate.) Any questions? (Conduct a final spot-check.)

For my overhead example, I have the "M" volume for Michelangelo. When I go to the end of the article, I see that the author is David Summers.[3] While I write my author on the overhead, everyone record your author on your green citation form. What does the form tell you to write first?

Student: The author's last name.

LMT: Correct. And please be sure to spell it correctly. If you don't want someone to spell your name wrong, be sure you do the same for someone else's name. (If time permits, you can tell the following anecdote about names.)

Pretend it is the first day of school and you are in my class. As you come into the room I begin to write down your names on the board to make a seating chart. While I'm writing you say, "Hey, that's not the way I spell my name!"

"Too bad," I answer. "That's how it sounds to me, so that's what I'll put!"

Class, can I do that? Can I just decide to spell your name wrong? Of course not! It's your name. If I spell it wrong, it's not even you anymore, it's someone else.

LMT: Do you see there is a comma after the last name? Next, write the author's first name. I'll record "David" here on the overhead because that is my author's first name. For the sake of demonstration, let's pretend this person has a middle initial, Q. Some of you do have a middle initial, or a middle name, so watch on the overhead while I write, "Q" in its proper place. It appears in the natural order in which it would follow after the first name. Someone raise your hand and tell me what would happen if the person's full middle name was used?

Student: Can't we just skip the middle name?

LMT: Isn't that the same as spelling the name wrong? Do you have the right to simply decide to leave off part of, or misspell, any person's name?

Student: No. I guess not.

LMT: Exactly. You simply don't have that right, any more than I have the right to simply decide to spell your name wrong. Make sense? Finally, do you see that the whole name line is punctuated by a period at the end? So do that for your author. (Write on the *Figure 6-4* transparency while students write on their forms.)

Let's move on to the next item, "Article title." Someone tell me what an article title is.

Student: The title of the article.

LMT: Yes, but what is that in particular, for your Renaissance project?

Student: Oh yeah, my artist.

LMT: Exactly. It's what you're looking up, your topic. Locate your article title either from the guide words at the top of the page or from the boldfaced words at the beginning of your article. When you find them, copy them exactly as they appear. I'll look up "Michelangelo." Do all of you know that he has a last name, Buonarroti? Who sees a problem with me looking up "Michelangelo"?

Student: Oh yeah! That's his first name. You told us we're supposed to look up someone's last name.

LMT: Very good. Artists' names don't always follow the rule, so I'll help you figure out what to look up. Finally, notice that the citation form again tells you there is a period at the end of this whole "Article title" line. Everyone with me?

The next item on the sheet is "Title of encyclopedia." Whew! Finally something simple! Well, not so fast. Here on the spine is an abbreviated name for this encyclopedia. But when we turn the book to the front cover, it states a full name. That is what you have to put. You must always look a book over and find the entire title, not to be confused with a series title. No shortcuts, or again you'd be simply deciding

to change the name. I usually tell students to look for the title on the title page, where it very clearly states what you're looking for. Copy down the title onto your form. (Model this by writing it on the transparency.) Finally, did you remember to do what the form tells you to do for the title of the book?

Student: Underline? But there's already a line on the form. Why do I have to underline it again?

LMT: That form line is just to write on. To show an underline, you actually have to draw it. Do you see the difference between the title of the article and the title of the book? They're both titles, what's the difference?

Student: The article title gets quotation marks and the book title gets an underline.

LMT: Maybe an easy way to remember is that you underline the title for the outside of a book, but you put quotation marks for the title found inside a book. Try to think of your own ways to remember things like that. Are we finished? (Purposely omit the period.)

Student: Oh. You forgot something. The period!

LMT: Good eyes! You're learning that correct punctuation is extremely important for an accurate citation. (You can tell the following punctuation anecdote, if time permits.)

Today is Tuesday. Suppose you walk into math class and say, "Hello teacher. It's Tuesday, and I've decided that for today, 2 + 2 = 5."

Just like you're looking at me now, your teacher would probably look at you like you're crazy. The reason I tell you this is that it is just as crazy for you to say, "Teacher, it's Tuesday, and I've decided for this project, I am not going to put a colon after the place of publication." You simply cannot do that! Who says so? MLA says so. This does not make your life harder. We are never expecting you to memorize all this. That is what this MLA citation form is for. Just copy it! Are you beginning to realize how this little piece of paper will save your life? The more you do bibliography entries correctly, the less difficult it will seem. It's no more weird than copying all the little bits and pieces of an Internet web site URL correctly.

LMT: Let's locate the remaining item, the "Year," inside the volume. (Hold up an encyclopedia volume so everyone can see.) Open up your volume to the title page. You can identify it because it has much more information on it than just the title.

A title page is a very handy thing to know about. All of the pieces of a print bibliography entry are found on the front and back. The title is usually at the top. Somewhere in the middle is the author of a book, but in an encyclopedia authors are located with their articles. At the bottom of the page is the publisher, and underneath that is the place of publication. Uh, oh. What if there is more than one place? Do you write down all of them? No, an easy rule to remember is that you pick only the first one and just ignore all the rest!

LMT: To locate the year, turn the title page over to the back. (Wait while students follow the direction.) Somewhere buried in all the small print is always a date. Look, we have a problem again. There are tons of dates here in this encyclopedia. Which one do you pick this time?

Student: The first one?

LMT: Not this time. Anyone else?

Student: The last one?

LMT: Yes, if you mean the latest date. Remember, doesn't it make sense that you're looking for the date this particular book was printed? The latest date refers to, of course, the newest information.

Student: Shouldn't I just look for the little circle "©" for copyright?

LMT: Yes, a book is usually copyrighted each time it is published. But just remember that you are looking for the latest possible date. While I write it here on the overhead, record the date of the encyclopedia onto your green form. Finally, the sheet calls for you to add the letters "ed" with a period. When you read this back it means "the 2000 edition."

Good, we're almost done. There is one last important item. Everyone draw a circle around the first letter of the author's last name. Do you see in the upper left corner where it says "Alphabetical order"? Write the letter you circled in that space. (Demonstrate on a transparency of *Figure 6-4.*) When everyone is looking back up, I'll know you have completed that instruction. Good. At the end of research, this makes it easy to put all your citation forms in alphabetical order to make a final citation list. Any questions?

Student: But I have an encyclopedia where there is no author. What do I put? "Unknown," because the author is unknown? Then do I write the letter "U" for "Alphabetical order"?

LMT: Great question! And the answer is no! MLA says to just skip the author space. Leave it blank if there's no author. Instead, go down to the next line, which is what?

Student: The article title?

LMT: Yes. If you have no author, circle the first letter of the article title and that becomes the way to alphabetize that entry.

Student: I have another question. In my last project, I had two citation forms with exactly the same author. I wasn't sure how to put them in alphabetical order. Should I just pick one?

LMT: Everyone needs to know the answer to that. If the author is exactly the same, start by putting both entries in the alphabetical position for the first letter of both authors' last name. For example, if I had two authors named Summers, I'd start by putting them both in S. Then look at the first letter of their first names and use that, if possible. If both books or articles are by the exact same author, look next at the first letter of the book or article titles. For example, I might label two articles by David Summers as "S-1" and "S-2." If this is confusing, I'll be showing you an overhead of a final citation list later in the project. It will demonstrate what I'm saying. Another hint for correctly alphabetizing entries is to skip small words beginning a title, such as "The," "A," or "An," and alphabetize with the first main word. I'm sure you've done that before.

CD-ROM Encyclopedias

Technology Proficiency

LMT: Set aside the green form for a print reference and put the blue CD-ROM form in front of you.

Student: But how can we fill this out if we haven't even been to the computers yet?

LMT: Good question. Once I demonstrate this to you on the overhead with my Michelangelo example, you'll be able to repeat it on your own. So just watch while I locate and record CD-ROM citation items, but don't write on your form. Pencils down.

It's easy to get citation items from a print encyclopedia, but where do they come from if you're using a computer? From a printout! First, look at the CD-ROM citation form and see what items we need to locate. (Refer to the *Figure 6-4* transparency while students look at their blue forms.) Much of it is the same as for the reference: the author, the article title, the CD-ROM title, and the year.

Now, let's look at a printout from an electronic encyclopedia, which I have also made into an overhead. Let's circle the citation items we've just identified. Here at the top is the article title. (Circle each item as it is named.) At the bottom the word "Contributor" identifies the author, and in fine print at the very bottom I'll circle the title of the electronic encyclopedia. What symbol indicates the year this was made?

Student: The little C in a circle. I see it! It's 2000.

LMT: Good. I'll copy what we've found onto the citation form. (Write the information on the transparency, but purposely omit some required punctuation.) There, looks pretty good to me!

Student: I think you forgot something. You forgot to put quotation marks around the article title. (Write on the transparency, as the student indicates.)

Student: Yeah, and you didn't put a period after the word "CD-ROM" or after the letters "ed." (Make this correction.)

LMT: Wow! You guys are getting good! Let's move on to the last example for today to prepare you to work independently. Of course, I'll always be here to help when you get stuck.

Internet Web Sites

Continue using the transparency of Figure 6-4 *for this section.*

LMT: Now put the pink Internet form in front of you, but keep your pencils down for now. The Internet is probably the easiest citation because, in middle school, there are really only three items I want you to be aware of. As with most electronic information, you will need a printout from the Internet to locate citation items. Let's look at an overhead transparency from a Michelangelo web site.

Technology Proficiency

Looking at the pink form, we need to locate the title of the web site, the date of access, and the URL. On this web site, I'll circle the title here at the top. Here in the lower right corner is the date of access. What in the world is that? Does anyone know?

Student: I think it's, like, the day you find your stuff?

LMT: Yes! It would be today if you located a web site for your artist during this class period. You can see the date of access on the lower corner of this printout. Unfortunately, that's not always there. It's better to get into the habit of recording citation information the day you get your printout.

Finally, locate the URL, which stands for Uniform Resource Locator, but you don't have to remember that. It's the web site address, just like your home address. You all live at a house address or an apartment number, right? Well, so does each web page on the Internet. URLs can sometimes be extremely long and complicated. Luckily for you, they are often on your printout, as we see here at the bottom. If not, copy it right from the computer. Either way, you usually have to copy a URL by hand onto your citation form. Let's do that right now. Watch while I attempt to copy this fairly long URL. (Students watch as the you write the string of letters and symbols, explaining what certain ones mean along the way.) It is extremely important to copy them correctly, or your teacher will not be able to get back to

that web site. Therefore, it would be called "unverifiable." (Carefully complete the URL.) There, I think that's it!

A computer lesson that I might arrange with your teacher, if time permits, is to teach you how to create a "Webliography." This is where you can capture URLs electronically simply by cutting and pasting between the Internet and a word processing program. That would eliminate mistakes from copying by hand.

Student: I think you forgot something again. The form says "angle brackets." What's that?

LMT: Music to my ears! You're getting very good at paying attention to the small details that are so important to an accurate citation. Let me ask you, are these angle brackets? (Draw parentheses "( )".) Are these angle brackets? (Draw square brackets "[ ]".) Perhaps these are angle brackets? (Draw angle brackets, "< >", and a few students should say, "Yes!") Right. I'll put them at the front and the back of the URL.

Finally, watch while I write the date of access. The day is written first, with no punctuation, then the month, abbreviated to three letters with a period. Then the year with no period, as the form says. Any questions? Don't forget that the web site title, like an article title, has quotation marks. Why? Because it is inside the Internet, just like an article title is inside a book or CD-ROM.

Accountability

LMT: Before the bell rings, your teacher and I are checking each of you off on the Tracking Sheet to indicate that you completed your citation forms for today. Any research step not completed will be carefully marked so that we know exactly where each of you is at all times. Sit quietly with your three forms showing while we finish.

Next, remember that your teacher and I collect everything! So put all three citation forms inside your research folder along with your Research Process and Research Checklist sheets. Stack your folders in the middle of your table. One student can then bring the stack up here to your teacher's bin. Remember, if you're absent and get behind, or feel you want to work outside of class, you can sign out your folder on the agreement that you bring it with you to class the next day.

Great! You learned a lot today! Be ready to tackle notetaking strategies tomorrow to learn what to do with the information in all of the sources you will be using.

Extension Lessons

Simple and Annotated Citations

This lesson is for all students at the conclusion of research. It is presented by the LMT, time permitting, or can easily be taught by the classroom teacher back in the classroom. It only takes a few minutes.

LMT: Now that you have completed notetaking and have used all of your sources, I want to take just a few minutes to show you how to create your final citation list. First, let me ask you an important question. (Hold up a group of the color-coded citation forms.) Are these the citations you turn in with your final report? No! These are only the practice forms to help you gather all the bits and pieces of a citation entry. The reason we were so careful to do what the forms said to do is that you need every little piece. If anything is left out, you have probably created a lot more work for yourself. The book you forgot to get a date for may be checked out later when you need it!

Lifelong Skills

The first step is to alphabetize all of your citations. You've made that job easy by circling the first letter of the author's last name on each citation form during your research. If there were two authors with the same last name, you used . . .

Student: . . . the first letter of the first name.

LMT: Yes! But if it was the exact same author, you used . . .

Student: . . . the first letter of the article title.

LMT: Yes, again! And if there was no author you used . . .

Student: . . . also the first letter of the article title.

LMT: Excellent! Everyone take a few minutes and alphabetize all of your color-coded forms. Good. Stack them up in alphabetical order. I'll put out a stapler and a three-hole punch so you can clip them into your three-ring binder.

We're ready for the next step, copying them into final form. Let's look at a previous student's final citation list. (Display a transparency of *Figure 6-5*.) This simple list of your sources in alphabetical order is all you need for the Renaissance project.

Fig. 6-5. Final Citations

Citations

Beck, James H. "Michelangelo." Microsoft Encarta '99 Encyclopedia. 2000 ed.

Harris, Nathaniel. Renaissance Art. New York: Thomson Learning, 1994.

"Michelangelo." 27 Apr. 2000 <http://www.craft.com/michel.html>

Partridge, Loren. Michelangelo: The Sistine Chapel Ceiling, Rome. New York: George Braziller, 1996.

Summers, David. "Michelangelo." World Book Encyclopedia. 2000 ed.

Student: But my science teacher said to put all the books together, all the encyclopedias together.

LMT: Good point. You are not the first student who has said that. Do you know what? Without being defiant, you may politely point out to your teacher that there is a more accurate way. It is inaccurate to group sources like that because there is no logical way of listing them. It is arbitrary. I think if you show that teacher an example of an accurately arranged citation list, he may see differently.

Student: My science teacher also wanted something called an annotated list, like where you tell about each thing.

LMT: Another good point! I just happen to have an example of one here, so everyone can see the difference. (Display a transparency of *Figure 6-6.*) Some projects, like Science Fair or History Day, require you to write a sentence or two telling how you used each source. (Read a few samples.) For the rest of the class period, finish transferring your own citation entry form into a finalized list.

Fig. 6-6. Final Citations: Annotated

Annotated Citations

Beck, James H. "Michelangelo." Microsoft Encarta '99 Encyclopedia. 2000 eds.
I used this CD-ROM for notes about two of Michelangelo's works of art.

Harris, Nathaniel. Renaissance Art. New York: Thomson Learning, 1994.
This book had a lot of information about the Renaissance subtopic.

"Michelangelo." 27 Apr. 2000 <http://www.craft.com/michel.html>
This was a good summary that made it easy to select some facts I was missing about his life and art.

Partridge, Loren. Michelangelo: The Sistine Chapel Ceiling, Rome. New York: George Braziller, 1996.
I got notes and a picture for the third work of art that I needed.

Summers, David. "Michelangelo." World Book Encyclopedia. 2000 ed.
I found good notes about all three subtopics.

Learning MLA Style

Based on Figures 6-7 and 6-8, *this lesson is for advanced seventh-graders or eighth-graders to prepare them for independent research in high school.*

MLA Examples for Print Materials

Literacy

LMT: I am passing out to you a handout of MLA-style citations for a wide variety of print and nonprint sources (*Figures 6-7* and *6-8*). Our goal in this lesson is for you to be able to understand all the parts and pieces of a citation entry so you can use this guide sheet on your own. We want you to achieve independence in information management.

Let's begin on the side that starts with "Books." Notice this sheet is divided by the formats we have been talking about. (Slide a marker down the sheet and read the format section titles.) Get ready to put check marks beside the print materials I think you will use most often:

- **Books:** Put a check underneath "Book" beside "One author." Like the example I have here (hold up a typical Renaissance nonfiction book), many of you will find the book you're using was written by only one person. Just in case the book you locate is different, look at the MLA sheet, and it shows you what to do if a book has two authors, more than two, or if it doesn't have an author at all but was put together by an editor or a corporate group. You need to be able to handle anything. This sheet will show you exactly what to do! Does that make sense?

- **Encyclopedias:** Put a check mark beside both encyclopedia article "with author" and "no author." For the sample activity we are going to do today the author will be very apparent. Unfortunately, sometimes you won't be able to find one; the guide sheet will help you in either case. These are the entries for a printed encyclopedia, but it's important to notice on the back of your MLA sheet that there are also encyclopedia entries for CD-ROMs and the Internet. Many of you will use those in this project and you need to be aware of which example to follow.

MLA Examples for Nonprint Materials

Technology Proficiency

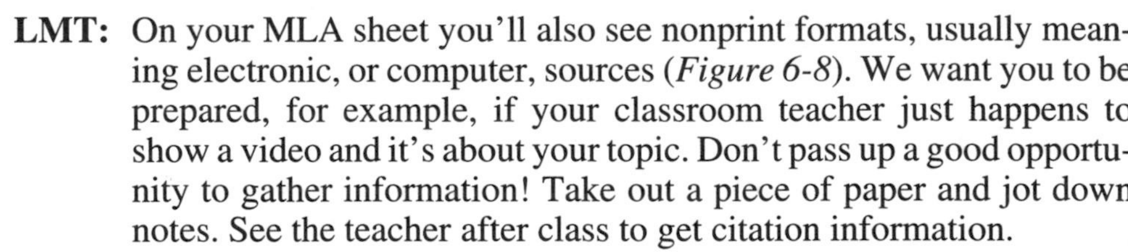

LMT: On your MLA sheet you'll also see nonprint formats, usually meaning electronic, or computer, sources (*Figure 6-8*). We want you to be prepared, for example, if your classroom teacher just happens to show a video and it's about your topic. Don't pass up a good opportunity to gather information! Take out a piece of paper and jot down notes. See the teacher after class to get citation information.

- **CD-ROMs:** Locate the CD-ROM section. Put a check beside "Encyclopedia article" because that is the principal kind of general CD-ROM source we have available in this library media center. However, we also have a topic-specific CD-ROM about

Leonardo da Vinci, one of the most famous Renaissance artists. Would everyone try to view it at some point during this research project? It may have information for your "Renaissance" subtopic. Did you also know that if you locate and use even one picture from a CD-ROM you can cite it as a source? Give credit for everything you use! Besides staying within copyright regulations, teachers think you're smarter the more sources you use. It's a win-win situation! And this piece of paper is your guide. (Hold up the MLA sheet.)

- **Internet:** The last item you see is the Internet. This is what everyone wants to use. Put a check mark here because we will make sure everyone has an opportunity, during your scheduled research time, to use the Internet so that we prepare you for high school. Exactly how to credit this source is part of our hands-on bibliography activity.

Notes

1. "Modern Language Association (MLA) Guide to Style" (Accessed 14 Jul. 2000), <http://www.wilpaterson.edu/wpcpages/library/mla.htm>.
2. "American Psychological Association" (Accessed 14 Jul. 2000), <http://www.apa.org/about/>.
3. David Summers, "Michelangelo," *The World Book Encyclopedia* (Chicago: World Book, 1999).

Fig. 6-7. Source Citations: MLA Examples

**All examples cited from the web site below except starred items.*
14 Jul. 2000 <http://ollie.dcccd.edu/library/Module4/M4-V/examples.htm>.

BOOKS:

No author*

People of Long Ago. Milwaukee: Rourke Publishers, 1986.

One author*

Newberry, Louis. Hair Design. Los Angeles: Newberry Press, 1986.

Two authors

Zwerdling, Alex, and Richard Voorhees. Orwell and the Left. New Haven: Yale UP, 1974.

Two or more authors*

Kingsley, Eric, et al. Ships. New York: Alfred A. Knopf, 1995.

Edited

Foster, Carol E., Mark A. Siegel, and Nancy R. Jacobs, eds. Women's Changing Role. The Information Series on Current Topics. Wylie: Information Plus, 1990.

By a corporation*

Dallas County Community College District. Richland College. Institutional Self-Study. Dallas: Richland College, 1993.

SPECIAL BOOKS:

Anthology or multi-volume set

"Fromm, Erich 1900-1980." Contemporary Authors.Vol. 29. New Revision Series. Detroit: Gale, 1990. 55 vols. to date. 1981- .

Atlas

Atlas of the World. New York: Oxford UP, 1992. Munro, David, ed.

Dictionary

"Hard Rock." The American Heritage Dictionary of the English Language. 3rd ed. Boston: Houghton, 1993.

Poem, play, or short story from an anthology

Chekhov, Anton. The Cherry Orchard. Trans. Avraham Yarmolinsky. Norton Anthology of World Masterpieces. Ed. Maynard Mack. 4th ed. Vol. 2. New York: Norton, 1979. 1192-1230. 2 vols.

ENCYCLOPEDIAS:

In print, with author

Landry, Tom. "Football." World Book Encyclopedia. 1991 ed.

In print, no author

"Industrial Architecture." New Caxton Encyclopedia. London: Caxton, 1977. 20 vols.

Fig. 6-8. Source Citations: MLA Examples

CD-ROM:

Encyclopedia article

Kumbier, William A. "Science Fiction." World Book 1997 Multimedia Encyclopedia. Deluxe ed. CD-ROM. 1997 ed.

Newspaper article

Birnbaum, Mary C. "Information-Age Infants: Technology Pushes the Frontiers of What Babies Know." Dallas Morning News 23 Aug. 1994: 5C. NewsBank CD News. CD-ROM.

INTERNET:

Web site

"Hank Aaron." 1996. Total Baseball. Tot@lSports. 6 May 1997 <http://www.totalbaseball.com>.

Encyclopedia article

Enfield, David B. "El Niño." Britannica Online. Vers. 98.2. April 1998. Encyclopedia Britannica. 1 Jul. 1998 <http://www.eb.com>.

Magazine article

Kluger, Jeffrey. "The Gentle Cosmic Rain." Time 9 Jun. 1997. 11 June 1997 <http://www.pathfinder.com/index.htm>.

Newspaper article

Johnson, George. "Don't Worry: A Brain Still Can't Be Cloned." New York Times 2 Mar. 1997, forums sec. 11 Jun. 1997 <http://forums.nytimes.com/library/ national/0302clone-review.html>.

E-mail

Jeser-Skaggs, Sharlee (sjs@dcccd.edu). "Keyword Quirks." E-mail to Gary Duke (gd@dcccd.edu). 28 Feb. 1995.

MAGAZINES:

Article, with author

Idelson, Holly. "Gun Rights and Restrictions." Congressional Quarterly Weekly Report 24 Apr. 1993: 1021-27.

Article, no author

"Stolen Art Treasures Found in Texas." Facts on File 22 Jun. 1990: 459.

NEWSPAPERS:

Article, with author

Moreno, Sylvia. "Senate Endorses Gun Bill after Brief Filibuster." Dallas Morning News 18 May 1993: 1A+.

Article, no author*

"Aiding the Arts." The Milwaukee Sentinel 15 Jan. 1997: 3B

MISCELLANEOUS:

Film and video

The Wrong Stuff: American Architecture. Videocassette. Dir. Tom Bettag. Carousel Films, 1983.

Interview

Face to face: Pei, I. M. Personal interview. 27 Jul. 1983.

Telephone: Poussaint, Alvin F. Telephone interview. 10 Dec. 1980.

Pamphlet

Treat like a book.

Chapter 7

Reading, Thinking, Selecting: Lesson 3, Part 1

Instructor Information

Student Lesson

"The students are so quiet! They're really reading those encyclopedias."
—Substitute teacher

Fig. 7-1. Research Process: Read/Think/Select

Topic *A good topic is "doable," but slightly challenging to your assessed abilities.*

A. Locate a topic in textbooks, library sources, or the teacher's topic list.
B. Check in the library media center for at least three formats of supporting information.
C. Cross-check in an encyclopedia to narrow or broaden a topic.

Subtopics *Ask yourself: What do I want to know about my topic?*

A. General subtopics may be brainstormed. Examples:
   Person: early life, education, work (be specific), later life.
   Place: origin, history, leaders, geography, economy.
   Thing: who, what, when, where, why/how.
B. Specific subtopics must be located in, for example, an encyclopedia's subheads.
C. The number of subtopics is based on the number of days of research.

Sources *A good source is any kind of supporting information that you can read.*

A. Format (the form information comes in) Examples include:
   Print: books, encyclopedias, magazines, newspapers.
   Nonprint: videos, laser disks, CD-ROMs, computer software, Internet.
B. Use at least three formats of information. Using one source is not research!
C. Credit sources using MLA-style citations.

Read/Think/Select *Good research promotes comprehension and evaluation.*

A. Read an entire "chunk" (a paragraph or a page) with your pencil down.
B. Think about what was read. What was important?
C. Select only a few key facts from each "chunk" to match your subtopics.

Notetake *A good note creates information ownership. This is learning!*

A. One note per card, titled with subtopic. Use as many cards as needed.
B. Record important keywords, facts, or a list, up to about 20 words (use your judgment).
C. No small words like *a*, *the*, *an*, *is*, *was*. Instead use commas and dashes.
D. No copying of sentences (without quotation marks and footnotes).

Sort and Number Notes *Good organization of notes makes writing easier.*

A. Sort notes by subtopic section, about five notes per paragraph (use your judgment).
B. Read notes in one section at a time and put in an order that makes sense.
C. Number notes consecutively through all sections without starting over at number 1.

Extension
   Write/Publish/Present
   Final citations list
   Technology integration

Evaluation Student tracking

Chapter Concepts

Promoting Literacy and Information Literacy

Educational reform can meet the literacy challenge of a diverse student population through the Research Process, which is structured so that students must read, then evaluate what was read to critically select information to proceed to the next step, notetaking. The reading, thinking, and selecting strategies in this chapter guarantee that the current dilemma of students either copying from print sources or printing electronic information and passing it off as their original work will not occur.

Students Must Read to Access and Comprehend Information

Refer back to *Figure 1-2* to see that opportunities for reading diverse materials occur at each step of the Research Process. Strategies for the reading of research information, which are different from those for pleasure reading, are the focus of this chapter.

Students Must Think About Reading to Evaluate Information

Thinking about information happens automatically when students match what is read to their topic and subtopics. Subtopics form a frame, making it easy to see what ideas and keywords to select and what to skip. Having a clear purpose for reading enables critical reading and thinking to occur easily and automatically.

Students Must Select Important Ideas and Keywords to Use Information

This step prevents plagiarism! Plagiarism may occur when students do not have the strategies to critically evaluate information not only to select what *is* important, but to know what to *leave out*. Without predetermined essential questions keyworded into subtopics, students do not have a frame of reference for information management. Without reading and thinking strategies, students do not have the tools to actively process information to sort it, select it, and change its form to make it their own. It is when information changes form that learning occurs.

Instructor Information

Points in this first part of the third lesson are often inseparably taught with the notetaking lesson in the student lesson scripts.

Reading

Literacy

The value of the Research Process to promote literacy across all grade levels, ability levels, interest levels, and language needs cannot be overstated. If the teachers

at your school had any idea how much breaking research down into these manageable steps, then teaching the students strategies for accomplishing those steps, ties into overall educational literacy goals, they would be beating down your door.

An example is an incident that occurred in my fifth year of collaborative research instruction. Although it was not in a middle-school class, the value of the literacy experience was the same. The class was seated in the library media center, the teacher was rotating among the students to assist with direction following. That day the site's reading specialist, who was also the Title I teacher, had scheduled to come and observe a student mainstreamed from the pullout reading program. She was seated inconspicuously to the rear of the class.

The students had been taught and had practiced the reading strategies illustrated in the following student lesson. The LMT had talked about how to read quickly through a "chunk" of text with pencils down. The students were all using a reference encyclopedia on this particular day and were seated in pairs. The classroom teacher had partnered high-level readers with struggling readers, so whenever necessary, a student was reading aloud to the partner. After reading, students discussed what they had just read. They decided what information matched the subtopics and what was important enough to copy onto their note cards. They then picked up their pencils and recorded their own notes.

Everyone was on task. Everyone completed the information gathering goal for the period despite the variety of reading ability levels for that kind of source. A check of students' notes reflected that information had been read, comprehended, selected, and recorded.

At the end of the lesson, the reading specialist came to me and said, "That was amazing! Do all the teachers at the school know about this? Do you know how much this ties in so completely with the reading strategies we teach them in special training? Those kids were reading not only because it had purpose but also because they were interested! How many times do you see students who are having fun reading an encyclopedia?" She went on to say that if more students were involved in an active library media program, there would not be as many reading difficulties. What a great asset to educational reform!

Information Literacy

My response was that this is the curriculum of all library media teachers! That is why this position is so important, not only for research and technology integration into the curriculum but also as she saw firsthand, to support the school's literacy program. In providing experiences for reading for purpose as well as for pleasure, or reading in a variety of print and electronic formats, library media teachers offer an unbeatable integrated curriculum of both literacy and information literacy.

Strategies for reading for research can include:

Purpose: Subtopics provide specific reasons for reading.

Speed: Skimming or scanning instead of reading slowly.

Amount: Reading a "chunk" without stopping. Depending on reading ability, this means a paragraph, a page, or several pages.

ELL/Special Modifications

Content-Area Standard

Of special significance is the adaptation of these reading for research strategies to the needs of special students, as evidenced by the Renaissance unit presented in this book, in which the ELL teacher teamed with the art and library media teacher specifically for that purpose. Reading specialists, Title I teachers, and ELL teachers are all able to include collaboration with the library media teacher on a research project as documentation in student IEPs (Individual Educational Programs). The regular classroom teacher is able to use examples of Research Process projects for site review or accreditation documentation for the integration of literacy (reading, writing, listening, speaking) and information literacy into the content-area curriculum.

Thinking

In my experience a common complaint among teachers in every subject area is "The students' work looks like they didn't even think about it!" Every day I see students come into the library media center who not only don't want to read for research, they don't want to think about information. Why should they?

"Don't push me." In this era of passive bombardment by outside stimuli, thinking requires the student to actively engage in pondering or discovering ideas and information.

"Don't waste my time." In a world promoting immediate gratification, too many "quick" solutions are available without thinking.

"Don't bore me." With media promoting constant excitement, it isn't fun for students to think about tasks they don't perceive to be meaningful or interesting.

"My son will sit for hours in front of the computer trying to figure out how to build a web site about his favorite wrestling hero, but I can't get him to finish his homework!"

The solution is to fight fire with fire! Engage students in a meaningful activity, which inherently seduces them into critically thinking without even trying. To understand how to do that, a difference must be established between "pleasure" thinking and "school" thinking. Both can be intense and difficult. Have you been in a video arcade lately? The kind of thinking required to play a video game is fun and exciting. Is the same true with research situations? Does it have to be? Remember the admonition of Seymour Pappert in this book's introduction. It *is* our responsibility to make schoolwork, especially the critical thinking involved in research, *not boring*! The teacher's presumption that kids "don't even know how to think" might not be correct. Perhaps it isn't the thinking that is the problem, it is the work!

The key strategy for seductively engaging students to think critically is purpose. Purpose is empowered by *choice!* Students need to have the opportunity to make choices, and this is inherent in each step of the Research Process: topic, subtopics, sources, and keyword facts for notetaking. In this lesson, when students learn the skills and are given the opportunity to make choices to evaluate information, it proves you really can teach students to think! "When can we come back for another research project?" is an astonishing but actual question from my students.

Strategies to evaluate information for research include:

Subtopics: Have subtopic choices sitting in front of you so you know what you're looking for.

Pencil down: Read without writing to automatically promote an uninterrupted sequence of critically thinking about and evaluating information.

Ask yourself: What is important? Facts related to the subtopics will pop out, all by themselves. It's like magic!

Selecting

Some of the points in this section are taught in the student lesson script for Lesson 3, Part 2 because they are embedded in notetaking strategies.

There is a little magic act that goes along with this segment to enhance student understanding. I stand in front of the class with a pencil in my hand and ask them what it is for. I explain that there is something in our brain that makes us use this instrument when we are holding it. So I make that pencil disappear! I set it down dramatically and proceed to read aloud a segment of text. Then I ask the class to tell me the most important thing they heard, which they do quickly and easily. Believe it or not, this bit of drama is a key to information management! Forcing students to read a specified amount of information before selecting keyword facts magically ensures critical thinking. Try it yourself! Ideas and information that are truly important practically pop right off the page.

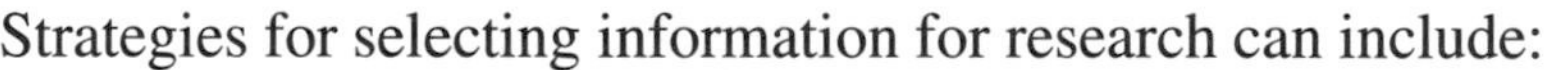

Strategies for selecting information for research can include:

- Choosing information that directly supports the topic and subtopics.
- Focusing on new information, not on obvious or prior knowledge, or small words your brain already knows.
- Using a book's table of contents or index to go directly to subtopic information.
- Using the bold subheadings of print or electronic encyclopedias to go directly to subtopic information.
- Skipping information not related to subtopics, at least until subtopics have been covered.

Specific strategies for selecting, excluding, or changing information are covered more explicitly in Chapter 8, on notetaking.

One of my collaborating teachers commented, "This is like riding a bicycle. It's easy to learn, and my students will never forget it. This [series of lessons] has changed their lives."

Instructional Strategies

I have heard it said that teachers are really frustrated actors. This lesson on selecting important information from context is one where I pull out all the stops on dramatic instruction to emphasize to the students certain points about information evaluation strategies. With only one chance to make a lasting impression, the dramatic technique of instructional hyperbole becomes very important. An example is when I demonstrate how to skim and scan. I come around from behind the overhead projector and stand right in front of the class. While holding a book open to a page of text, with exaggerated facial expressions, voice intonations, and gestures, I actually say things such as:

Literacy

I'm quickly skimming quickly down the page . . . read, read, read, read. When I get to the bottom, I ask myself, "What was on this page? Absolutely nothing! So I flip to the next page and do it again.

I do not feel I am insulting students' intelligence by using words and gestures as if I were acting out the activity in a play. I think this play-acting enables me to make the same points lesson after lesson with the same sincerity and vigor. My exaggerations rivet their attention, and the students focus on what is being said whether they intend to or not. The students' ability to repeat evaluation strategies when working on their own testifies that something is working.

What's interesting is the effect of the lesson on the class's instructor. Although I may repeat the same research lesson five times in one day, the same collaborative teaching partner not only remains with the students but often comes up to me after each lesson to reflect on a different point or impression that he or she realized helps students gain these lifelong skills.

Lifelong Skills

As seen in the following student lesson script, the attention span of middle-school students requires that explanations of strategies, no matter how dramatic, for reading, thinking, or selecting information, be interwoven with supporting activities. For that reason, although isolated in this chapter for emphasis, this chapter's material is actually embedded in the notetaking lesson. In a teaching situation, to make meaning for middle-schoolers, it is difficult to separate purposeful reading strategies from the goal of notetaking. Therefore, the notetaking lesson is merely a logical extension of reading, evaluating, and selecting information.

Adaptations for Special and Advanced Students

Depending on the learning level of the students, the instructor precedes this lesson with some transitional re-teaching to create articulation from the previous lessons to enable better student comprehension. Reading, thinking, and selecting strategies for special needs students are intertwined with the entire Research Process.

ELL/Special Modifications

Second language and special education students benefit from:

- Topics pre-selected from available and readable sources.
- Subtopics with apparent and abundant support material. Fewer subtopics than required for the project for average students.
- Sources preselected for specific reading levels. Fewer sources than required for the project for average students.
- Reading from smaller "chunks." Evaluating for fewer keywords.
- Fewer notes required on a daily basis for the project for average students.
- Fewer pages for a rough draft written from notes.
- Project requirements that can be completed during class time instead of as homework, perhaps in special, but inconspicuous, LMC seating areas.
- Primary language tutor being available for research lessons. Partnering or grouping for peer assistance.

Problem Solving

Gifted and talented students benefit from:

- Challenging and/or independent topic choices.
- Subtopics requiring more extensive pre-searching for supporting information. More subtopics than required for the project for average students.
- Sources that are more challenging, even off-campus. More sources than required for the project for average students.
- More information read and selected for notetaking.
- More notes than required for the project for average students.
- More pages written from notes for the rough draft.
- Project requirements that need extra time to be completed, perhaps before and after school or as homework.

Student Lesson

Transitional Re-teaching

Optional section, depending on time and the ability level of the class.

LMT: Let's make some sense about what we've done for the last two days by looking back at the first few steps on your Research Process sheet (*Figure 7-1*). You may be surprised how much you've learned in a short time.

Look at the first step, "Topic." For the rest of your life you'll have strategies for selecting a good topic by yourself. Challenge yourself and stretch your intellectual ability, but choose a topic with information within your physical limitations, such as after-school activities or not having transportation to the public library. Do not choose a topic so easy you learn nothing, or so difficult you get frustrated and cannot adequately complete the task.

Lifelong Skills

Next, think what you learned about subtopics. First, you know that they are the keywords to essential questions your research will answer and that you absolutely can't proceed without them. They are the backbone of your research, without which you have no idea what you are doing! Second, you know that they will tell you what information to select and what information to skip. Remember that controlling your subtopics is how you control information. At any time during research you can combine, change, add, or toss them out. But you must have them!

Yesterday, we looked at the "Sources" step of the Research Process. You now understand how important it is to give credit to an author. Best of all, you know how to locate all of the little parts and pieces of a citation entry and how to convert them into a final citation list.

Are you beginning to feel like a competent information manager? Wait, there's more! Today you are going to learn what to do with information from the sources you so carefully selected. I am going to use actual work samples from previous students to teach you effective strategies for reading, thinking about, and evaluating information to select keywords and facts for notetaking.

Information Literacy

Fig. 7-2. Purposeful Reading Cartoon

"It's an 'audio alternative' called reading."

Reprinted with permission of H. L. Schwadron as appearing in *Phi Delta Kappan*. January 1997, Volume 78, number 5.

Reading

Timing: 10 minutes.

Literacy

LMT: (With a transparency of the *Figure 7-2* cartoon on the overhead, hold up a fat book about the Renaissance.) Once you find a good source, guess what you have to do? You actually have to read! Yes, I know how you feel. Like the boy in the cartoon, there are many other things you'd rather do! Do you think that I am asking you to read an entire book like this? No! That's the good news. This whole book may be about your topic, but what about those wonderful subtopics that tell you what to include and what to leave out?

Problem Solving

Do you begin to realize that subtopics will save your life? Instead of having to read this whole book, you simply turn to the table of contents (open and display this) or to the index (again, demonstrate), and you will see very quickly exactly what you need.

Later, while researching, a student locates a subtopic in the table of contents of a book and says to his buddy, "Hey! Here is a whole chapter on my subtopic about the personal life of my artist. That's great. I have plenty to do this library period, so don't talk to me!"

Student: What if this chapter is still more than I need?

LMT: Excellent question. Let's say the chapter is 30 pages long and you have only 20 minutes left in the period. Do you have to sit here and try to read all 30 pages? Not unless you want to. There are a few, I'll call them "reading management," strategies that will save you from either unnecessary work or being overwhelmed by too much information. Does that remind you of what we decided about copying out of a book?

Literacy

Student: Yeah, when kids are confused they don't know what to pick out so they just take everything. It's plagiarism.

LMT: Very good! Let's get "unconfused" by first deciding what we mean by "reading." Is that what you're really doing during research? No, reading for this Renaissance project is not the same as relaxing at night with your favorite scary novel. What we should call this, instead of "reading," is "skimming," which is reading quickly for the general idea, or even "scanning," which is glancing over text for quick ideas or answers to questions. Because both of these are much faster than reading, the first strategy is speed.

The next strategy has to do with how much to read. Your Research Process sheet (*Figure 7-1*, letter A) says to read an entire "chunk" before selecting facts. What in the world is a "chunk?"

Lifelong Skills

Student: A piece of something.

LMT: Right! Reading a "chunk" means to read a piece at a time. It's like dividing a pizza up into slices so it's easier to eat. Let's take an example from a Renaissance book. I have an overhead transparency of a page from a book about Michelangelo. Look here and you'll see that a "chunk" in middle school may depend on how well you read. Your teacher knows you and can help you decide how fast and how much you can read.

For a second-grader, a "chunk" might be only a sentence. That's only as much as he or she can read and think about at one time. For a fifth-grader, it's probably a paragraph. But for you in seventh grade, it's at least a paragraph, maybe even a whole page, depending on how long the chapter is. The more you practice doing research, or the older you get, the bigger a "chunk" gets. (Adjust the examples to empower slow readers and challenge fast readers.) Does that make sense?

ELL/Special Modifications

Lifelong Skills

Here is a very important strategy that will help you read a whole "chunk." See this pencil in my hand? Put it down! (Demonstrate.)

Did you know that if you physically have a pen or pencil in your hand when you get ready to read, you will automatically do what a pencil was intended to do: write! But when you put that pencil down, you will automatically, magically, read that whole paragraph. In the beginning this is very hard to do. You'll have to force yourself. Hold your hand behind your back! (Gestures are very effective here.) Someone say back to me what the advantage is of that pencil being down.

Literacy

Student: You read.

LMT: That's it!

Thinking

Timing: A few minutes.

Problem Solving

LMT: The good news is, you do more than just read. Your brain automatically, without you even trying, starts to think about what that "chunk" is saying. Facts about your subtopics begin to jump out at you! These facts are the important words, which we call "keywords" because they are "key" information that matches your subtopics. I'll ask you to remember this in a few minutes when we talk about taking good notes. But the best news is, guess what you get to do with all of the information that doesn't match your subtopics? You get to skip it! It's wonderful!

With your pencil down, by the end of the "chunk," you're automatically saying to yourself, "I saw two facts that were important to my subtopic."

When facts jump out at you, without even trying, you are doing what's called "evaluating" information. It would be like your friend asking you to tell about a horror movie you just saw. Very easily you'd probably pick the scariest part to tell about. This is what happens when you read with your pencil down. It's simply magic!

Selecting

Timing: 5 minutes or less.

Problem Solving

LMT: When you evaluate information, what you are automatically doing is selecting what's important. Let me demonstrate how easy this is:

Here's a page about Michelangelo. I skim a paragraph with my pencil down . . . read, read, read, read. . . . When I get to the end, I think about my subtopic and automatically say, "Hmmm. There's nothing really important here!" So guess what I do? Skip it!

Do you realize what has just happened? Without consciously trying, I read quickly, I thought about what was in this paragraph, and I selected what was important, which in this case was nothing.

I do the same thing for the next paragraph, but automatically, all by themselves, two important facts jump right off the page. They almost pick themselves!

LMT: Let me emphasize again, if you are writing while you are reading, you lose the ability to make judgments about information. Everything looks good. You stop reading quickly for general ideas, you stop evaluating for what is important, and pretty soon the bell rings and you've spent the whole period copying everything out of the book. While you sat there using 45 minutes to copy a few pages in one book, your neighbor, who remembered to put her pencil down, used three sources! It's not brain surgery to know which student is going to end up with more research accomplished in less time.

Important Idea

Do you see that by asking you to read your sources, we are not asking something unreasonable? The reading strategies just covered, skimming quickly and dividing text into chunks that you read with your pencil down, will help you any time you are confronted with the task of reading and evaluating information. These are tools to help you meet your teacher's goal for you to use your time wisely. Better than that, it meets your goal of learning to do research *F-A-S-T*. You want to finish this project, right?

Problem Solving

Chapter 8

Notetaking: Lesson 3, Part 2

Instructor Information

Student Lesson

"I have ten notes in all of my subtopics. Can I take some more?"

—Eighth-grader

Fig. 8-1. Research Process: Notetaking

Topic *A good topic is "doable," but slightly challenging to your assessed abilities.*

A. Locate a topic in textbooks, library sources, or the teacher's topic list.
B. Check in the library media center for at least three formats of supporting information.
C. Cross-check in an encyclopedia to narrow or broaden a topic.

Subtopics *Ask yourself: What do I want to know about my topic?*

A. General subtopics may be brainstormed. Examples:
   Person: early life, education, work (be specific), later life.
   Place: origin, history, leaders, geography, economy.
   Thing: who, what, when, where, why/how.
B. Specific subtopics must be located in, for example, an encyclopedia's subheads.
C. The number of subtopics is based on the number of days of research.

Sources *A good source is any kind of supporting information that you can read.*

A. Format (the form information comes in) Examples include:
   Print: books, encyclopedias, magazines, newspapers.
   Nonprint: videos, laser disks, CD-ROMs, computer software, Internet.
B. Use at least three formats of information. Using one source is not research!
C. Credit sources using MLA-style citations.

Read/Think/Select *Good research promotes comprehension and evaluation.*

A. Read an entire "chunk" (a paragraph or a page) with your pencil down.
B. Think about what was read. What was important?
C. Select only a few key facts from each "chunk" to match your subtopics.

Notetake *A good note creates information ownership. This is learning!*

A. One note per card, titled with subtopic. Use as many cards as needed.
B. Record important keywords, facts, or a list, up to about 20 words (use your judgment).
C. No small words like *a, the, an, is, was*. Instead use commas and dashes.
D. No copying of sentences (without quotation marks and footnotes).

Sort and Number Notes *Good organization of notes makes writing easier.*

A. Sort notes by subtopic section, about five notes per paragraph (use your judgment).
B. Read notes in one section at a time and put in an order that makes sense.
C. Number notes consecutively through all sections without starting over at number 1.

Extension

Write/Publish/Present
Final citations list
Technology integration

Evaluation Student tracking

Chapter Concepts

The Key to Information Ownership

Learning occurs when information changes form. Notetaking accomplishes this. Through the selecting and recording of keywords or facts, students must process the original information into a note, which is then reprocessed into the writing of a rough draft. Information changes form twice and plagiarism is impossible!

The Key to Literacy and Learning

Creating a good note, both in content and in form, necessitates that the student read and comprehend sources to evaluate and select information that matches the subtopics and supports the topic. These automatic and sequential steps are literacy and learning.

Teaching Notetaking Strategies

Middle school teachers are overwhelmed with their own content-area curriculum. Teaching research strategies is not in their standards. Therefore, the library media teacher should respond to the information literacy mandate to give direct instruction in information management strategies, including notetaking. Teaching notetaking is accomplished most effectively through a flexible balance of direct instruction, guided practice, and hands-on activities.

Notes Should Look Like Notes

This section explores what a note is. Recording only keyword facts on separate note cards is one way to eliminate plagiarism. Copying sentences is allowed only with quotation marks and endnote or footnote citations. Paraphrasing and summarizing are also legitimate forms of gathering information, but are not addressed in this book. Alternative forms of notetaking for middle-schoolers beyond note cards are offered.

The Advantage of Good Notes

This section explores what makes a note good. Speed, accuracy, and amount of information gathered are the direct benefits of good notetaking, enabling students to use more sources, gather more information, and sort notes more easily to write a better-balanced and more internalized report. Simply put, good notes empower good writing!

Instructor Information

The Key to Information Ownership

Lifelong Skills

Notetaking is the "front line" of information ownership. It is the means by which information leaves the source and transitions to the user. In other words, it is

the essential step for converting information ownership from the author to the student. That transition involves all the evaluation, critical thinking, and problem solving skills that we desire students to learn to become independent thinkers and lifelong learners. With this in mind, the implications of what it means to simply "take a note" are enormous. It means that a student has a viable topic, has subtopics to guide the search for information, has appropriate sources, has read pertinent information, has comprehended what was read, has used critical thinking to select something important, and has understood a means of recording it into the form of a note. Wow!

Yet an incredible dilemma is continuing to occur. I have heard adults, even other teachers, say that for lack of instruction during their own school days, they simply "came up with" their own method of doing research and taking notes. Is this being perpetuated among our students today?

No, in this sense: In the middle and high schools where I have taught, it has been the language arts, GATE (gifted and talented education), and AVID (Advancement Via Independent Determination) teachers who have made the time and have the interest in teaching notetaking skills to their students. To their credit, they teach many different kinds of notetaking to meet the needs of reading, writing, and listening learning situations.

Content-Area Standard

Yes, in this sense: Curiously, it is the social science, science, and health teachers who, although they assign more research projects, do not often teach the research skills needed to complete those projects, as we saw in Chapter 1 in *Figures 1-5* and *1-6*.

Information Literacy

This continuing information literacy crisis is a call to arms for library media teachers to take up the banner of teaching information management and critical thinking, especially through direct notetaking instruction. Happily, this is accomplished through the Research Process, which also ensures that notetaking meets collaborating teachers' specific needs for standards-based research.

The Key to Literacy and Learning

Literacy

The positive goal of this chapter is to demonstrate that notetaking begins with reading and ends with learning. The negative goal is to prevent plagiarism. Notetaking is a process skill that enables students not only to manage information independently but also to learn how to learn. Two parts of notetaking, content and form, are presented in this lesson.

Content

Problem Solving

Content comes from deciding what information should be in a note. It involves the cognitive act of notetaking. Information from a source is accessed by reading and comprehending, evaluated by processing and selecting, then changed or reduced into keywords and facts to create information ownership. Most important, the entire process begins with reading, thus the focus on literacy. The process ends with information changing form through notetaking, which is learning. In the student lesson script, I call notes "shrinky dinks," which are later expanded by

prior knowledge and imagination into good writing. When students copy, no learning occurs because information is not processed through critical evaluation but is merely repeated in its original form. Thoughtful information ownership strategies include:

- Selecting new information, not something the student already knows.
- Selecting keywords or facts to distill the essential meaning of context.
- Changing the order in which information originally appears while maintaining the accuracy of the data.
- Combining words, phrases, and facts from the same source, or a variety of sources, to creatively meet a specific purpose.

Form

Form is the physical act and appearance of notetaking. It's what makes notes look like notes. It is the recording of information in a form different from the original narrative to enable both speed and accuracy, but mostly to provoke the most memory for future writing from the fewest words. Notetaking strategies include:

Lifelong Skills

- Carefully selecting words for maximum meaning.
- Recording phrases and facts including numbers and nouns, as well as adjectives and adverbs, that expand the student's vocabulary. I tell the students to take "fat, juicy notes!" by leaving out small, unimportant words and replacing them with commas or dashes to connect similar information.
- Listing related words or terms that are scattered over a paragraph, page, or chapter in a source, connected with commas.
- Summarizing or paraphrasing. This usually requires quotations and a footnote citation because it is borrowing heavily from the original author. (This strategy is not presented in this book as a notetaking tool for students at this stage of learning the Research Process.)
- Quoting sentences and creating proper citations to credit the author. (This form of notetaking is not required in this Renaissance unit.)

Teaching Notetaking Strategies

The concepts of notetaking explained in this instructor section are not belabored in the following student lesson script. Middle-schoolers need action! Therefore, direct instruction about notetaking is quickly followed with the students' real-time preparation of their own note cards to begin hands-on research. The student lesson is divided into parts enabling each student to:

- Prepare his or her own individual, genuine note cards through specific labeling directions. Students will understand that the purpose of good labeling is simplicity, speed, and accuracy.
- Learn the reading/thinking/selecting strategies it takes to extract and record information so notes look like notes.

- Learn what both the content and form of a note should be through many student samples. Both content and form make it obvious to the instructor whether the note is good or bad.
- Learn that the purpose of taking notes is to write, and write well! Good notetaking is goal-driven. The more students relate their own notes to their own writing, the less you will hear the following:

"Teacher, is this a good note?" asks a seventh-grader.

"Can you make a sentence out of it?" asks the LMT. "Or better yet, could you make either one fantastic sentence, or several good sentences? Whose paper is this, and whose note?"

"Oh yeah, I get it. I need to change this a little."

The ultimate purpose is independent information management!

Notes Should Look Like Notes

Why note cards? Despite the many excellent ways to teach and take notes, I strongly believe that note cards are the method that should be taught first in Research Process instruction. In my experience, cards for notetaking can and should be used from grades three to nine. I have used them as early as first grade, I use them exclusively in middle school, and some high school teachers prefer to use cards if students have had little previous instruction in notetaking.

Information Literacy

Figure 8-2 represents a condensed template of blank note cards that I use, by teacher request, with students who might lose lots of individual cards. These attached cards are used in the same way as separate cards: titled with subtopics, coded with sources, recorded with keyword notes, then cut apart for the final step of sorting and numbering. However, most middle-schoolers are quite capable of managing separate cards with the help of a good storage system. I either save their work in class folders or provide a three-hole punch so storage bags can be kept in their three-ring binders.

The purpose of using cards is not so much to teach a specific system or a methodology of recording information as much as it is to teach students how to think! There is a sequential logic to note card notetaking that, once learned, becomes a permanent part of the student's information management skills.

A transitional form of notetaking that is appropriate for middle-schoolers is specialized note sheets. It is discussed at the end of this chapter.

Preparing Note Cards

On this third day of research lessons and activities, capture students' interest quickly by kicking off with an activity for preparing genuine note cards (*Figure 8-3*), not samples. Middle-school students can easily use blank cards made from old, recycled catalog cards or from chopped up, recycled computer printer paper. These don't have all the circles and lines seen on the overhead transparency, and it is important for students to understand the rationale for note card labeling so this potentially tedious job makes sense and they'll want to repeat it independently:

Title: A subtopic appears at the top center of each card as a guide to what the note is about. This reinforces for students why research questions are reduced to an essential keyword or two. The subtopic title not only tells the student what to look for in a source, but later makes the card information self-sorting to prepare notes for writing. Having all cards pre-titled is a mandate I insist upon in middle school so that students have the added benefit of knowing each day of research exactly how many remaining notes to take for each subtopic. This is a great time-saver and organizer.

Initials: This is a simple tool for the identification of cards. Instruct students to record their initials in the upper right-hand corner of all cards.

Source Code: For novice researchers, a simple "B" for book, "R" for reference, "CD" for CD-ROM, "I" for Internet, etc., should appear in the lower left-hand corner of each card. For experienced researchers, or when more accurate citations are required for quotations and footnotes, a more specific citation code can be taught (see *Figure 8-20*).

Sequence Number: Students should leave this space blank. It is very important that the upper left-hand corner is left blank during notetaking because that is where the sequence number of the note will be recorded during the final step of sorting note cards to prepare for writing.

Note Space: The entire center of the card is also left blank for notetaking, as demonstrated when the student lesson script goes on to cover "What is a note?" and the difference between "good" and "bad" notes.

Fig. 8-2. Template of Student Note Cards

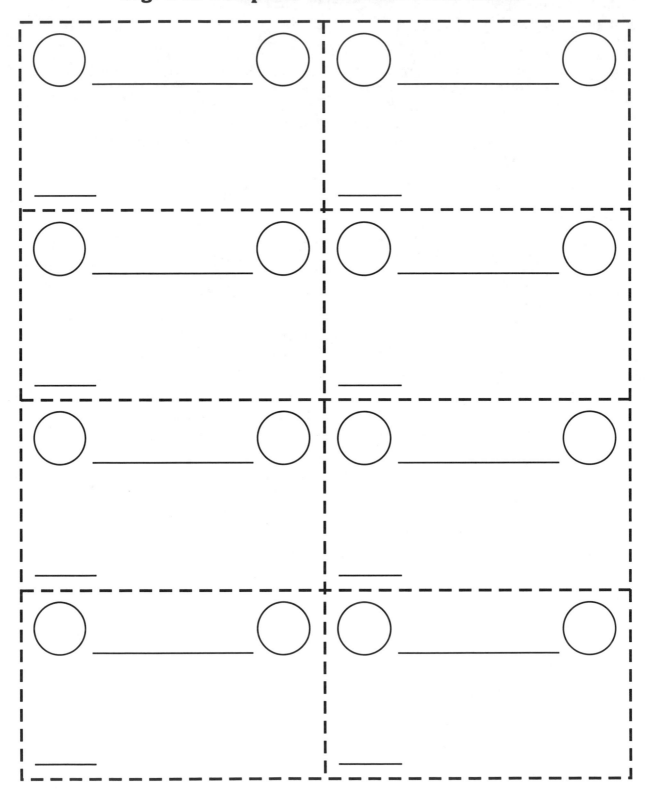

Fig. 8-3. Note Card Setup

Sequence Number
(during sorting)
Subtopic
Student's Initials
Source and/or Page Number
Keyword Note:
• main idea or fact
• one note per card
• up to 20 keywords (use judgment)
• no small words
• use commas or dashes
• no sentences (without quotes/footnotes)

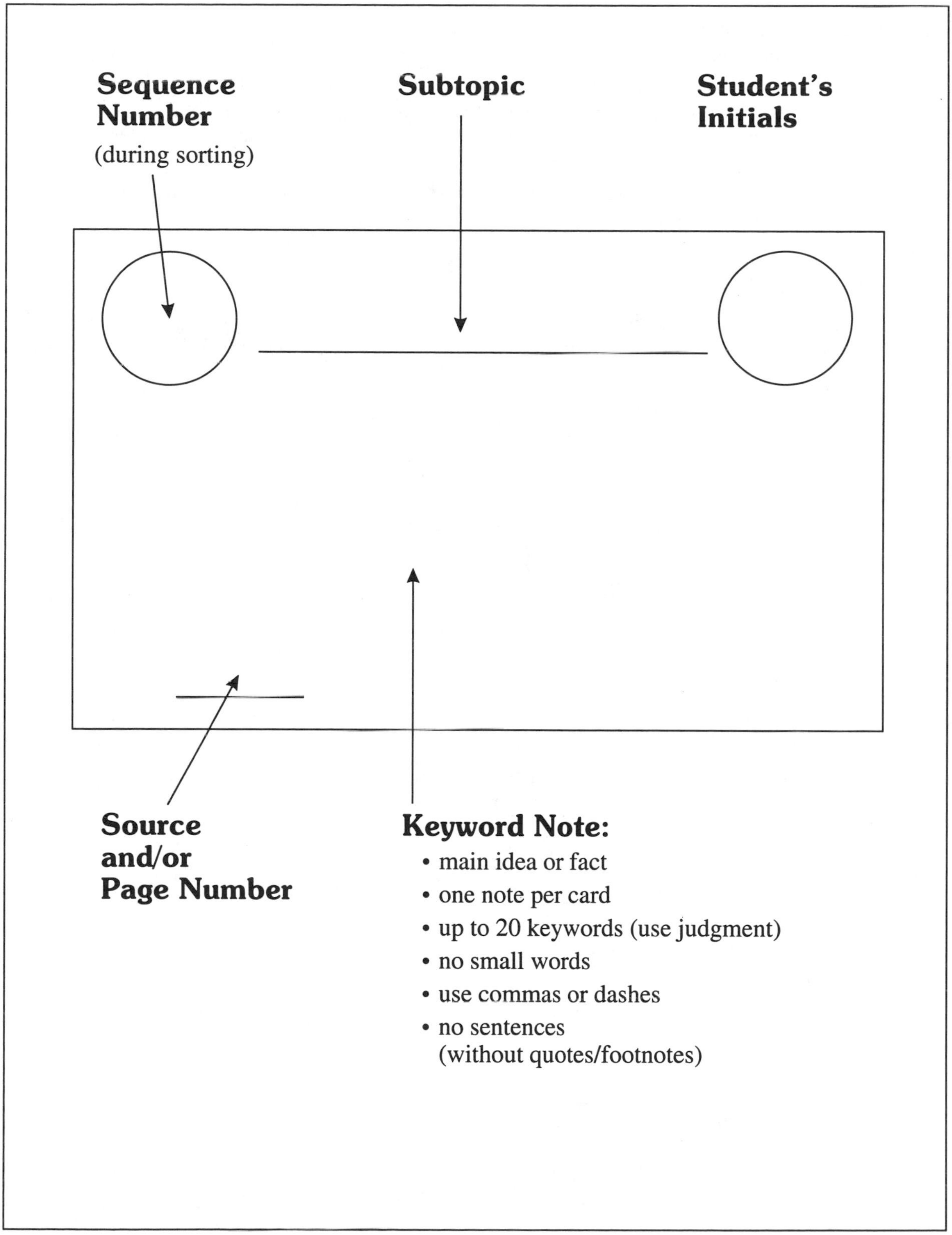

Setting Reasonable Expectations

Information Literacy

What the Research Process does that may be different from other information management systems is to set goals, specific numbers of things, that can be reasonably accomplished by the average student in the research steps (*Figures 8-4* and *8-5*). This adjustable formula is based on years of collaborative lessons with all levels of students. Giving students tangible daily goals is part of those doable bites that enable the Research Process to translate abstract information literacy standards into concrete information management. "Can't I do more?" some students even ask! "Of course," replies the LMT. "Just finish 10 notes in each subtopic first, and be sure you've used each of your sources."

ELL/Special Modifications

Ten notes per day is the number an average student can reasonably be expected to complete in one class period. Keep in mind that this includes locating a source; reading and comprehending the information; then evaluating, selecting, and recording notes. Advanced students may be expected to take more than 10 notes per day. Special students may take fewer.

The collaborating teacher sets the number of research days (*Figure 8-4*). Based on that number are the goals students can reasonably attain in each step of the Research Process. Time is the key to all expectations.

Important Idea

The minimum number of notes—10 per day for the average middle-schooler—multiplied by the number of days spent in the LMC equals a reasonable total number of notes that students are expected to complete successfully.

The minimum number of notes can also be a guide for a reasonable expectation of the number of pages the student later writes. Ten good notes should equal about a page of writing. For the Renaissance unit, with 30 notes, each student should produce at least a three-page paper.

Setting practical expectations results in greater student success. So when teachers say, "My students need to write a 10-page paper," I gently guide them into doing the math! Once they walk through what it physically takes for a student to be able to perform research and produce a product, they usually say, "Oh! I had no idea. I guess I really would rather have something shorter and more genuine."

Fig. 8-4. Aligning Notetaking with Research Expectations

Subtopics	Sources	Research Days	Notes	Pages Due
3	3	3	30	3
4	4	4	40	4
5	5	5	50	5

Special student: Reduce each number according to ability.
Advanced students: The above expectations are a minimum.

Fig. 8-5. Notetaking Goals

Notes per Subtopic	Notes per Day	Notes per Source*
10	**10**	**10**

Special student: Reduce each number according to ability.
Advanced students: The above expectations are a minimum.

*The number of notes per source is sometimes a lesson goal, and sometimes it is negotiable, depending on the sources.

The Advantage of Good Notes

"I never really understood the value of note cards until now. It's so easy to move information around so writing makes sense."
—Workshop attendee

The simple fact is that good notes empower good writing. All of the previous research lessons and all of the demonstrated strategies are targeted to that intuitive goal. I firmly believe that the instructor must gently (or strongly, with middle-schoolers!) push students through all of the Research Process steps, especially coercing them through the seeming drudgery of note card notetaking, to the point where they must sit, in class, with only their note cards in front of them and write that paper. That is the moment of realization.

With access to their past sources entirely cut off and the prospect of writing a three-page (or more) paper looming large, light bulbs go off in their heads:

"Can't I just look back at that one book I was using?"

"I just need three more notes for my 'Renaissance' subtopic."

"But I wasn't done with my CD-ROM printout!"

These are the pleas from students for whom the idea that all those little note cards really do add up to something hadn't quite jelled.

"Make do with what you have," says the wise instructor. "Next time you take notes you'll do a much better job!"

What good are all those little scraps of information, anyway? Lots of good!

Instructional Strategies

Lifelong Skills

Be patient. Good notes are not achieved the first time through the Research Process. But when their notetaking improves, students are so excited their faces absolutely glow! This success is developed only with practice in every year of schooling. Over time, good notes can be achieved through the following strategies, which are presented more simply or dramatically, concretely or abstractly in the student lesson depending on the students, the time, and the instructor's techniques:

- **Humor:** Many thanks go to Hoest and Reiner (*Figure 8-9*) for the introductory cartoon. Appropriate humor, from professional humorists or from the instructor, form a transition between research steps or smooth the bumps of the often rocky road of information management.

- **Instructional delivery:** Are you wild and crazy or polite and subdued? Making meaning for middle-schoolers can often depend on the manner in which an instructor delivers the message. You really can make a silk purse out of a sow's ear!

- **Student samples:** Although student samples are used in each of the Research Process lessons, they are especially effective in this lesson on notetaking. Instructors would do well to save strategic samples of student work (no names please) and use them to make important points. Classes really understand what a good or a bad note is by seeing what previous students have actually done. "Seeing is believing" decreases their own error rate while increasing their notetaking and writing success.

- **Sharing:** Be sure to take some time at the end of the first notetaking lesson for students to practice. While they are reading and making those early, tenuous attempts, walk among the students to view their progress. Ask to share different kinds of good examples. Without embarrassment, students having problems will more quickly make adjustments.

- **One-on-one intervention:** Quietly ask the student who is still copying sentences what he or she could do to change the note into a keyword fact. Suggest ideas, guide the cross-outs, help locate the important words, help insert commas and dashes. Presto! A good note emerges from the ruins. Coming back later, you'll see the student is recording all notes appropriately.

Adaptations for Special Students

ELL/Special Modifications

Middle-school students genuinely are "caught in the middle." Although learning and maturity levels range from elementary to middle school to high school, usually the Research Process modifications seen in each of the lessons work quite well. However, there are some students with learning and language disabilities for whom that is not enough. Two examples of special adaptations are given on the following pages.

The first example, *Figure 8-6,* was created for a unit with special education students who were able to handle the note card format but were overwhelmed and confused by separate, individual cards. The previously mentioned research modifications were made. They had an "easy" topic, fewer general subtopics, fewer and easily read sources. The students had a very concrete learning level, so during the planning stage the LMT and teacher decided that students should try to locate two notes for each of the three subtopics in each source. Students still had an element of true information searching in the sense that the instructors did not always know exactly which sources would contain all three subtopics. Therefore, these sheets were pre-formatted for books, references, CD-ROMs, and the Internet so students had a choice of hunting in all formats to locate their three subtopics. Their success in accomplishing this task was so empowering that they eagerly approached the writing task and produced some wonderful products, which were then enhanced with technology integration. Students were so happy that many selected the report for their portfolios. They loved it and learned a lot!

Problem Solving

Technology Proficiency

The second example, *Figure 8-7,* was created for special education students with more severe mental and physical limitations. Some students could barely read and write; indeed, they functioned at a lower level than upper-grade elementary students. But in meeting the educational requirements to not "dumb down" the content of what is taught, we forged ahead with a unit on the biographies of famous African Americans. Anticipating such an eventuality, I had stocked the library media center with a good selection of elementary-level biographies, so the students actually had a choice, the first point of empowerment! Only the tool for gathering the notes was truly adapted. In fact, it came straight from a unit I had done years earlier with second-graders. Very simple notes were recorded on the two-tiered, pre-ruled line spaces. Again, it worked. An appropriate tool reduced or eliminated information-gathering frustration, and students were able to produce most satisfactory products, which were embellished with color image insertions. They were proudly displayed at Open House!

Literacy

Fig. 8-6. Notetaking Adaptation for Resource Specialist Students

Notetaking

(Reference) Encyclopedia: MLA-Style Citation

AUTHOR"S NAME (last, first, middle) ______________________________ (period).

ARTICLE TITLE (quotation marks) ______________________________ (period).

TITLE of reference (underlined) ______________________________ (period).

YEAR ______ (period). Followed by edition, abbreviated to: ed ______________________________ (period).

Example: Summers, David. "Michelangelo." The World Book Encyclopedia. 2000 ed.

○ Life ○	○ art ○	○ Renaissance ○
○ Life ○	○ art ○	○ Renaissance ○

Fig. 8-7. Notetaking Adaptation for Special Education Students

Name:

Topic:

What was the artist's (life) like?

-
-
-

What was the artist's (art) like?

-
-
-

What was the (Renaissance) like?

-
-
-

Fig. 8-8. Note Sheet Notetaking in AVID Format

Name: ______________________ Teacher: __________________ Pd.: _____

Topic: Michelangelo

Notetaking

1. Part A: Record subtopic on line space below "Subtopic."
2. Part B: Record one note per bubble. Important words only. No capitals, periods, or small words. Copy sentences only when using quotation marks.
3. Part C: Record source codes: B = book, E = encyclopedia, I = Internet.

*Line space before "Subtopic" and bubbles will be numbered later when notes are sorted.

Part A: ____Subtopic	Part B: Keyword notes	Part C: Source code
__________	○ ______________________________	__________
	______________________________	
	○ ______________________________	__________
	______________________________	
	○ ______________________________	__________
	______________________________	
	○ ______________________________	__________
	______________________________	
	○ ______________________________	__________
	______________________________	
	○ ______________________________	__________
	______________________________	
	○ ______________________________	__________
	______________________________	

Beyond Note Cards

The use of note cards can be, and should be, a choice based on the needs of the collaborative teaching that evolve during the initial planning meeting. Although note cards are important to train students to organize their thinking as well as their information, there are times when other methods of information gathering are appropriate. Other factors may include:

- **Teacher's time:** A two-week research unit pictured in the *Figure 2-6* lesson plan calendar is simply not always possible in the busy schedules of both the library media teacher, who struggles to accommodate the needs of all teachers and all students on campus, and the collaborative teacher, who likewise struggles to cover all required standards-based curricula for which the students will be accountable on year-end testing. When a unit needs to be condensed into an incredibly tight one-week time frame, a notetaking sheet similar to the example in *Figure 8-8* can be an excellent compromise.

Two important points must be made regarding such a notetaking form: (1) This style of notetaking must never take the place of initial training with note cards, and (2) a note sheet must be devised for each of the source formats being used in a project. This note sheet example with an encyclopedia citation at the top would be accompanied by others written for the Internet or for a book if those formats were also being used, even on a short project.

- **Students' experience:** There comes a point when students grow beyond note cards. Depending on their level of training in research when they arrive in middle school, this point can come in either seventh or eighth grade. Once students begin to develop logical thinking patterns for information management and show signs of independent use of research skills and strategies, the use of specially designed note sheets in middle school hastens the progression toward the notebook paper notetaking taught to high-schoolers and explained in *Practical Steps to the Research Process for High School.* One particularly effective note sheet is the AVID (Advancement Via Individual Determination) sheet in *Figure 8-8.* This sheet allows tremendous flexibility in meeting different teachers' content-area needs while supporting a powerful program for assisting low-income students to make college dreams a reality.

Lifelong Skills

Notice that *Figure 8-8* incorporates several research steps into one form: Section A reflects chosen subtopics; section B allows two lines for recording notes in keyword form with blank circles for the later step of sorting and numbering notes; section C is a simple way to cite a source for every note. It's quite a handy and flexible tool!

Fig. 8-9. Notetaking Cartoon

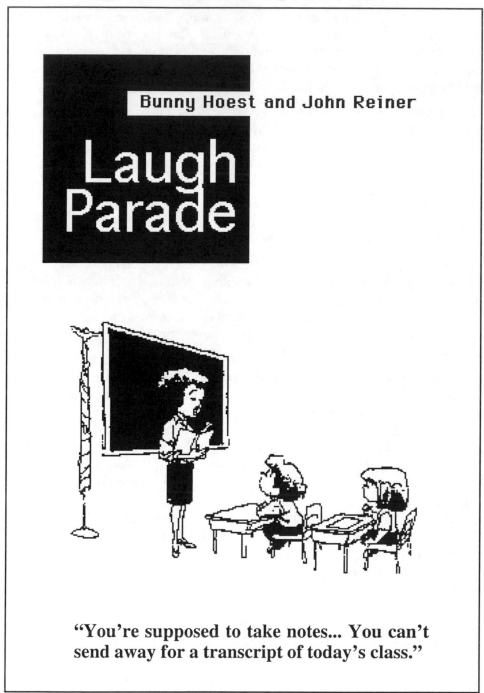

"You're supposed to take notes... You can't send away for a transcript of today's class."

Student Lesson: Notetaking Strategies

Timing: 20 minutes.

The Key to Information Ownership

LMT: To move you into the next step of the Research Process, let's look at the cartoon on the overhead (*Figure 8-9*). The teacher is telling her two little cyber-cherubs that they're "supposed to take notes." Why is she saying that?

Student: The kid is just gonna download stuff and turn it in, probably.

LMT: You're probably right! Curiously, as soon as all your teachers construct a web page, it would be easy, even helpful, for you to sit at your home computer and print out a copy of that day's lesson. But is snatching information electronically a good way to solve today's research problems?

Technology Proficiency

Now think about it. Downloading could be a form of copying, which we just learned in yesterday's lesson about "Sources" is illegal! More important, you don't learn anything that way. Just like the teacher in the cartoon, I'm going to tell you to take notes to prevent you from copying. So today's lesson is about notetaking. I hope you will see that it will make research easy as well as help you learn! Easy learning? Sounds impossible. But, believe it or not, something occurs in your brain when you take notes that is the secret to "information ownership," making information your own. First let me ask you, what are some ways that you have gotten information in the past?

Student: Copy out of the book.

LMT: Very honest! Your answer could be taken in two ways. Literally, it means information from a source goes right into your report. Maybe you changed a few words so you could tell your teacher you "wrote it." But I think you mean that you need to transfer information from one place to another. Right? Some of you copy to transfer information because you might not know any other ways, right again? So let's dig into the Research Process toolbox one more time and we'll find some notetaking tools, the strategies, which will allow you to evaluate and select information so that it becomes yours, not just the author's.

Fig. 8-10. Research Checklist: Notetaking

LMT/Teacher Tracking:	**Date Due:/Points:**	
Topic *Michelangelo*	*10/31*	*5*
Subtopics	*10/31*	*5*
I. *What was his personal (life) like?*		
II. *What was his (art) like?*		
III. *What was the (Renaissance)?*		
IV. ______		
V. ______		
Sources	*11/3-8*	*30*
A. At least 3 formats. Circle choices: (book), (reference), CD-ROM, (Internet), other: ______ B. Total number of sources: *3*		
Read/Think/Select	*11/3-8*	*5*
A. A "chunk" is *a paragraph.*		
Notetake A. At least *10* notes for each subtopic. B. Total number of notes: *30*	*11/3-8*	*30*
Sort and number notes		
Write rough draft from notes		
Teacher Grading: Title Page		
Typed Report		
Final Citation List		
Image/Chart		

Preparing Note Cards

LMT: There are a few simple directions to prepare for notetaking. The first thing I want you to do is get out your Research Checklist (*Figure 8-10*). Why?

Student: Because you told us to have our subtopics ready.

LMT: And if anyone didn't do that, you are really stuck today! You absolutely cannot go on to this step of notetaking, or do any research at all, without subtopics. I'll say it again, without them, you have no idea what you're doing! Also, remember you're being evaluated at each step. While I'm talking, your teacher is coming around with the Tracking Sheet (*Figure 12-1*) and he'll give you a minus if you don't have all three subtopics.

In the middle of every table is a small box filled with cards that you will use for your notes. This is how we recycle here in the LMC. Some of them are old card catalog cards. You probably don't even remember those ancient things. But most of it is recycled paper from the computer printers or copy machine that we chopped up.

I want you to count out 30 cards. Why 30? Because that will be the notetaking goal for this project on the Renaissance. You're scheduled for a total of three days in the library media center for hands-on research. You are supposed to take at least 10 notes each day. That will be 10 notes for each of the three subtopics. Three times 10 equals 30. Get it? So on your Research Checklist sheet in the "Read and Notetake" section, write "30" in the blank space after letter B. Is everyone clear on the minimum number of notes expected?

ELL/Special Modifications

Will you be allowed to take more than 10 cards per subtopic, or per day, when you start your own research? Of course you can! Whose paper is this?

Student: It's my paper!

Information Literacy

LMT: Yes! I want you to begin to feel empowered with the idea that you are learning ways to take control of the information that goes into your project. That is called information management, and it will be very important to you in all of your school years.

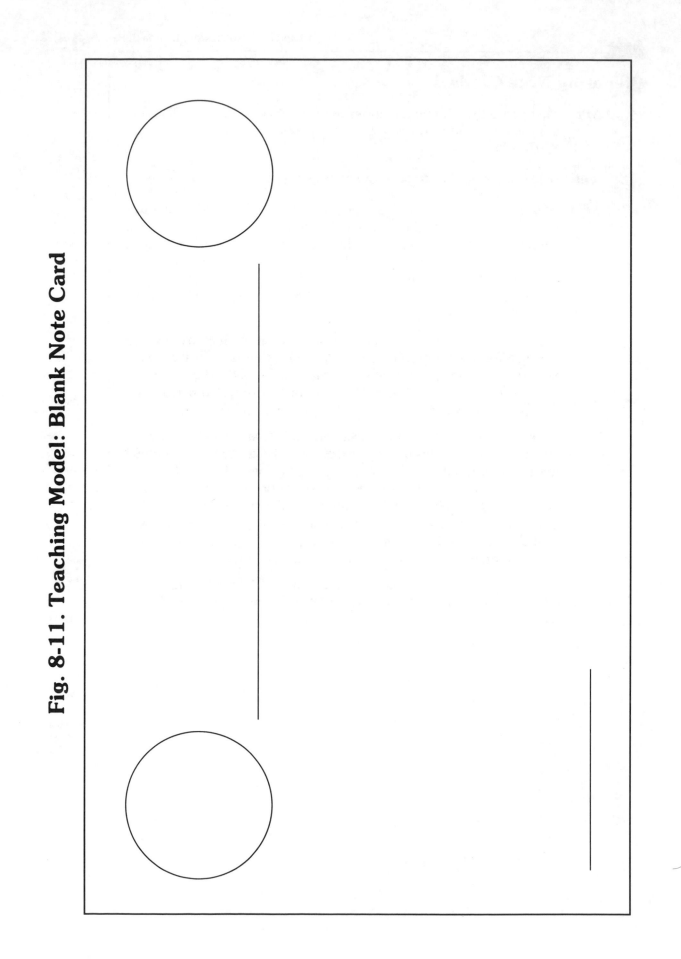

Fig. 8-11. Teaching Model: Blank Note Card

LMT: The next thing I want you to do is to prepare your cards for actual notetaking. Up here on the overhead I have a giant note card. (Use a transparency of *Figure 8-11.*) The lines and circles you see are just to show you where to put certain things as you label your own cards. Let's try it.

Put your initials here in the upper right-hand corner. (As an example, write your initials on the transparency.) I'm going to give you a few minutes to write your initials on each of the 30 cards. The signal that you are done and ready for the next direction is to look up at me, even a quick glance. It's important to prepare all your cards at the beginning so you have a definite goal for your research.

Most of you seem ready. Next, count out 10 cards and write your first subtopic on the top line, like a title. Why 10?

Student: Because that's how many notes we're supposed to take for each subtopic.

LMT: Correct. Does that mean you have to take all 10 notes in one subtopic before going on to the next one? No, because you don't know how many, or what kind of, notes you will find in each source. Using one source each day, simply aim for at least 10 notes that day. You could end up with three "life" notes, five "art" notes, and two "Renaissance" notes.

If there is still time left in the period, stop taking notes in that source after those 10 notes and go on to another source. So, 10 notes is also your cue to move to the next source! Wow, 10 is really important, isn't it? Yesterday in our "Sources" lesson, why did we say to move on to another source even if there is more information to take notes about?

Student: So we don't get everything out of one place and do plagiarism.

Student: To force us to use lots of kinds of sources, not just one or two.

LMT: Very good. Now finish titling your note cards by putting the second subtopic on 10 more and the third subtopic on the last 10 cards. (It is important to give most students time to complete each task.) If you don't get done, finish it for homework.

Fig. 8-12. Sample Note Card

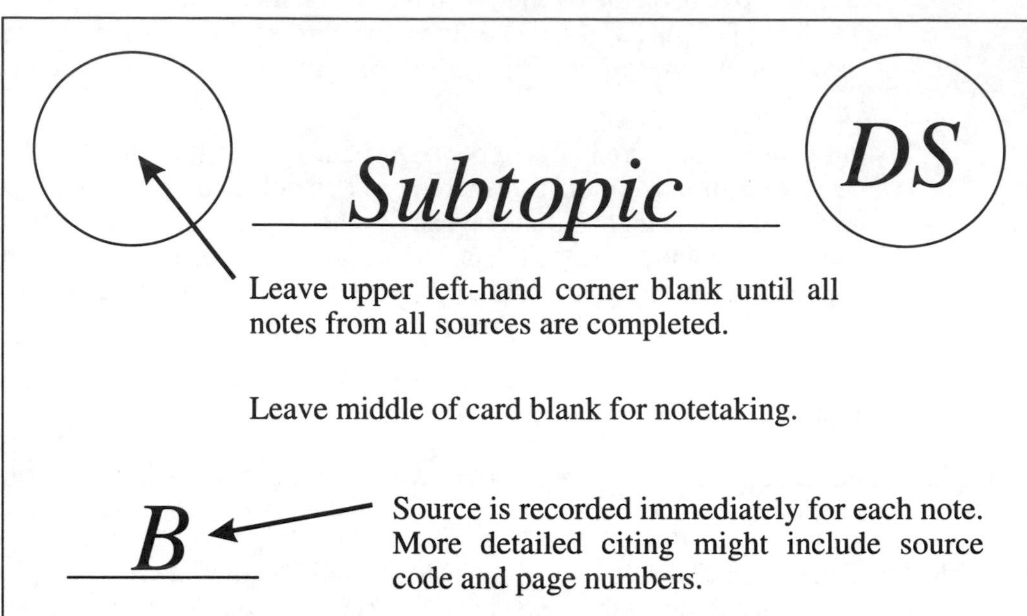

Citing Sources on Note Cards

For this exercise, write on a transparency of Figure 8-11. *The result is reflected in* Figure 8-12.

LMT: One last direction about setting up your note cards. Down here in the lower left-hand corner (*Figure 8-11*), I want you to always indicate what kind of source you have used. For example, if you're using a book for research today, write a "B." If you're reading and using a CD-ROM printout another day, what would you write?

Student: "C?"

LMT: Yes. Actually "CD" is fine. How about an encyclopedia?

Student: "E?"

LMT Or "R" for "reference." You're actually giving yourself a code to identify your source. It proves that your information came from three formats. Your note cards will be incomplete and receive less credit without that source citation. So, here's what your completely labeled cards will look like. (Display the labeled *Figure 8-11*.) Your teacher does not have to spend much time to see at a glance that all the parts are there.

Notes Should Look Like Notes

If time is short, teach only this important section. Don't refer to the Research Process sheet with less-mature or less-experienced students.

LMT: We've labeled and prepared our note cards, but we haven't tackled the main issue: What in the world is a note? In the Research Process (*Figure 8-1*, letter A), the first thing to remember is that there is only one note per card. If you have more than one idea or piece of information to write down, simply get a new card. Each card is titled with a subtopic telling what the note is about. That is *really* important! You'll see why in a few days when you need to sort your cards to use them for writing. If you have more than one idea or piece of information to write down, simply get a new card. Do you begin to see that is why taking 10 notes for each subtopic is so easy? Notes are short!

Problem Solving

Let's think about how to make good, short notes. We just learned about those important words called "keywords" a few minutes ago when we talked about some reading strategies. Who remembers the single most important thing that will make those keyword facts jump right off the page at you?

Lifelong Skills

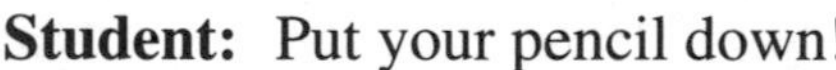

Student: Put your pencil down!

LMT: Wow. I think you've got it. That's exactly right. Pencil down forces your brain to read an entire "chunk"; then you automatically make decisions about what is important. Works like a charm!

Literacy

If you're looking for important keywords, then another very important thing in the Research Process (*Figure 8-1*, letter D) is "no copying of sentences." That means you cannot copy from anything, whether it's a book or the Internet, without using quotation marks and giving credit with something called a footnote or an endnote. Ever heard of those? You're lucky because that's not part of your teacher's requirements this time. You won't be required to do something that hasn't been taught to you in a lesson. That means, then, in your entire Renaissance project, there won't be quotation marks. But think, if there are no quotes, that means you cannot copy even one sentence from any source you use!

This brings us back to where we started. If you can't copy, what is a note? It's your turn to tell me the answer by telling me what you see. Here is an example of a student's note card from the semester before you. (Place a transparency of *Figure 8-13* on the overhead.) What do you think?

Fig. 8-13. Copied Note

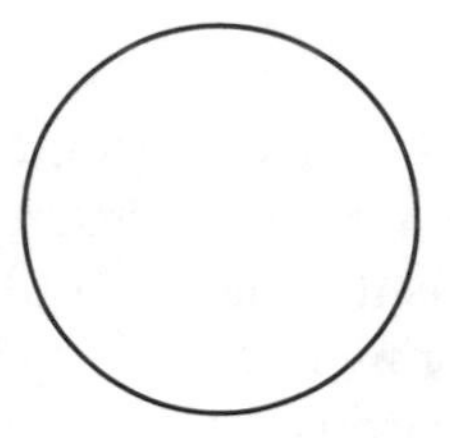

Life

DS

Michelangelo was born on March 6, 1478. His full name was Michelangelo Buonarroti and he came from a respectable Florence family.

R

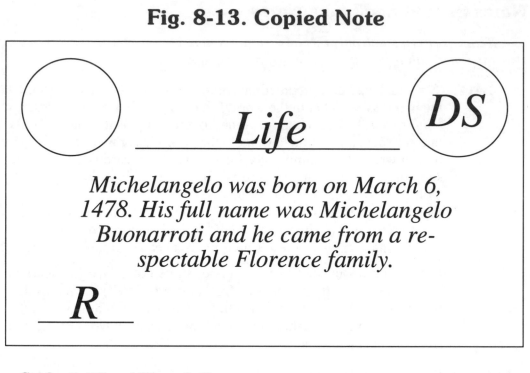

Student: Whew! He copied!

LMT: What makes you say that?

Student: I see sentences.

LMT: Which you can easily tell by the capital letters at the beginning and the periods at the end, unless it's for a name. (Circle those items, as in *Figure 8-14*.) So get rid of them in your notes. They are very obvious! Also, you said "sentences," so there's more than one. That's another problem, huh? This person has two notes stuck together on one card. (Draw a slash mark to separate the two sentences.) What else is wrong?

Student: I see small words that aren't important: "was," "on," and "for."

LMT: Very good. Remember, the Research Process sheet says, "Discard small words like *a*, *the*, *an*, *is*, and *was*. Use commas and dashes instead." Let's do some surgery. Let's cut out everything unnecessary and see what we have left. I'm going to start at the beginning. The first thing I'll cross out is "Michelangelo" (*Figure 8-14*). Why? Because that's this student's topic!

Fig. 8-14. Changed Note

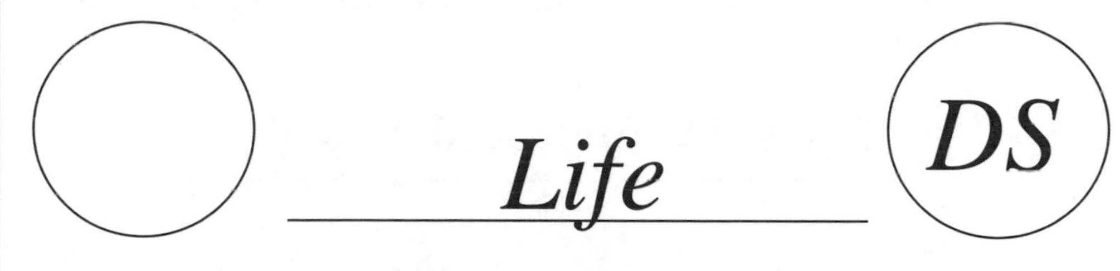

LMT: Why in the world would you waste time writing something you already know, and the most obvious thing you know is your topic? This leads us back to the question: What are notes for? The answer: new information! Use your very short library time to write down only things your brain has never heard of before.

Okay. Let's go on. Let's get rid of "was" because as a verb, that automatically makes this a sentence. "Born" is important, so let's leave it, but cross out "on." We'll replace it with a dash, not a comma. What do you think is the difference? Both commas and dashes seem to take the place of missing words.

Student: Um, I'm not so sure. The dash is replacing words you took out, but not the comma. It's just linking things that go together.

LMT: Interesting observation! That seems to make sense. The important thing is that you are making the choices of what to leave out, what to keep, and how to connect them. Those "keepers" are the keywords. They are the most important, essential words that make meaning for you later. They are like the keys to your brain that let all the information you read or remember come pouring out later on when you look back at your notes.

LMT: Let's finish repairing this note card. We'll put what's left of the two sentences on two cards and we'll take out all the small words, leaving only keyword facts. Here's what we have left: two greatly improved notes (*Figure 8-15*).

Fig. 8-15. Improved Notes

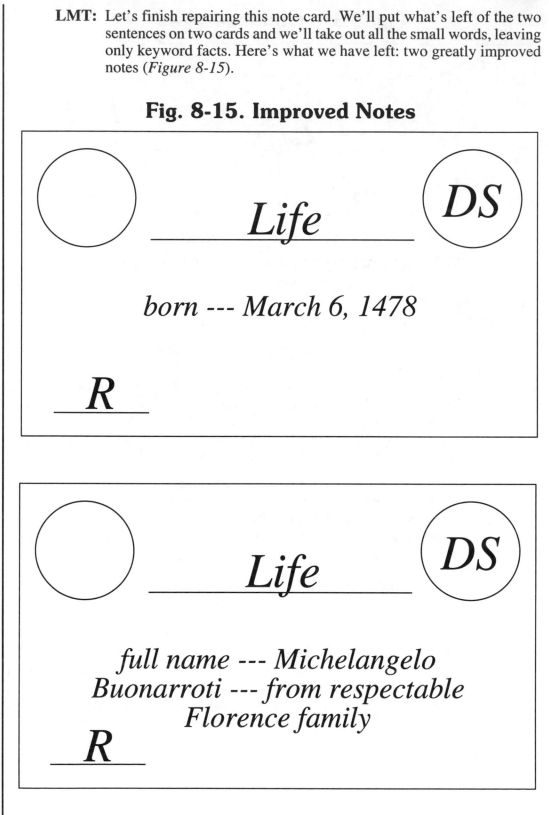

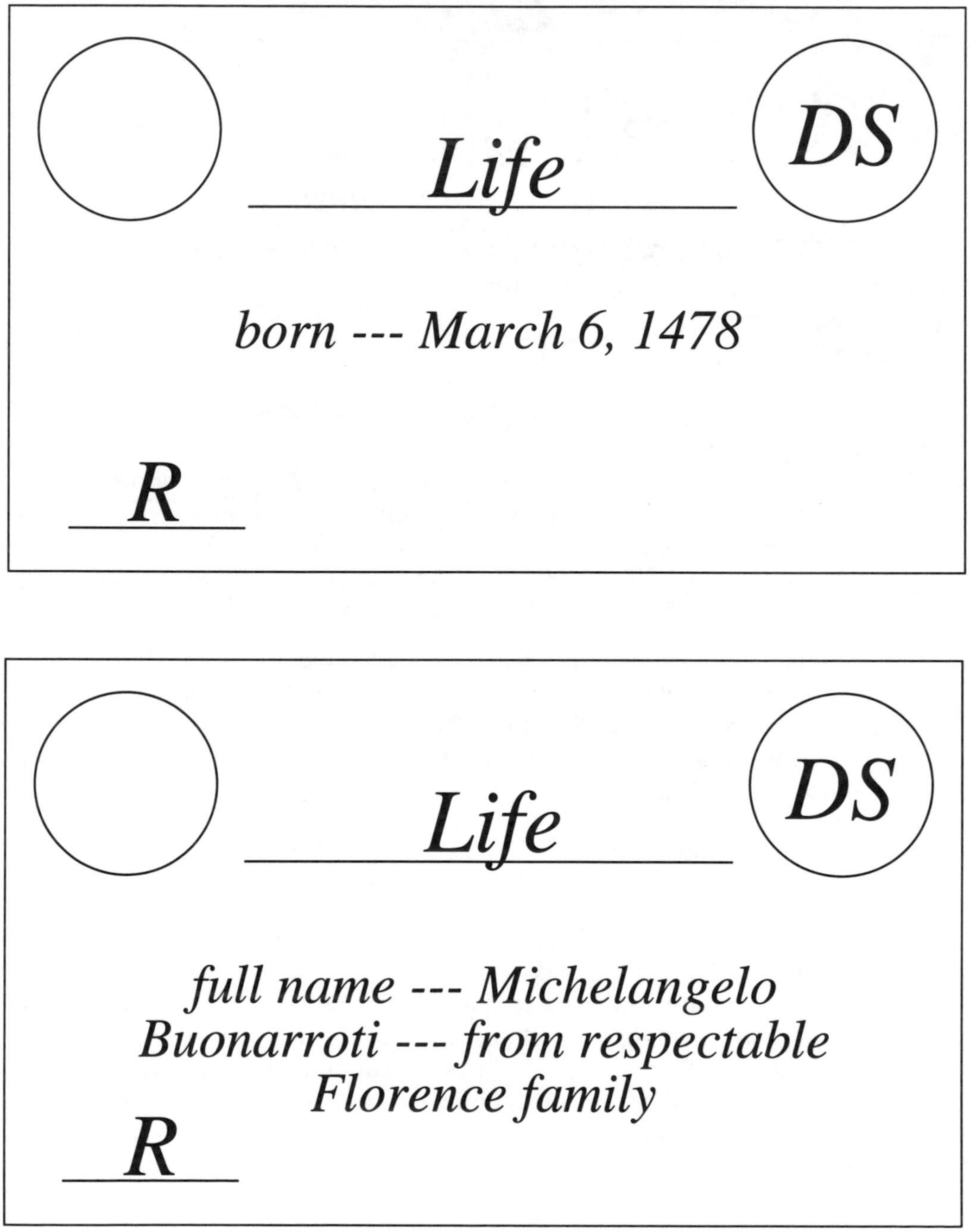

Life — *DS*

born --- March 6, 1478

R

Life — *DS*

full name --- Michelangelo Buonarroti --- from respectable Florence family

R

Fig. 8-16. List Note

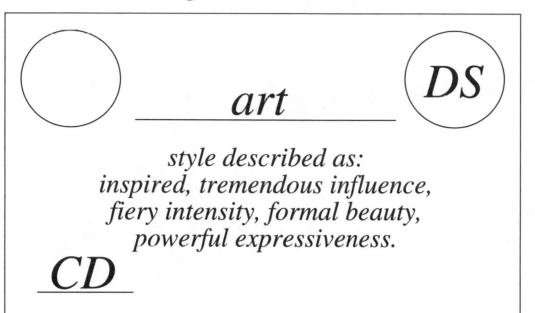

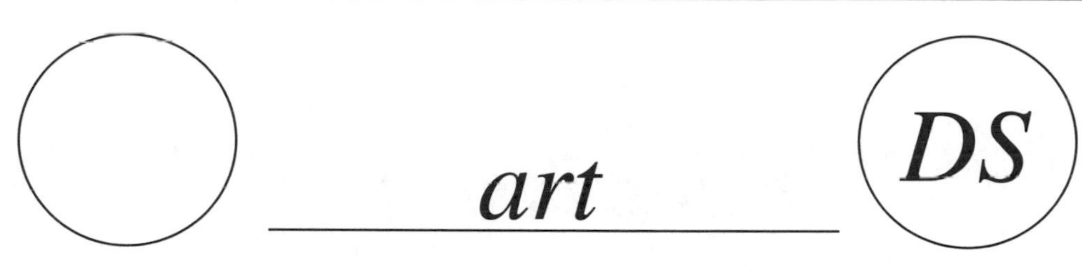

style described as:
inspired, tremendous influence,
fiery intensity, formal beauty,
powerful expressiveness.

CD

Notes in List Form

LMT: There are other ways to make good, short notes. Letter C on the Research Process sheet says, "Up to 20 words per card, [but] use good judgment." Twenty words is a lot! If we know you're never allowed to copy out of a book, unless it's a quotation, then there must be some special ways to select important words to keep the note short. As a matter of fact, the Research Process sheet even mentions one way—a list! For example, if you find several pages that describe Michelangelo's art, perhaps you could pick out words scattered all around those pages and connect them into a list, like this. (Display *Figure 8-16.*)

Student: That seems like an awful lot. Why isn't that copying?

LMT: Excellent question. Remembering that these words were scattered over several pages of a CD-ROM printout means this person had to read the whole chunk, decide what was most important, and then create this list. Reading and evaluating information to make choices about what to select is a very personal decision. When this student combines these particular words with another similar list that may have been found in an encyclopedia, for example, it is magically transformed into this person's own work.

Fig. 8-17. Too Brief Note

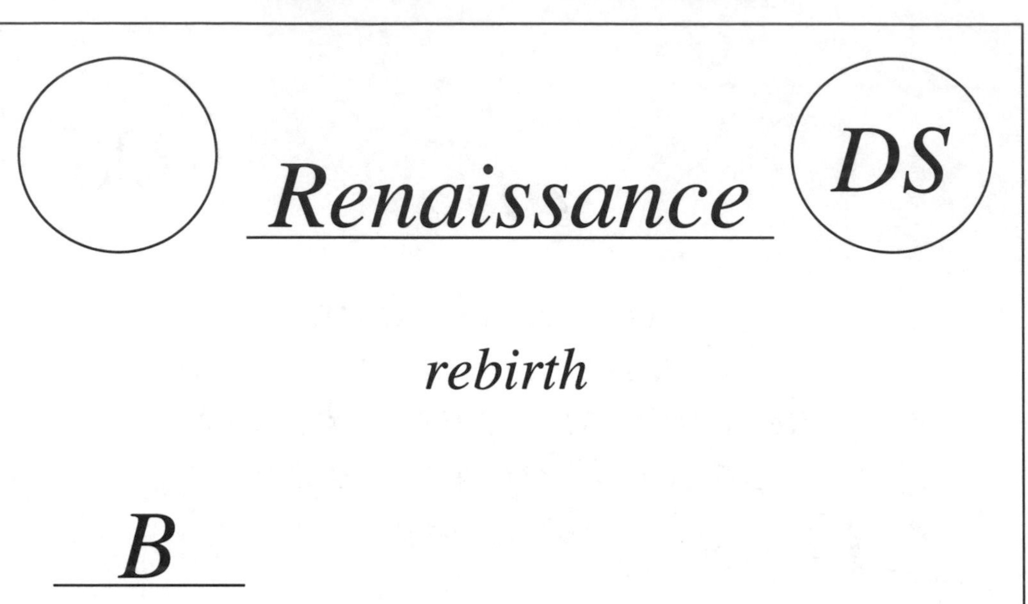

Notes That Are Too Brief

LMT: After a notetaking lesson last year, I had one class who was working so hard on trying to take good notes that a few of them got carried away. Look at this example and tell me what you think. (Use the overhead to display a transparency of *Figure 8-17.*)

Student: That's a note?

LMT: Yes. This is what a student actually wrote. Let me ask you the same question: "That's a note?" Who can remind us what makes a note good?

Student: By how much you can write with it.

LMT: Yes. Learn to be your own best judge. This note is fine if the student can make at least one good sentence out of it. But this particular student raised his hand and, get this, asked me what this note meant! I gave him a funny look and said, "Whose note is this?" He blushed and said, "Oh, yeah." Isn't it obvious that the most useless note would be one that even the student who wrote it couldn't understand? This student learned the hard way that a bad note is one that gives no help at all in writing a paper.

Fig. 8-18. Fat, Juicy Note

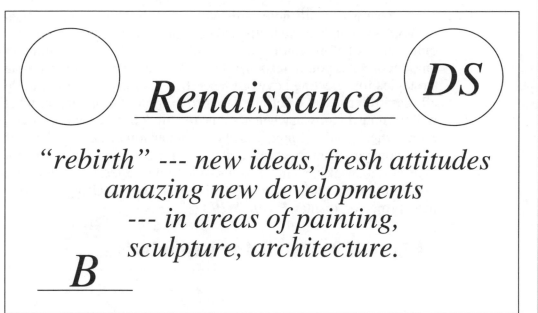

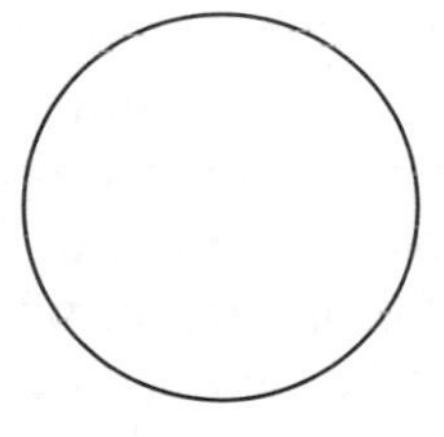

Renaissance *DS*

"rebirth" --- new ideas, fresh attitudes
amazing new developments
--- in areas of painting,
sculpture, architecture.

B

Notes That Are Fat and Juicy

LMT: Now this note looks better! (Using the overhead, display *Figure 8-18.*) Look at all the information that has been added to give meaning. This is what I call a "fat, juicy note"! Give yourself exciting adjectives and other interesting words that will help make better writing. But why is all this allowed on one card?

Student: Because it's all about "rebirth." And it's tied together with dashes.

LMT: Excellent. You're really beginning to understand what a note should be. Let's take it a little further. Remind us what looks good about this note, and what you see that could still be improved.

Student: There's no capital letter or period. So it doesn't look like a sentence.

Student: Yeah, it looks more like a fact, but I still see small words like "in" and "of."

LMT: Very observant! You are already doing a better job of critically evaluating information. You're recognizing strategies that will terrifically speed up your own notetaking.

The Advantage of Good Notes

LMT: You've learned to title note cards with subtopics, so you know what the note is about. You've learned to take the time to prepare all the required notes before you begin research as a guide to the minimum amount of notes you're responsible for. You've learned some simple strategies for selecting keyword facts. But it's most important to do all these things with a definite purpose in mind. For example, what will the note do for you when it's time to write? In other words, if you know where you're going, you'll do a better job of getting there. If you know you want to write a better paper, take better notes! Let me give you a sneaky example to test what you've learned. Based on everything we've talked about, is this a good note? (Using the overhead projector, display *Figure 8-19*.)

Fig. 8-19. Use Prior Knowledge

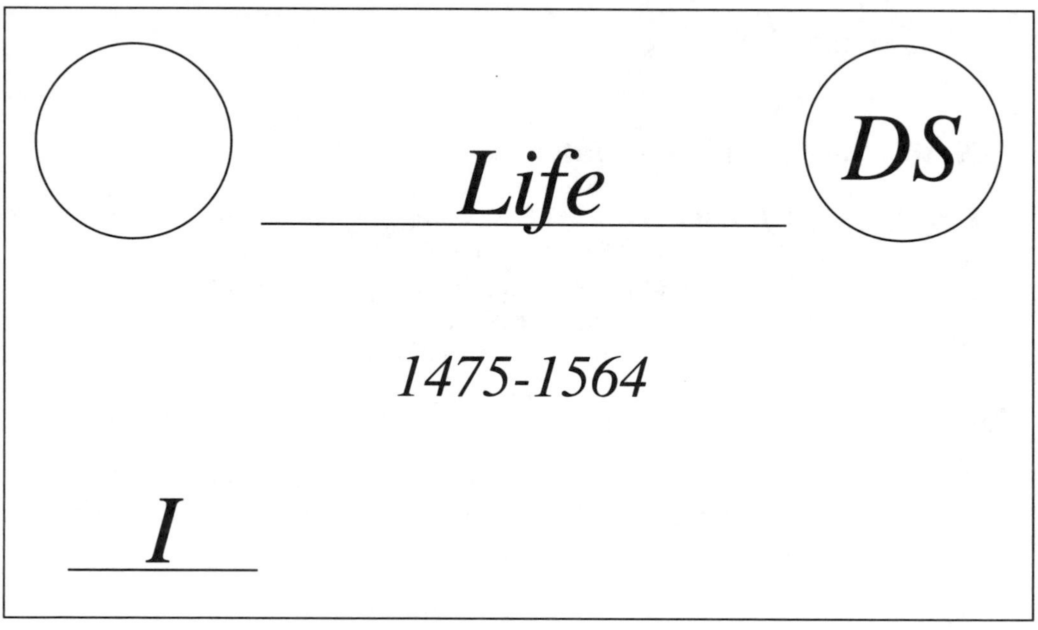

Student: No! It's way too short.

LMT: Ahhh. But let's think about that. Why does a good note make a good sentence? Because of the amount of memory it gives you. That must mean an excellent note can make a really excellent sentence, or better yet, it can make many sentences. Right? So what can we do with these dates, 1475 to 1564?

LMT: I'll say the sentence that comes to mind and write it here on the overhead.

Michelangelo Buonarroti was born in the year 1475, and he died in the year 1564, which made him 89 years old when he died, a very long life at that time.

See what you can do! Think back to all the things you have read during your research, or that you just know in your brain, that you could add to the facts in your note. In this case, I did some simple math to arrive at his age. That wasn't part of the note. Are you allowed to add stuff into your sentences that's not recorded on a note card? Yes, you're supposed to do that! That's where good reading and good research make good writing. It's also called learning because you're combining new facts with old information, called prior knowledge, about your topic, which the keywords in the note cause you to remember.

Literacy

Because notes are supposed to expand into good writing, I call them "shrinky dinks." Your brain is the water. Add your brain to a keyword note and out pops a wonderful sentence, maybe more than one sentence. Write as much as you can think of!

Lifelong Skills

Accountability

LMT: Okay, let's try it. During the next 15 minutes, I want you to begin to read from the source in front of you and practice locating and recording a few good notes. I won't actually start recording your note count until tomorrow, when you'll have your first full period of notetaking with 10 notes due. While you're working, I'm going to walk around and share some good examples.

Extension Lesson for Advanced Students

Fig. 8-20. Full Citation Note

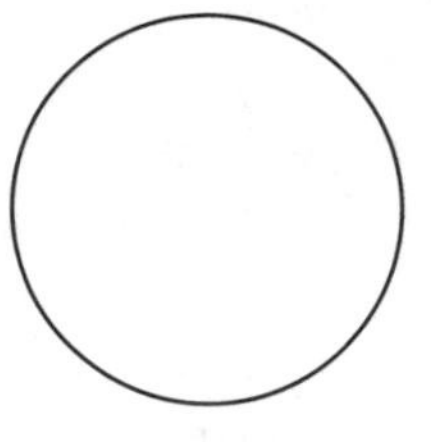

Life

DS

"He came from a respectable Florence family, and he was born in the village of Caprese, where his father was a government agent."

B#3, p. 58

Citing Sources in Notes

Literacy

LMT: Yesterday you learned that you need to cite your source even before you begin reading. Today, we'll learn to create a "rough" citation list. First, you need to record the source on each note card. This is not complicated. In fact, it's very quick and easy. You've been doing a good job all along using the color-coded citation forms. If you have several in each format, give them a temporary number, perhaps in the order you used them. For example, take the first book form you filled out and call it book one, call the second book two, and so forth. Those books will actually end up in a very different order later in your final, alphabetized citation list. So what would you do if you were using a third book for notetaking?

Student: I guess I would say it's "B3" on the note cards.

Information Literacy

LMT: Yes, it's just a way to save you time. More than a simple "B" for book or "I" for Internet, that temporary number lets you quick-code the note for easy, but more accurate, identification, as in this example (*Figure 8-20*). Keep using all the sources you want, cite notes easily, and worry about alphabetizing later.

LMT: But wait, besides a longer source citation, there's something else that's different about this note from the note we saw before. (Switch back to the copied note, *Figure 8-13.*)

Student: They're both copied sentences, but I see quotation marks in one.

LMT: Yes. In this example (*Figure 8-20*), the student has copied, but is carefully giving credit. The teacher must be requiring footnotes in the final paper, and that's an excellent skill to learn for high school. With quotation marks on the note, you also need to record the page number. See "p. 58" written on this card? You must tell exactly where the quote came from so that later you can accurately create a footnote or endnote. Your teacher needs to be able to look up this quotation and find it right where you said it was, and that's called validation. Validation is also important for an accurate citation list at the end of your project. But hey, life's not so bad! The quick codes on each note card that we've been discussing will make writing those final citations a snap!

Lifelong Skills

Now let me ask you a really important question. When these students copied from the source, did they really think about their information? Let me ask it this way. Has the information changed in any way from the way it appeared in the source? Ah-ha! Then the student didn't really have to think about what was copied. Do you see what I'm getting at?

Important Idea

Student: This is teaching us to think.

LMT: Now you've got the picture. Maybe taking good notes means good thinking. Let's see if this all makes sense according to the Research Process sheet (*Figure 8-1*). You found a topic, right? You found some good sources, okay? You read chunks of information that matched your subtopics, yes? Now to take a note you have to: think! If you can't copy, you have to change the information. This is the secret of our lesson today. Changing information means learning.

Lifelong Skills

So let's get busy and practice some of the strategies for changing information that we talked about. If you need help, refer to the large chart about research and notetaking steps over there on the bulletin board (*Figure 8-21*).

Fig. 8-21. General Notetaking Chart

Locate sources

- Find and use one good source each day.
- Don't waste time looking for many kinds of things.

Prepare for notetaking

- Label all note cards or note sheets in advance.
- Title each card or each note sheet with a subtopic.

Cite sources

- Write a source code on each note.
- Use MLA style citations to give credit for information.

Use reading strategies

- Break reading into "chunks" such as a paragraph or page.
- Keep pencil down while reading.
- Skim and scan to locate information.

Use evaluating strategies

- Match "chunk" information to subtopics.
- Select only new and important information, not what you know.
- Skip what's unimportant unless you add or change subtopics.

Use notetaking strategies

- Record only one note per card or per space marked on note sheet.
- Record only keywords and facts.
- Leave out small words, beginning capitals, and ending periods.
- No sentences without quotations and footnotes or endnotes.
- Aim for a minimum of 10 notes per subtopic.

Chapter 9

Sorting and Numbering Notes: Lesson 3, Part 3

Instructor Information

Student Lesson

"What a great system for handling all that information."

—Tutoring assistant

Fig. 9-1. Research Process: Sort and Number Notes

Topic *A good topic is "doable," but slightly challenging to your assessed abilities.*

A. Locate a topic in textbooks, library sources, or the teacher's topic list.
B. Check in the library media center for at least three formats of supporting information.
C. Cross-check in an encyclopedia to narrow or broaden a topic.

Subtopics *Ask yourself: What do I want to know about my topic?*

A. General subtopics may be brainstormed. Examples:
   Person: early life, education, work (be specific), later life.
   Place: origin, history, leaders, geography, economy.
   Thing: who, what, when, where, why/how.
B. Specific subtopics must be located in, for example, an encyclopedia's subheads.
C. The number of subtopics is based on the number of days of research.

Sources *A good source is any kind of supporting information that you can read.*

A. Format (the form information comes in) Examples include:
   Print: books, encyclopedias, magazines, newspapers.
   Nonprint: videos, laser disks, CD-ROMs, computer software, Internet.
B. Use at least three formats of information. Using one source is not research!
C. Credit sources using MLA-style citations.

Read/Think/Select *Good research promotes comprehension and evaluation.*

A. Read an entire "chunk" (a paragraph or a page) with your pencil down.
B. Think about what was read. What was important?
C. Select only a few key facts from each "chunk" to match your subtopics.

Notetake *A good note creates information ownership. This is learning!*

A. One note per card, titled with subtopic. Use as many cards as needed.
B. Record important keywords, facts, or a list, up to about 20 words (use your judgment).
C. No small words like *a*, *the*, *an*, *is*, *was*. Instead use commas, and dashes.
D. No copying of sentences (without quotation marks and footnotes).

Sort and Number Notes *Good organization of notes makes writing easier.*

A. Sort notes by subtopic section, about five notes per paragraph (use your judgment).
B. Read notes in one section at a time and put in an order that makes sense.
C. Number notes consecutively through all sections without starting over at number 1.

Extension

Write/Publish/Present
Final citations list
Technology integration

Evaluation Student tracking

Chapter Concepts

The Importance of Sorting Notes

Before notetaking, developing subtopics creates a frame for sorting out sources of information that support the topic. This helps students to *access* information. During notetaking, titling note cards or note sheets with subtopics provides guidelines for sorting relevant from irrelevant information. This helps students *evaluate* information. After notetaking, using reading/thinking/selecting strategies to sort notes helps prepare information for writing. This helps students *use* information. Thus, sorting is a component of critical thinking inherent in each part of the information literacy process. Sorting information is another way in which information changes form. This is learning.

Reading Notes

Only after notetaking from a variety of sources do students get a global picture of the information they have found. Besides promoting literacy, reading notes cumulatively provides the motivational step of prewriting for Process Writing, leading to composing. Furthermore, reading their own notes strengthens students' ties to prior knowledge and to recently read, new information.

Thinking About and Sorting Notes

Sorting notes involves a series of personal decisions for evaluating and interpreting them. Redundancy, irrelevancy, even missing pieces become apparent. This critical review increases ownership of information. Personal reflection promotes personal growth in knowledge of the topic and validates research strategies that were used well or calls attention to those that could be strengthened. Research novices probably should sort notes by subtopics, identified with Roman numerals, to create the paper's outline of information. Notes within subtopic sections can be further sorted into subsections, even paragraphs and supporting sentences.

Numbering Notes

Numbering notes is last! Have students number notes consecutively from subtopic section to section, never starting over at number one. One stack of consecutively numbered note cards equals a report that simply writes itself.

Instructor Information

The Importance of Sorting Notes

Why devote an entire section in a thoughtful process like the Research Process (*Figure 9-1*) to a seemingly mechanical step where the whole point is to flip cards around? First, this step requires as much critical thinking as any previous

step. Sorting notes to prepare for writing is very much a part of the Research Process because it deals directly with managing information. It involves both the evaluation and use of information prescribed in information literacy standards (*Figure 14-1*).

Second, sorting notes provides closure, which validates the entire research process. Carrying something through to its logical conclusion not only gives the teacher a logically assembled product to grade but also equips the students with information management tools to do what they set out to do.

Once the steps of information management are completed, writing the report, using technology enrichment, and assembling a creative project are considered extensions beyond actual research and are therefore addressed separately in the following chapters.

Reading Notes

Literacy

Critical reading produces better notes, which must in turn be read critically to produce writing. The experienced research teacher knows that students do not take perfect notes the first time around, or even the second time. Reading sources to take notes is a skill that definitely improves with age and practice. But reading notes to sort them for writing provides immediate feedback. "This doesn't make sense!" you'll hear students say to themselves. Students quickly become their own best critics.

With the return to original information cut off and the goal of good writing now facing the students, reading their own notes triggers a sequence of criticism and evaluation in which students recognize the quality and quantity of information they have gathered. "This is easy!" is a comment you'll hear from students who have trustingly followed and completed each of the previous research steps. A feeling of calm confidence permeates the room as those successful students slide easily from reading to sorting their notes. "Research isn't so bad after all!" The tie-in to literacy is obvious as students continue to bond with their new information as they read and reread notes for sorting. Title I and ELL teachers just love this. New knowledge sticks to prior knowledge, building Velcro™ in the brain. This is learning!

Thinking About and Sorting Notes

Problem Solving

Critical thinking about notes is a natural consequence of critically reading notes. The instructor knows reading notes jogs memory and causes students to ponder their information. Students may realize that they don't like some of the things they have recorded or that they've left some important items out. Critical thinking continues as students evaluate which notes to include or exclude and then which come first, and next, and next. Almost inadvertently, what is occurring is the transformation of information into knowledge as students digest the content-area material.

Numbering Notes

Figures 9-5 through *9-8* show students how to number notes consecutively. Relevancy is provided with the example of asking students to remember how they connected dots when they were little, which resulted in an animal "popping out of" the page. Out of the numbered notes pops their final paper, which practically writes itself. It is clear that they have just connected the dots!

> *Wow! If I'd only known this when I was a kid! It's so logical and organized. I love it.*
>
> *—Classroom teacher*

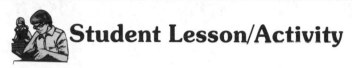

Student Lesson/Activity

Timing: 10 minutes.

The Importance of Sorting Notes

Lifelong Skills

LMT: Hello, class. You've been working well the last few days on your note-taking. We will begin today with one last lesson. I promise this will be brief, but it is very important. Now that you have completed your research, you need to prepare your notes for writing a rough draft. What's due today?

Student: Our notes. But I was absent and didn't get finished!

LMT: And no excuses! There are a few of you with whom we need to make some special arrangements, but see me in a few minutes. You can still participate in the lesson. I need everyone to pay attention. I promise this will make so much sense to you that, ready or not, you will be able to do it on your own. Before we start, please have your Research Checklist sheet handy (*Figure 9-2*).

Student: Why can't we just take our notes home and write our report?

LMT: Excellent question. Many of you are probably used to doing just that. However, it is my experience that when notes go home before writing begins, they sometimes don't find their way into the paper. Learning to write from notes involves building your confidence in combining what's on the notes with what's already in your heads. That takes some guided practice and time in class to share what we have written.

Let's begin this way. Spread yourselves out so you have plenty of table space. Put all backpacks and notebooks on the floor beside you, so there's nothing in your way. The only thing in front of you is your stack of note cards—whatever you have. Ready?

The first thing is to take your stack of mixed-up notes—you should have at least 30—and "play cards" with them. By that I mean to simply sort them into three piles. Why three?

Student: Oh, I get it. The three subtopics.

LMT: Exactly! I'll give you a minute to finish sorting so that your piles look like this: (Using the overhead projector, display a transparency of *Figure 9-2*, or simply draw three empty boxes with an overhead pen.)

Fig. 9-2. Sort Notes by Subtopic

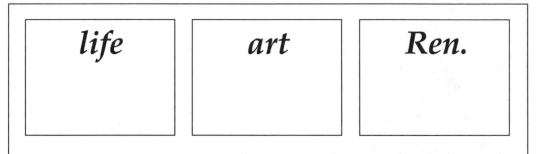

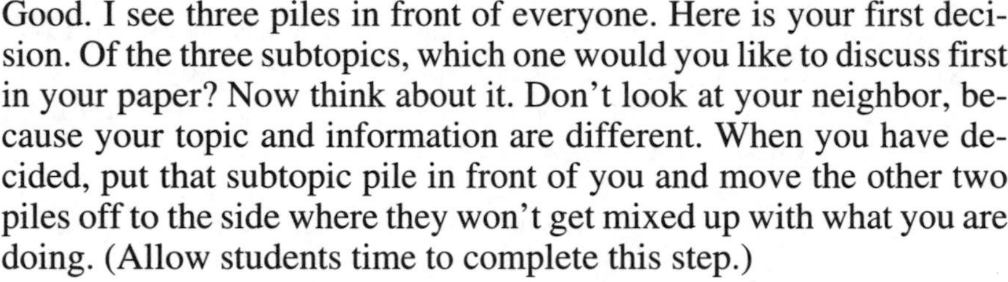

Problem Solving

Good. I see three piles in front of everyone. Here is your first decision. Of the three subtopics, which one would you like to discuss first in your paper? Now think about it. Don't look at your neighbor, because your topic and information are different. When you have decided, put that subtopic pile in front of you and move the other two piles off to the side where they won't get mixed up with what you are doing. (Allow students time to complete this step.)

Information Literacy

Lifelong Skills

Congratulations! You have made the first important decision in managing the information you have gathered. No one is telling you which subtopic to pick. That is entirely your choice. Can you relate this to the choices you've been making during research? You selected sources, you selected subtopics to guide your reading, then you selected important information to record on your note cards. Now you're choosing the order of notes for writing. I'm purposely saying this long list to show you how much control you have over all of the steps of research. You are really learning to be good information managers.

Fig. 9-3. Research Checklist: Sort and Number Notes

LMT/Teacher Tracking:	**Date Due:/Points:**	
Topic *Michelangelo*	*10/31*	*5*
Subtopics	*10/31*	*5*
○ *What was his personal (life) like?*		
○ *What was his (art) like?*		
○ *What was the (Renaissance) ?*		
○ __________		
○ __________		
Sources	*11/3-8*	*30*
A. At least 3 formats. Circle choices: (book), (reference), CD-ROM, (Internet), other: ________		
B. Total number of sources: *3*		
Read/Think/Select	*11/3-8*	*5*
A. A "chunk" is *a paragraph.*		
Notetake	*11/3-8*	*30*
A. At least *10* notes for each subtopic.		
B. Total number of notes: *30*		
Sort and number notes	*11/9*	*15*
Write rough draft from notes		
Teacher Grading: Title Page		
Typed Report		
Final Citation List		
Image/Chart		

Fig. 9-4. Prioritize Subtopic Sections

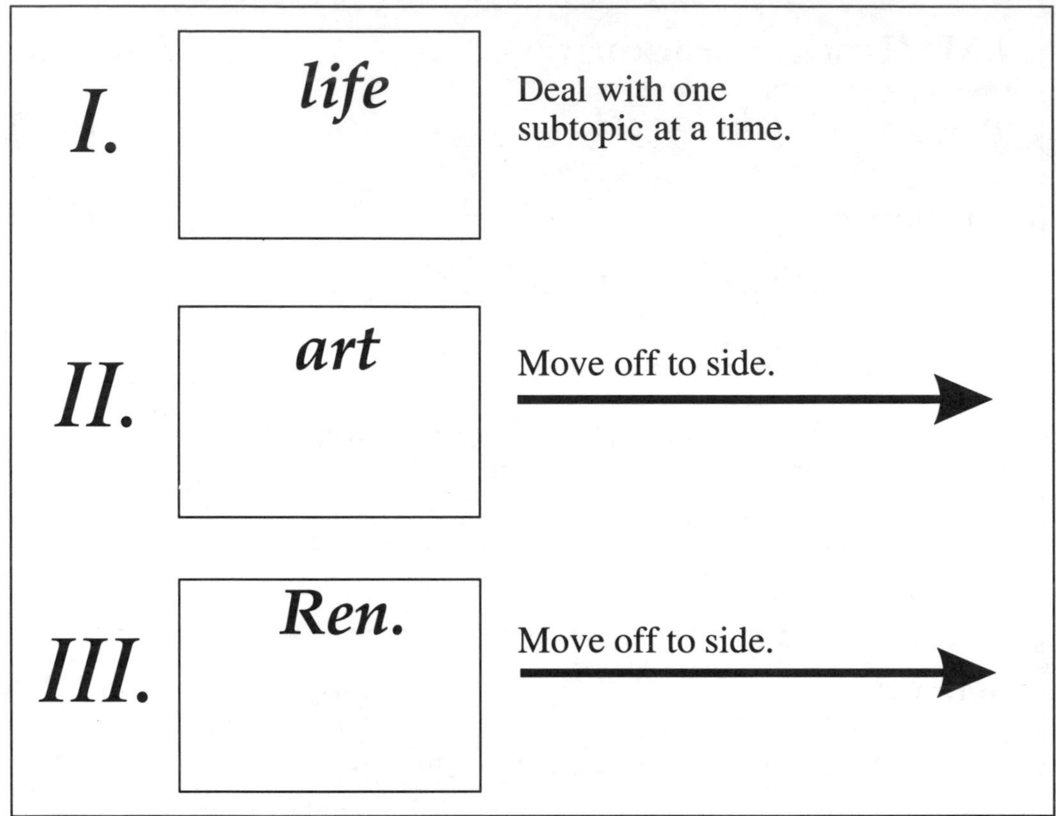

LMT: Getting back to the first pile in front of you, this is obviously subtopic number one, so I am going to write a Roman numeral one here beside this box (*Figure 9-4*). I'll draw arrows leading away from the second and third note stacks to show that they should be moved to the side.

Let's flip back a minute to your Research Checklist (*Figure 9-3*), to remind you that you recorded subtopics in Roman numeral order way back when you first thought of them, only they weren't in any particular order at that time. What do Roman numerals remind you of? An outline? Who remembers or has used an outline in any of your other classes?

Student: In social studies we sometimes outline the chapter we're reading.

LMT: Good! Then it's something you should be familiar with.

You do not have to go through your notes and put Roman numerals on all of them. But here on your Research Checklist sheet is where I want you to switch the Roman numerals to match the order you have now selected for your written paper. (Use an overhead pen to change *Figure 9-2*.) This is now your final outline. It is the frame, like the skeleton, of your paper, on which you will hang the "meat," which is the subtopic sections and all of your good notes! You can't write a paper if you don't know what order the information will go in. Otherwise everything will just be very confusing, like nonsense!

Reading Your Notes

LMT: Okay, we're ready to move on. I want you to take this first pile of notes—there should be at least 10—and spread them out in front of you. You need to be able to see every note. (Allow students time to complete this step.) The next thing you need to do is, guess what? Just like when you found your sources, you have to read!

I have a transparency here on the overhead projector (*Figure 9-5*), so you can follow the steps as you sort your note cards. We're down to step 4, which says to "Read notes in that section," so I'm going to be quiet for a few minutes while you read all of the cards in this first subtopic stack. I'll know you're done when you look back up at me.

While he was reading, a student of mine raised his hand and asked, "Teacher, what does this note say?" I looked at him with a funny expression and said, "Whose note is it?" "Oh yeah," he said as he crumpled it up.

Thinking About and Sorting Your Notes

LMT: Reading all your notes together enables you to make judgments about your information. While you were reading, a few of you started to do what comes naturally. I know you were making decisions in your heads because some of you started moving your cards around. That's the next step. The very first thing I want you to decide is what is the very first note you want to kick off your paper. When you've found it, physically pick it up and put it up at the top of a row I want you to make. (Use an overhead pen to draw lines on *Figure 9-5* to show how cards are moved into descending order from top to bottom, as illustrated in *Figure 9-8*).

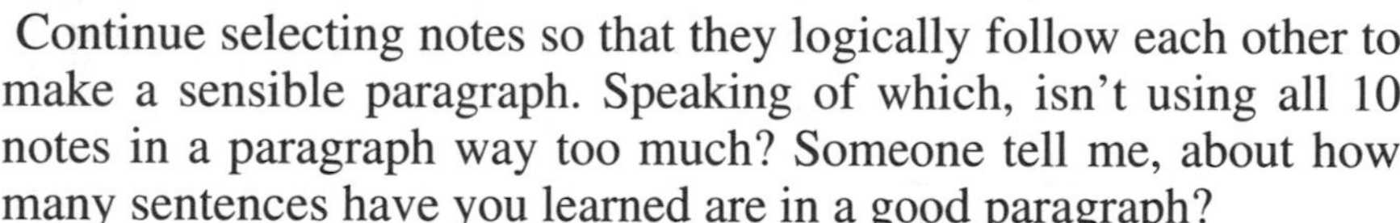

Continue selecting notes so that they logically follow each other to make a sensible paragraph. Speaking of which, isn't using all 10 notes in a paragraph way too much? Someone tell me, about how many sentences have you learned are in a good paragraph?

Student: About five or six?

LMT: That's fine. So let's do that. If each of your notes can make at least one good sentence, then let's say that about five notes will equal a paragraph. But remember, it doesn't always have to be like that. Sometimes four of your notes, or maybe six, will more logically fit together. Only you can make that decision. The main point is that while you are deciding which sentences follow each other, you are also deciding which can be grouped together into a good paragraph. See the dotted line on the overhead? (Point to the transparency of *Figure 9-5*.)

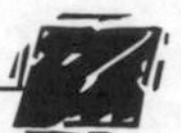

Fig. 9-5. Teaching Model: Sorting the First Subtopic

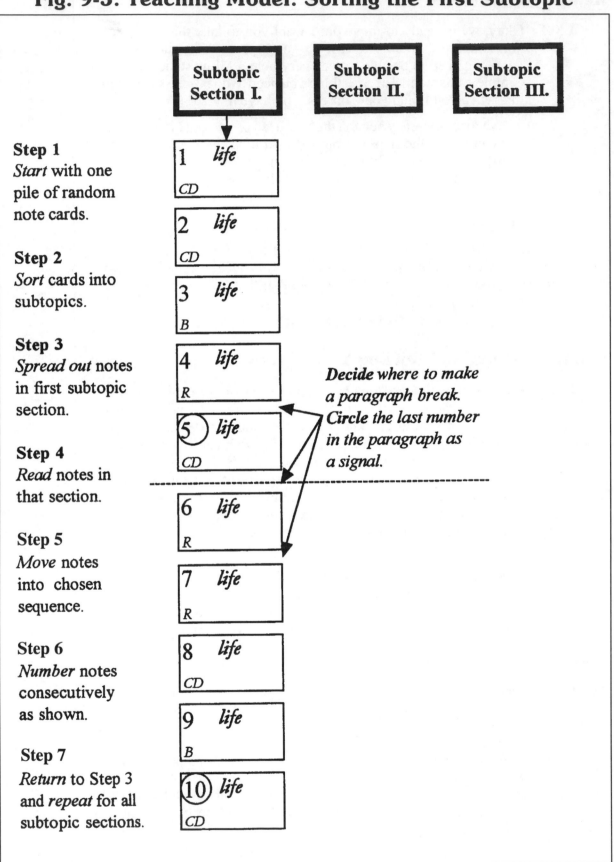

The way you can show yourself which notes belong together is, again, by giving yourself a code. See up here on my overhead how I've just done a simple thing like circle the number on the card which will be the last note in that paragraph? That's fine. You could have a star, or anything. Just keep it simple, but put it there! It will greatly help you in your writing later. (Allow students time to sort and move cards around.)

Important Idea

"Do I really have to use both of these notes? They say they same thing," said a student last year.

"Whose paper is this?" I replied.

"Oh, I get it. They're my notes to do whatever I want with."

Numbering Your Notes

ELL/Special Modifications

LMT: Most of you seem ready. Some of you have more than 10 notes and it will take you a little longer. That's great! Just listen and follow along with us while you finish. You'll be very glad you have all those notes when it's time to write. Those of you who didn't find enough notes may be beginning to see that you won't have enough to write with. Do you see why I was pushing you during notetaking? It wasn't for me, it was for you! You'll want to take more notes next time because you know the reason why they're important.

Once your cards are in an order that makes sense, the very last thing you do is to number them. Remember, I told you earlier never to number notes during notetaking because you hadn't gathered all of your information yet. Something you may have given number one when you were researching has very little chance of being the first fact discussed in that section of your paper. Does this make sense?

Look again at the overhead. Notice that you put the number in that blank spot in the upper left-hand corner of each card. Now you understand what that space is for! Remember to number in pencil just in case you want to change your mind later. Are you allowed to switch note numbers?

Student: Yes! It's *my* paper.

LMT: When that section is sorted and numbered, gather the cards back up into one pile with number one on top and number 10 on the bottom. Set that pile off to the side and, of course, put your second subtopic pile in front of you.

Guess what you get to do? Repeat the same thing you just did. Look up here at the next overhead (*Figure 9-6*), and follow it along through each of the steps: Spread out your cards, read them all, decide how they can be moved around to make good connecting sentences, divide those sentences into at least two paragraphs, and then number the notes.

Stop! What's going to be different when you number them? Are you going to start over at number one the second and third stacks? After all, you're beginning new subtopics. The answer is, no! You are going to begin numbering at the next consecutive number. For example, if the last pile ended with note number 10, then start the next pile with note number 11. Get it? That way if you sneeze and your notes fly everywhere, you can put them all right back in order again without wasting any time.

I actually did have a student who dropped all his cards on the way out the door one day. With the bell about to ring, whew, was he glad they were numbered! When you're finished with each stack, simply add it onto the bottom of the first pile to finish up with one numbered stack of notes (*Figure 9-8*).

Student: I have too many cards to finish this period. Can I finish for homework?

LMT: Of course. For everyone, your task is to arrive here tomorrow with all your cards sorted and numbered so we can move on to the next important thing, writing!

Lifelong Skills

Let me ask you one last important question. Do you have to do this exact system forever? No. As you get older and have more experience with research, you might want to come up with a system that will work better for you. That's wonderful, because then you will understand how to manage information. A research project in high school will not be such a dreadful, overwhelming task!

Fig. 9-6. Teaching Model: Sorting the Second Subtopic

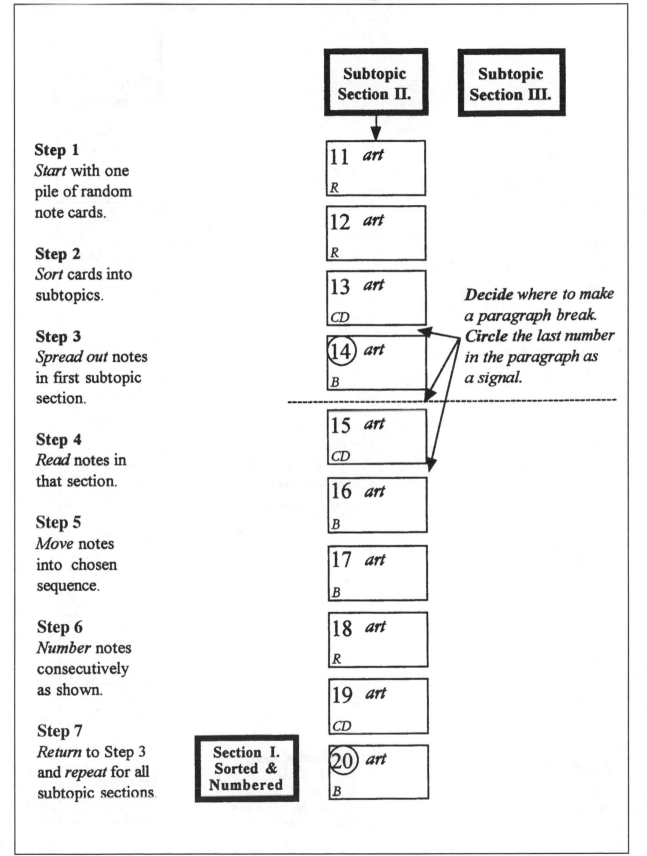

Step 1
Start with one pile of random note cards.

Step 2
Sort cards into subtopics.

Step 3
Spread out notes in first subtopic section.

Step 4
Read notes in that section.

Step 5
Move notes into chosen sequence.

Step 6
Number notes consecutively as shown.

Step 7
Return to Step 3 and *repeat* for all subtopic sections.

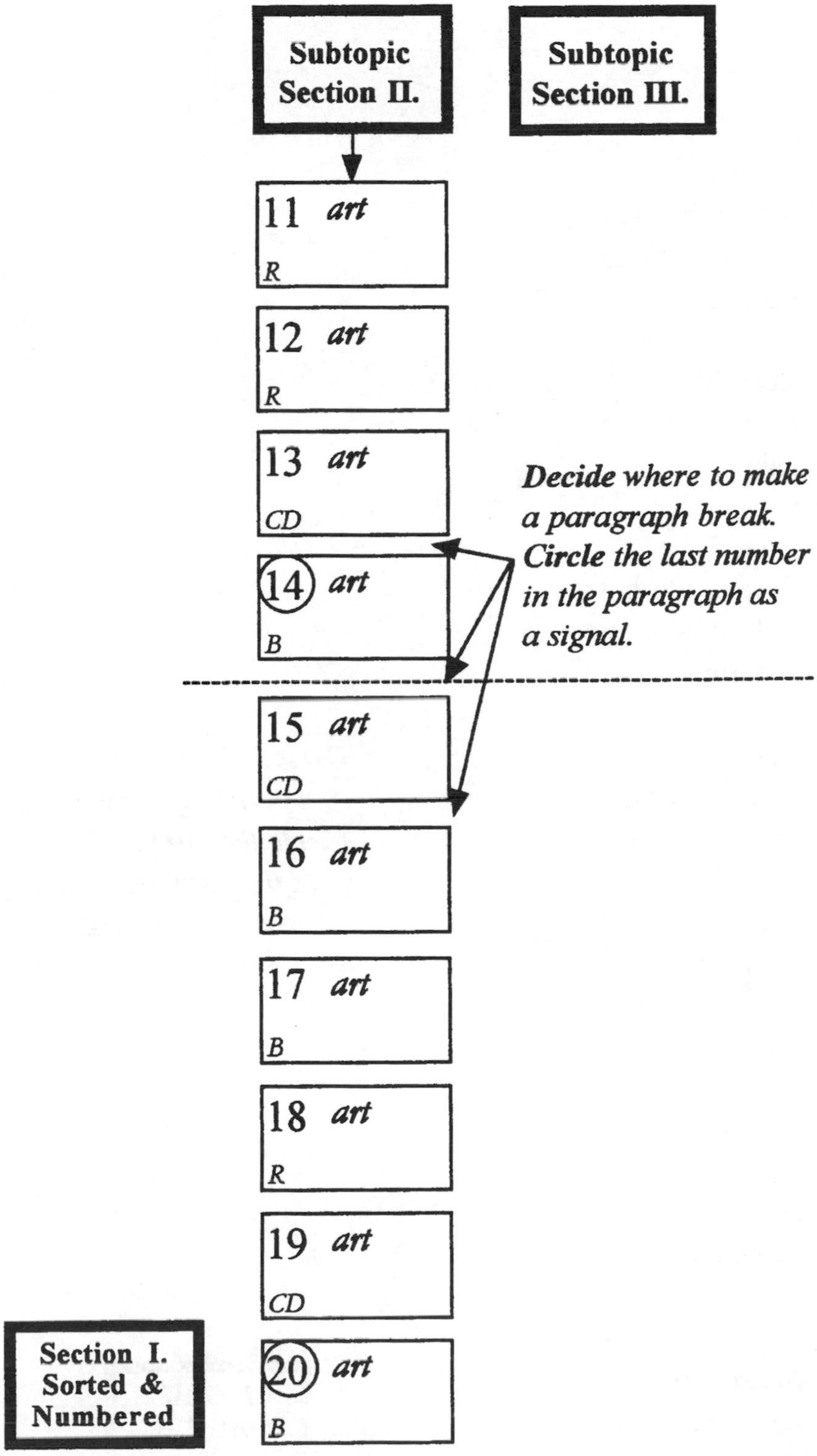

Subtopic Section II.

Subtopic Section III.

11 *art* — *R*
12 *art* — *R*
13 *art* — *CD*
(14) *art* — *B*

Decide where to make a paragraph break. Circle the last number in the paragraph as a signal.

---

15 *art* — *CD*
16 *art* — *B*
17 *art* — *B*
18 *art* — *R*
19 *art* — *CD*
(20) *art* — *B*

Section I. Sorted & Numbered

Fig. 9-7. Teaching Model: Sorting the Third Subtopic

Step 1
Start with one pile of random note cards.

Step 2
Sort cards into subtopics.

Step 3
Spread out notes in first subtopic section.

Step 4
Read notes in that section.

Step 5
Move notes into chosen sequence.

Step 6
Number notes consecutively as shown.

Step 7
Return to Step 3 and *repeat* for all subtopic sections.

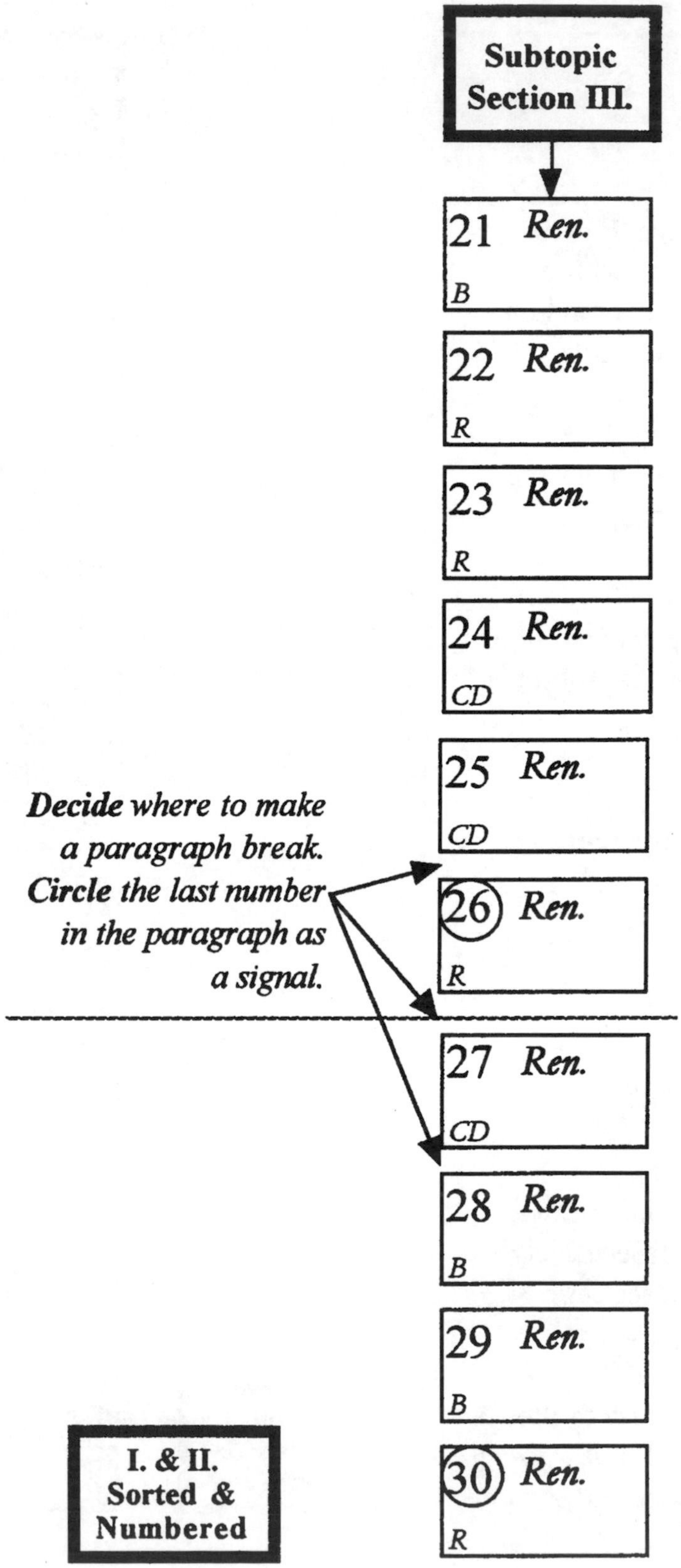

LMT: The last transparency here on the overhead (*Figure 9-8*) has fewer cards because I ran out of room, but it's just to show you that you started out with one pile of completely mixed up notes. You now have in your hand a pile of completely sorted notes. Do you realize that all of the hard work for writing a research paper is done?

Remember doing "connect-the-dot" puzzles when you were a little kid and out came an animal? Well, out of these numbered notes comes a fully written term paper. It's amazing! You'll see for yourself how well this works as you begin writing a rough draft.

LMT: When you come back tomorrow, you may find this will be the easiest paper you've ever written. Going from note to note will be exactly like connecting the dots. In the future, when other kids who don't know how to do this are sitting there, completely frustrated and overwhelmed and copying out of a book, you'll be sitting there with a paper that's practically already written! Here is the formula. You'll see what this means tomorrow. Don't miss it!

Lifelong Skills

Numbered notes
Prior knowledge
+Creative brain

Best-ever project and learning!

Fig. 9-8. Sorting and Numbering Note Cards

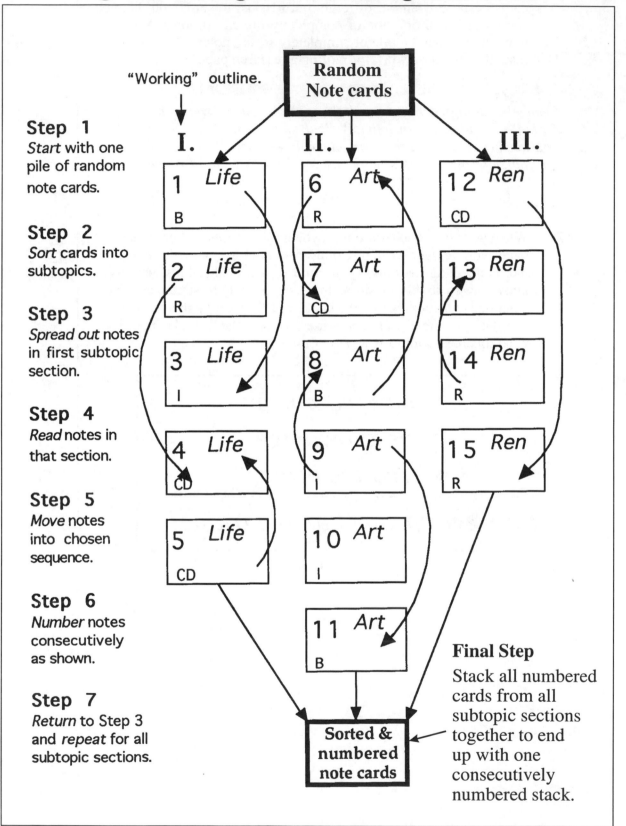

Step 1
Start with one pile of random note cards.

Step 2
Sort cards into subtopics.

Step 3
Spread out notes in first subtopic section.

Step 4
Read notes in that section.

Step 5
Move notes into chosen sequence.

Step 6
Number notes consecutively as shown.

Step 7
Return to Step 3 and *repeat* for all subtopic sections.

Final Step
Stack all numbered cards from all subtopic sections together to end up with one consecutively numbered stack.

Section 3

Application and Accountability

Chapter 10

Hands-on Research: Locational Directions

Instructor Information

Student Lesson

"There's a flipchart of pathfinders between the computer stations in case you get stuck."

—LMT

Fig. 10-1. Dewey Decimal System

000-General Works
000 Monsters, Computers
010 Bibliographies
020 Libraries
030 Encyclopedias
050 Periodicals
060 General Organizations. Museums
070 Journalism, Newspapers
080 Special libraries
090 Rare Books

100-Philosophy and Psychology
110 Metaphysics
120 Knowledge, Purpose of man
130 Supernatural, Astrology, Dreams
140 Philosophical viewpoints
150 Psychology: Senses, Feelings, Friends
160 Logic
170 Ethics
180 Ancient, Oriental Philosophy
190 Modern, Western Philosophy

200-Religion
210 Natural Religion
220 Bible
230 Christianity
240 Christian Morals
250 Religious Orders
260 Theology, Church work
270 History of Religion
280 Christian denominations
290 Other Religions

300-Social Sciences
310 Statistics: People of the World
320 Political Science: Gov't, Civil Rights
330 Economics: Money, Energy
340 Law: Constitutional, Criminal, Social.
350 Presidents, Weapons, Military
360 Social Problems: Alcoholism, Disabilities
370 Education: Careers
380 Commerce, Transportation, Metric
390 Customs, Etiquette (398.2 Fairy tales)

400-Language
410 Speech and Language Books: Dictionaries
420 English
430 German
440 French
450 Italian
460 Spanish
470 Latin
480 Greek
490 Other: Rosetta Stone, Hieroglyphics

500-Natural Sciences / Mathematics
510 Mathematics
520 Astronomy: Space
530 Physics: Air, Magnets, Electricity
540 Chemistry: Water, Rocks/Gems
550 Geology: Weather, Earthquakes
560 Paleontology: Dinosaurs
570 Life Sciences: Biology, Ecosystems
580 Botany: Plants
590 Zoology: Animals, Insects, Fish, Birds

600-Technology
610 Medicine: Body, Drugs, Diseases
620 Engineering: Machines, Cars
630 Agriculture: Farm, Garden, Pets
640 Home Economics: Cook, Sew, Children
650 Management: Business, Secret Codes
660 Chemical Engineering: Gas and Oil
670 Manufacturing: Metals and Textiles
680 Make it Yourself: Instruments, Printing
690 Carpentry: Building things

700-The Arts
710 Landscape
720 Architecture
730 Sculpture
740 Drawing, Decorating, Design
750 Painting
760 Prints /Printmaking, Engraving
770 Photography
780 Music
790 Sports: Indoor & Outdoor

800-Literature and Poetry
810 American (811 Poetry, 812 Plays)
820 English (822 Shakespeare)
830 German
840 French
850 Italian
860 Spanish
870 Latin
880 Greek and Hellenic
890 Other

900-Geography and History
910 Geography, Countries of the World
920 Biography, Flag books
930 Ancient World: Egypt, Greece, Rome
940 History of Europe: World Wars I and II
950 History of Asia
960 History of Africa
970 History of North and Central America: Native Americans,State Books
980 History of South America
990 History of island nations

Instructor Information

Balance Instruction with Work Time

Direct instruction in information management strategies, presented in the previous six chapters, must be equally balanced with hands-on library time for students to perform each sequential research step in which the strategies are embedded: Teach about topics and subtopics, and give students time to find them; teach about citations for different formats, and fill in some citation forms together in a target-taught lesson. Are students then ready to go off on their own? Almost. Don't forget to teach reading, evaluating, and notetaking strategies. Hands-on research does not follow the six steps; as the position of this chapter would indicate, it is the independent practice part of each of these lessons. The purpose in separating out this chapter is to emphasize the need for *time* to perform research tasks as they are presented. The goal of these lessons is student independence in following the guide sheets and applying information literacy strategies to build lifelong skills for research success. This success is observable!

Lifelong Skills

On the first day of hands-on research, students come in eager to get started. That in itself is sometimes a change. Have you noticed in the past that without this degree of preparation, students approached research halfheartedly or were not quite sure of what they were supposed to do, leaving them little choice but to copy information? Now, when students hear that there are just a few instructions before they get started, they may actually complain, "But I'm ready, I'm ready!"

Information Literacy

Impatient to get started, students don't realize they have not received equipment access directions. These are the library skills which, in the past, have been mistaken for research instruction. Part of the paradigm shift for educational reform is putting the hardware and software in their rightful place as tools to support the information literacy strategies of accessing, evaluating, and using information. Briefly, at the beginning of this hands-on research day, demonstrate to students some simple equipment procedures.

Technology Proficiency

Dewey/Boolean Handouts

If time and student attention span permit, give a brief explanation of *Figure 10-1*, the Dewey Decimal System, for print materials, and *Figure 10-2*, Boolean Logic, for the Internet. Regarding Dewey, it has been my staggering experience that students often arrive in high school without card catalog access skills! Catch them now in middle school. Regarding the Internet, I do not expect students, or even teachers, to have a working knowledge of logical operators. Awareness of Boole's techniques is a start. It's handy to have these guide sheets posted around the library media center for quick referral.

Fig. 10-2. Boolean Logic

George Boole was a mathematician who devised a system of logical operators to retrieve information.

And

cars and red

Type the word *and* to tell your search tool that you want specific information. For example, typing only cars will give you all colors unless you specify: *cars and red*. Now you'll get only red cars.

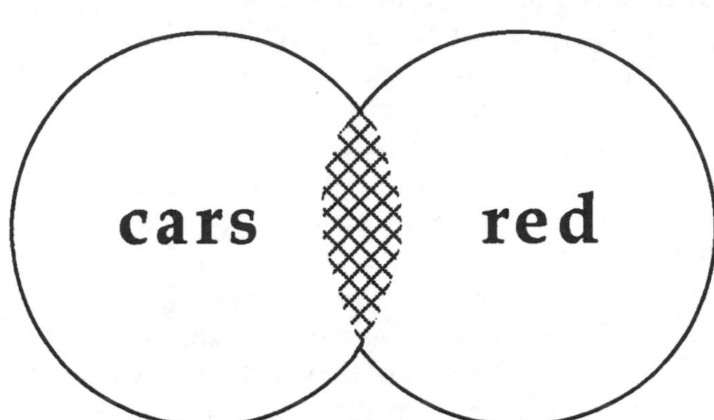

Or

cars or red

Type the word *or* to tell your search tool that you would be happy with either item. For example, you might be searching for pictures of all colors of cars *or* pictures of red cars, which means you'll be happy with pictures of both.

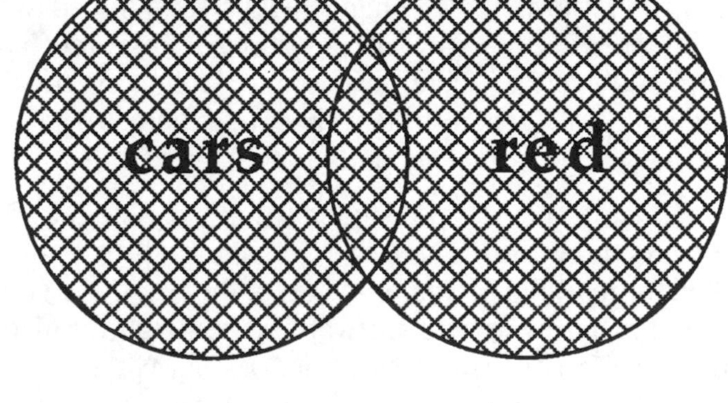

Not

cars not red

Type the word *not* to tell your search tool that you want to specifically exclude something. For example, typing *cars not red* will give you all colors of cars except red ones.

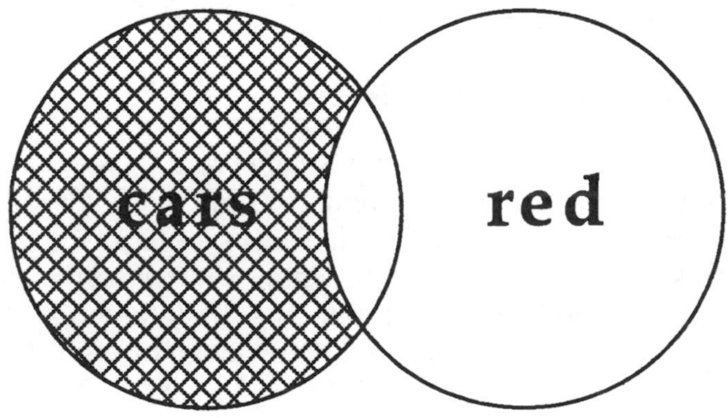

Student Lesson: Locational Directions

Print Sources: Using Dewey

Timing: 5 minutes.

LMT: This will only take a few minutes, I promise! I know you're anxious to get started today on your own research. Does anyone remember where you start first?

Student: An encyclopedia.

Literacy

Student: The card catalog, on the computer.

LMT: You're both right. However, there are not enough computers for everyone to begin using the card catalog to look up books on your topic, so some of you should head immediately back to the reference area. When you do get to the electronic card catalog and locate good sources, how do you find the book? (Blank stares!) Someone must remember! What does every item have on it?

Technology Proficiency

Student: A white tag on the back?

LMT: Which is called a "call tag." And it contains? Remember orientation in September, when we located the nonfiction resources in this room, and I told you how to find them?

Lifelong Skills

Student: Numbers.

LMT: Whew! Yes, that will be true for the nonfiction books for your Renaissance artists. Look at the Dewey sheet. Back in the 1800s, Melvil Dewey came up with a system to locate every kind of nonfiction book by assigning a number to its subject. On the sheet, do you see the 10 major subject classifications? It's obvious for your Renaissance project that you would probably not head off to the 200s because that's about religion. Or the 600s, which is about technology. Right?

Let's see how well you can read and follow this guide sheet. If you wanted a computer book, where would you go?

Student: Zeros.

LMT: Good. A book on insects?

Student: The 500s.

LMT: More specifically?

Student: The 590s.

LMT: The Renaissance?

Student: The 940s? Is that right?

LMT: Possibly. Go check out the history of Europe, particularly Italy. But you are here because the Renaissance is an important part of which of your other classes?

Student: Of course! Art!

LMT: This is a little tricky, but look over the sheet carefully and see if there's another subject area where you'll probably find the most books on the Renaissance as a period in art history.

Student: Well, the 700s are about art, of course. Would it be in the 750s for painting?

Content-Area Standard

LMT: Good thinking! I want each of you to check and see. The other obvious thing you can do is search in the electronic card catalog, or even just look at the call tags on the Renaissance books I've put on this cart. Sneaky, huh? But effective.

There's one other very important thing I'd like to call your attention to. Let's say you find a good book on the Renaissance in the 750s. What happens when you go to the reference area of the library media center? Do you have to look up "Renaissance" all over again? The good news is that it will also be there in the 750s! Does that make sense? How about if you went to the "Oversize Books" area?

Student: The 750s.

LMT: Absolutely. Videos?

Student: The 750s again.

Lifelong Skills

LMT: Perfect. This will help you for the rest of your life in every library that uses the Dewey system. Once you locate a source's call number, it will be the same in every format, or kind, of information. Works well, huh?

These Dewey guide sheets are always available here in the library. It's like picking up a directory in a huge warehouse store. You can find what you want without wasting any time. Hasn't that been one of the main points in all of our research lessons? Locate a book simply by walking around the library and matching the numbers on the sheet with the shelf labels, then with the call tags on book spines. This is one of those handy-dandy things of life. You'll wonder how you ever lived without it!

Electronic Sources: Using Boolean Logic

Timing: 5 minutes. This handout is more effective with advanced students.

Technology Proficiency

LMT: Now take a look at the Boolean Logic sheet (*Figure 10-2*). Boolean Logic is for computers. It's specifically helpful for a few of our computer search tools as well as for the Internet. Full Internet orientation and instruction will be on another day. Let me give just a few quick pointers for you to be aware of.

The top of the sheet says, "Boolean Logic." (Read the sentence about George Boole.) Like Dewey, Boole came up with a way to search for information. Back in the 1800s, he would never have dreamed that we would be using his method a hundred years later with computers and the Internet. But his system of combining words in ways to either include things or leave things out has turned out to be surprisingly useful when you're trying to expand or narrow a search for information in something as enormous as the Internet.

Most of you think it's easy to use the Internet: Type your topic into a search engine and up pop some hot links to web sites. But there's really a lot more to it than that. This sheet tells you how three very common words—*and*, *or*, and *not*—can be used to tell a computer search tool or the Internet how to hunt for your topic more effectively. Cars are used as an example here, but let's use a Renaissance artist instead. We've been using Michelangelo all along. If you type that into a search engine, you'll get back absolutely every web site about that word, within the limitation of how many "hits" it displays at one time. But many of those web sites might not even be about the artist! In other words, you'd waste a lot of time sifting through restaurants or art stores, web sites that have nothing to do with what you really want to know. No one has time for that.

Problem Solving

So let's say you want to know only about Michelangelo's painting, not architecture or sculpture. Type in "Michelangelo and painting". It's confusing in the sense that you think you'd be getting both of those circles, but the word "and" is actually narrowing your search down only to very specific information about paintings by Michelangelo. Nothing else. So the word "and" is the most limiting of all the Boolean search tools. It narrows your search. Does that make sense?

Let's look at the next example, for the word "or." Let's say you want to know everything about Michelangelo and you also want to know everything about painting. That's a huge amount, by the way. Believe it or not, you'd type in "Michelangelo or painting".

Student: Doesn't that seem opposite to type "or" to get both items instead of each one separately?

LMT: When you type in two keywords connected by *or*, you're really telling the Internet search tool that you'd be happy with both! You'd be happy getting all of the web sites all about Michelangelo, or you'd be happy getting all of the web sites all about painting. On the diagram, you're getting both circles of information. So "or" is the most inclusive of the Boolean words.

The last one is "not." Let's say you wanted to learn about Michelangelo, but you don't want anything at all about painting. Type in "Michelangelo not painting". This makes a little more sense. If it's a Michelangelo web site about painting, it will be weeded out of the search. That was pretty quick, but we need to get busy. So please ask questions when you get stuck. I'm here to help!

Chapter 11

Writing the Rough Draft: Optional Lesson

"I can't believe what this student has written! She was hardly able to write a few sentences."

—English teacher

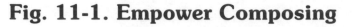

Fig. 11-1. Empower Composing

For the Student

Voice: The writer

- The imprint of ourselves on our writing.
- An engaging voice will hold the reader's interest.

Audience: The reader

- To whom is the writing directed?
- The intended reader determines the tone of the writing.

Sharing: Critiquing

- Sharing aloud separates the *content* from the *mechanics*, so students distinguish revising writing from editing errors.
- Criticism guidelines: A suggestion for improvement should be preceded by a positive observation.
- Hearing and responding to each other's work is the single most powerful tool to empower students' composing.

Reading: Literate Learning

- Read to write! Immersion in reading will build vocabulary, concepts, and interest in writing.
- Read outside sources: a variety of genres, fiction, and nonfiction, to increase knowledge for writing.
- Read student work: Reread your own and other students' rough drafts to revise and edit for self-improvement and for peer validation.

For the Instructor

Teacher: The empowering agent

- Question constructively to empower writing.
- Establish boundaries and strategies for student questions.
- Topic, content, and intent can be good sources of questions.

Environment: The empowering situation

- A risk-free environment comes from constant sharing and encouragement to promote fluency and creativity in writing.

Making Time

What is the most important way to validate the entire Research Process? A simple question addresses the urgent need to encourage good writing and prevent plagiarism:

Do you make time for student writing?

Whether you teach science, history, math, or language arts, scheduling one period to kick off writing the rough draft validates all steps of the Research Process and empowers students to write from notes. With the teacher as facilitator, all of the Empower Composing elements (*Figure 11-1*) can be present. Without scheduled time, perhaps none of it will occur, and yet the expectation of an excellent product remains.

Education is in the midst of a literacy crisis, and the only way for students to learn to read and to improve reading is to engage in reading. Writing is very much a part of literacy, and the same situation exists: The only way to learn to write and to improve writing is to write. Following the instruction of research strategies, both of these needs are met by allocating time. When the teacher/facilitator schedules time to begin the rough draft, more than writing occurs. The ingredients of validated notes, teacher questioning, time to write, and student sharing and feedback magically combine into creative empowerment. I believe this is putting our "money where our mouth is" for educational reform.

Process Writing

Teachers may not make time for writing for the same reason they don't teach practical research steps: They may be unfamiliar with strategies for promoting good writing. A well-known, comprehensive source of sequential writing strategies is a course in process writing. As a classroom teacher, I had the fortunate experience of attending a branch of the Bay Area Writing Project. This was a seminal, life-changing event for me. My whole approach, not only to the teaching of writing but to teaching in general, was forever changed.

I count my classroom experience with process writing as one of the critical areas of training that made me a better library media teacher. Whenever possible, I advocate adding process writing as a preservice class for library media teacher credentialing. Because I knew *where* I was heading with good research, I had a much better idea of *what* I needed to do to bring students to that point. Prior to teaching middle school, I had library media teacher experiences in elementary and high schools. Especially in elementary and middle school, my collaborative teaching partners were delighted to make time for me to kick off composing the rough draft following the completion of notetaking. First-time collaborative teachers were often astonished that an LMT would do this, but if time permits, isn't this a logical extension? There are strategies for students' successful use of notes that validate the entire Research Process.

A quick look at the steps of process writing (*Figure 11-2*) shows that the only writing stages appropriate to the library media teacher would be the prewriting step and, briefly, the composing step. Beg for that!

Fig. 11-2. Process Writing

Prewriting
Notetaking/Motivational lessons and reading

Composing
Information + Creativity + Time = Fluency

Revising
Changing the content

Editing
Correcting the mechanics

Publishing
Audience other than the writer

Getting Started

If the teacher allows the LMT a period to begin writing the rough draft with students, hopefully it is preceded by a period of direct instruction for sorting, sequencing, and numbering notes. Once students understand these strategies, what isn't finished in class is easily completed as homework. What's important is that they arrive on writing day with notes entirely processed and numbered. Remind them to bring a couple of sheets of notebook paper to class. Arrange not to share the LMC with another class that day because writing requires quiet thought. With these things in place, students are physically ready to write, but are they mentally ready?

Writing the Introduction

"Is your first note the first sentence in your research paper?" Depending on the content area, the answer is no. With this question, I kick off these valuable moments of helping students convert their hard-earned research into a rough draft. Students often respond to this question with blank stares. Without instruction, the usual student reaction to *every* step of the research is this exact same confusion. This alone is validation for the collaborative teaching of Research Process strategies.

Important Idea

Students should have their Research Checklist (*Figure 9-2*) in front of them, which lists their topic and subtopics. This sheet is where the first paragraph comes from, so ask them to turn their pile of note pages or note cards upside down. (You should see the looks that instruction gets!) "Does anyone know how your paper should begin?" I ask. What I am leading up to is the need for an introduction: "You need to tell the reader what your paper is going to be about. It's like reading the summary on the back of a novel to decide whether to read the book." To save time, give specific instructions for creating an introductory paragraph:

Step 1: The first sentence or two of a research paper should state the topic and define it for the reader.

Step 2: Each of the subtopics becomes a separate sentence, telling what will be covered in each section of the paper.

In other words, students should write at least an entire introductory paragraph before they begin writing from their notes. I find this guided exercise, with much sharing aloud, very helpful in helping students set writing goals. They then write with greater confidence.

Prewriting

Prewriting is the mental motivation to compose. Because writing time with students is so limited, the primary tool is, of course, their notes. It is also extremely beneficial to read samples of previous students' papers. Here are a few simple steps to proceed with prewriting:

Step 1: Allow a minimum of five uninterrupted minutes for students to begin reading notes they have designated as subtopic, or section, one. They should read the notes in numbered order. The only sound permitted at this time is paper shuffling as they locate notes. Call "time" no matter how far students have gotten.

Literacy

Step 2: Have students use the person next to them as a partner. Allow five minutes for the first person to begin "telling" his or her paper to the partner, composing aloud from sequential notes. Allow another five minutes for students to reverse roles. Remind them: "If you can say it, you can write it."

Composing

ELL/Special Modifications

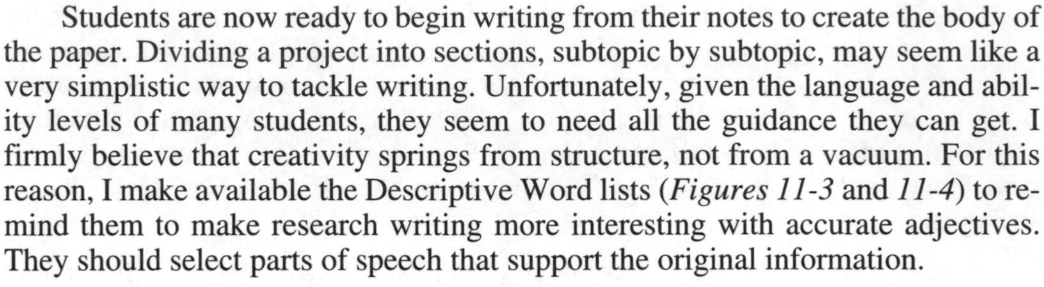

Students are now ready to begin writing from their notes to create the body of the paper. Dividing a project into sections, subtopic by subtopic, may seem like a very simplistic way to tackle writing. Unfortunately, given the language and ability levels of many students, they seem to need all the guidance they can get. I firmly believe that creativity springs from structure, not from a vacuum. For this reason, I make available the Descriptive Word lists (*Figures 11-3* and *11-4*) to remind them to make research writing more interesting with accurate adjectives. They should select parts of speech that support the original information.

Important Idea

For the remainder of the period, alternate 10 to 15 minutes of quiet writing with a few minutes of sharing time. This is the most important thing that could happen in the entire period. Call for volunteers who would like to read their introductions to the class. Model clapping when each reader has finished, and students will join in. Make a positive comment about the way something was done, and ask what someone else may have noticed that was working well. You'll immediately see the positive effects of this sharing time. Some students appreciate validation of their own work; others absorb ideas for improvement. The point is, they learn best from each other. When the bell rings, students will have a great start on an original piece of work! The LMT's work is done.

Fig. 11-3. Descriptive Word List, A–I

absurd
abundant
abusive
accurate
adventurous
affectionate
aggressive
agitated
aimless
ambitious
ample
ancient
animated
annoyed
appealing
artificial
attractive
austere
awkward
babbling
barbaric
beastly
beautiful
befuddled
believable
belligerent
beneficial
benevolent
biased
bickering
blazing
blotched
bloodthirsty
blubbered
blundered
busybody
calm
capable
cantankerous
candid
charming
cheerful
chilly
childish
clashing
clever
clobbered
clumped
comical
comfortable
commendable
commotion
compassionate
complex
competitive
conceited
complicated
confused
consistent
conservative
considerate
continuous
crushed
courageous
critical
curious
dainty
dashing
dawdled
dangerous
dazed
debatable
decent
dedicated
defective
deliberate
delicate
delirious
delightful
dependable
deplorable
depressed
descriptive
destroyed
destitute
determined
detected
devoted
disastrous
discouraged
disgraced
disobedient
disputed
dreary
dreadful
dreamy
dramatic
dribbled
dumbfounded
earnest
eager
eccentric
ecstatic
effective
eerie
elaborate
elated
embarrassed
emerged
emotional
encountered
endless
encourage
energetic
enduring
enjoyable
entangled
enormous
enthusiastic
envious
essential
especially
exaggerated
excessive
exhausted
exquisite
extravagant
fabulous
faded
familiar
fantastic
fascinating
fateful
feeble
filthy
fictitious
fierce
fidgety
flamboyant
flawless
flexible
flimsy
foolish
forceful
foreign
forgiving
fragile
freaky
fortunate
frail
frenzied
frustrated
frightened
frumpy
gallant
gentle
genuine
ghastly
gleaming
gloomy
glorious
griped
growled
gulped
hasty
harsh
heroic
hesitated
hopeless
horrible
howled
hotheaded
humorous
hypocrite
ideal
ignorant
illustrated
imaginative
immense
imbecile

Fig. 11-4. Descriptive Word List, I–Z

immortal
impatient
imply
mposing
impressive
impressionable
improper
impulsive
inappropriate
inarticulate
incredible
incompatible
inconsolable
indecisive
indifferent
indignant
indulge
inevitable
inexcusable
inferior
infallible
informal
ingenious
inflammatory
inflexible
innovative
initiative
inquiring
insincere
insensitive
insignificant
insufficient
insulting
intelligent
intimidating
investigate
irritating
irrational
jealous
jittery
justified
kooky
knowledgeable
laborious
lavish
legitimate
lenient
lighthearted
liberated
lively
logical
lonesome
lopsided
lovely
luxurious
magical
magnificent
malicious
manipulated
manufactured
marvelous
mature
meaningless
melodious
memorialize
merchandise
merciful
meticulous
meddling
migrated
mingled
miniature
mischievous
miserable
misfortune
misunderstanding
mistaken
mocked
moaned
modern
monotonous
modest
morbid
motivated
mournful
muffled
multitude
mumbled
mysterious
narrow
nasty
nauseating
neglectful
nimble
noble
nonsense
notable
noticeable
nuisance
nutritious
obedient
obese
objectionable
obligated
obnoxious
obscene
obscure
observed
obsolete
obstacle
occasionally
occupied
offensive
officially
ominous
opinionated
opportunity
oppressive
opponent
optimistic
optional
organized
ornate
outrageous
outspoken
outwitted
overacted
overlapped
oversight
overwhelm
painful
panted
paraded
pardoned
participant
particular
passionate
patriotic
perceived
pessimistic
persuaded
pitiful
pleasant
pondered
positively
precious
presumably
profound
provocative
punctual
quarrelsome
quiet
radical
random
reasonable
recognizable
refreshing
reliable
relevant
remarkable
respectful
restless
reckless
rowdy
sarcastic
satisfying
scholarly
scenic
scavenge
secluded
sensitive
serious
shocking
successful
tedious
terrifying
truthful
uncontrollable
vulgar
vulnerable
wallow
wisdom
yield
zoom

Chapter 12

Tracking and Evaluation

"Student projects were much better this time. I can't believe what a difference the tracking made."

—Collaborating teacher

Student Accountability

The Importance of Tracking

Important Idea

Chapter 1 suggests that instruction in specific and sequential, yet simple, strategies to accomplish research steps is often a "missing link" in information management. Emphasizing the steps of research helps teachers to focus on process as much as product (*Figure 1-6*). This supports the way in which information literacy divides information management into access, evaluation, and use.

That's great for teachers, but what is the incentive for students to accomplish either the process or the product? Teachers know that the surest way to encourage task completion is strict accountability. After all, it is human nature to alter situational responses according to positive rewards or negative consequences. Therefore, accountability is a critical component of the entire Research Process, as seen in an accountability section at the conclusion of each student lesson.

ELL/Special Modifications

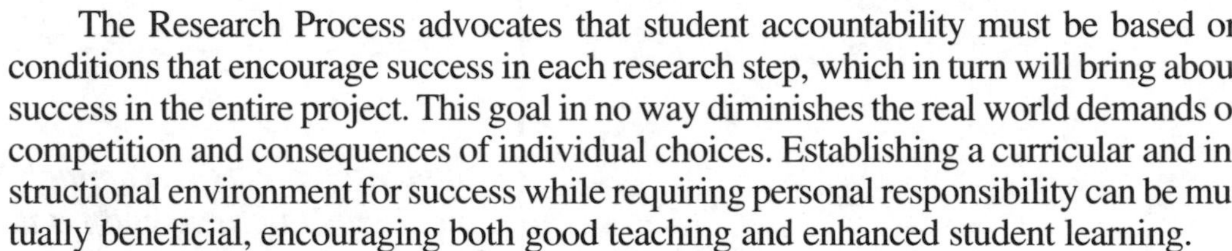

The Research Process advocates that student accountability must be based on conditions that encourage success in each research step, which in turn will bring about success in the entire project. This goal in no way diminishes the real world demands of competition and consequences of individual choices. Establishing a curricular and instructional environment for success while requiring personal responsibility can be mutually beneficial, encouraging both good teaching and enhanced student learning.

Prerequisites for Effective Tracking

The previous chapters elucidated the following basic conditions for student success in research:

Information Literacy

Teaching: The bottom line is that it's useless to track what hasn't been taught, but important to track what hasn't been learned. How can educators teach information literacy in an already overcrowded schedule? Hopefully, this book has shown that the fundamental purpose of the Research Process is to provide practical strategies embedded in real, live lessons for library media teachers and classroom teachers to do just that: teach information literacy standards through meaningfully integrated content-area units of study.

Lifelong Skills

The very nature of an articulated school curriculum is that, as students mature in their learning ability, they are exposed to new and more complex information and learning situations requiring increasingly higher order thinking skills. This reflects the role of the Research Process as a forum for the teaching and learning of new units of curriculum through increasingly complex information management strategies. Indeed, the same research steps can and should be taught in every year of schooling with increasing degrees of complexity, especially given the current environment of the exponential explosion of information access through technology.

Making time: Do you find that students aren't given class time to apply what they've learned about research strategies unless the teacher makes time? Teachers don't make time if they don't understand why it's important. So let's bring the message closer to home. Have you been in a teachers' lunch room lately? Aren't they often heard to "discuss" the many, genuine demands on their time that far exceed their physical ability to comply? Do they understand that in some cases their program expectations impose those same frustrating conditions on their students? This can happen in research situations unless teachers carefully analyze the time it takes for students to complete the parts of a project. But who has the time to do that? Hence, the dilemma. Not to worry! The Research Process solves this problem for time-stressed teachers. Time to apply information literacy strategies to complete a meaningful content-area project is fundamental to each step in the process.

Content-Area Standard

Collaborating: Two heads are better than one! It is a major advocacy proposition of the library media program that the collaborative process reduces teacher/student ratio, enabling more responsive intervention for student success. This concept is being echoed throughout educational reform initiatives. One example is the state-mandated California class size reductions, beginning in the primary grades, to increase literacy success for an increasingly diverse student population.

In an effective library media program, class size reduction can take many practical forms. Examples include whole-class instruction with two teachers in the room, or half-class instruction with the LMT in the library media center swapping groups with the teacher in the classroom.

Another popular method is research or technology student "stations" conducted by certificated or volunteer facilitators. Whole classes are divided into small groups and rotated through task-specific stations. This proves highly effective in a library media center environment as well as in a resource-challenged classroom.

ELL/Special Modifications

Setting goals: Specific student expectations at each research step are established in such a way that the task matches and slightly exceeds the ability of the student to perform that task. Students must stretch to grow! This concept is seen in current educational reform initiatives such as Cross-Cultural Language and Academic Development (CLAD) training, whereby second language students are placed in learning situations one step higher than their current language and learning ability, to promote growth. There are many ways to mix and match the specific number of subtopics, sources, notes, and report pages to meet the needs of students with learning (dis)abilities. The important thing is to use the Tracking Sheet (*Figure 12-1*) to monitor whatever progress has been accomplished.

Class, if you were told you must save $500.00 this year for your class trip and given no guidelines about how to do that, it is doubtful that many of you would succeed. But if you were each assigned a specific money-earning job, then told to set aside about $10.00 each week, and were rewarded with recognition for accomplishing that step, I bet the majority of you would achieve your goal!

Balancing process with product: It is usually new collaborating teachers who might say, "Oh, I don't want to be bothered tracking the research. I'll just grade the final project." The best testimony to the necessity of monitoring the process is to compare student products between tracked and non-tracked research projects. I can tell you, the differences are often enormous:

> *Wow! The difference in what the students achieved compared to last semester's project is so incredible! Thanks for doing the tracking. We'll always use it from now on.*
>
> *—Cooperating teacher*

Fig. 12-1. Research Tracking Sheet

Teacher: ___________ Period: __________ **Student Names**	Topic Subtopics	Sources	10 Notes	10 Notes	10 Notes	10 Notes	10 Notes	Rought Draft	Citations	Enrichment	Final Project	**TOTAL**

Scoring: **3 = Independent** **2 = Needs assistance** **1 = Deficient** **0 or (ab)**

The Role of the LMT in Student Tracking

Technology Proficiency

Flexibility of tracking methods is essential to a successful library media program. The library media teacher must be willing to bend and must adjust tracking to fit the unit needs and the accountability style of the teaching partner. Having the computer skills to design and tweak different tracking forms is a definite advantage for a successful LMT. During the initial collaborative planning meeting, show the teacher a Research Tracking template such as *Figure 12-1* and perhaps offer the following:

- To assist with tracking student progress at each step. Teachers will tell you right away if they don't want you involved. Some eagerly accept. For teachers whose research involvement is limited to simply assigning and collecting a project, this is a novel idea! LMT tracking may convert a teacher from a product to a process focus. But it's a win-win situation when students improve in both the content-area project and their understanding and use of information literacy strategies.

- To type the class rosters into a template for each of the teacher's classes. This is a service that can be accomplished by dependable student assistants, reaps an enormous harvest of gratitude, and gains converts to information literacy training.

- To adapt the tracking template to the time frame of the unit as well as specific daily or research step goals. The computerized template can be easily altered by adjusting the number of columns and retyping the header titles.

- To adjust the coding of student progress to match each teacher's style and needs. Some teachers want a quick minus sign, check mark, or plus sign to mark progress. Others prefer the 0-1-2-3 number code at the bottom of the sheet. *Figure 12-2* shows a more precise system of recording exactly how many sources students used and exactly how many notes were taken. This sounds like a lot of work, but it's not! I guarantee this is easily accomplished in the last few minutes of class, especially if you divide the tracking with the teacher. Instruct the students to have their notes counted. Then you can walk quickly among the students without even disturbing them. The potential of this daily tracking to produce a better quality product with a higher rate of both learning and creativity cannot be overstated.

Fig. 12-2. Recorded Student Tracking Sheet

Teacher: __________ Period: __________ Student Names	Topic Subtopics	Sources	10 Notes	10 Notes	10 Notes	10 Notes	10 Notes	Rought Draft	Citations	Enrichment	Final Project	TOTAL
A	+/+	3	12	23	31							
B	+/+	2	9	19	ab							
C	+/+	3	10	21	33							
D	+/+	3	5	16	30							
E	+/+	2	9	17	29							
F	+/+	2	13	25	35							
G	+/+	3	10	20	31							
H	+/+	3	8	19	28							
I	+/+	ab	3	12	19							
J	+/+	2	14	26	30							
K	+/+	3	10	21	30							
L	+/+	3	10	19	ab							
M	+/+	3	11	22	32							
N	+/+	3	7	18	29							
O	+/+	2	8	21	30							
P	ab	2	5	12	21							
Q	+/+	ab	10	20	30							
R	+/+	3	8	14	23							
S	+/+	ab	8	17	28							
T	+/+	3	10	22	33							
U	+/+	3	10	24	35							
V	+/+	2	16	29	40							
W	+/+	3	8	11	30							
X	+/+	3	6	ab	ab							
Y	ab	2	9	21	31							
Z	+/+	2	10	22	31							

Scoring: 3 = Independent 2 = Needs assistance 1 = Deficient 0 or (ab)

Unit Accountability

Information Literacy

The apparent value of the library media program to promote literacy and information literacy through collaboration in standards-based units of study does not exempt it from site and district accountability. Quite the opposite: Like every other field with a genuine curriculum, accountability both validates its successes and points to areas of improvement.

Content-Area Standard

Experience in the field suggests that the form of evaluation should match the program. In this case, the Research Process is only taught, and is therefore evaluated, through the curriculum of other subject areas. The desired advantage is an overall increase in content-area standardized test scores over a reasonable period of time. The greatest disadvantage is the obvious lack of the ability to accurately identify information literacy training as a positive factor. Therefore, upon completion of a unit with a collaborative partner, anecdotal references often may be of greatest value in determining the success of integrated research units.

Important Idea

The gathering of this kind of non-numerical data immediately causes a chronic adversary of research instruction to again rear its ugly head: time! Teachers absolutely do not have time to fill out paperwork. As stated in the first few chapters, an LMT who wants to kill off collaboration very quickly will give teachers forms to fill out. Therefore, it may be advantageous for the LMT to debrief with teachers informally, perhaps in the same "I'll catch you at lunch" manner used in the initial unit planning. Then, with a simple evaluation template such as *Figure 12-3* in hand, jot down notes during the conversation about what worked and what didn't. Later, the LMT takes that information back to the computer and tweaks the original lesson plan. The unit is amended, printed out, and put in the collaborating teacher's mailbox. The teacher will love it and so will the LMT!

In this way, over time the LMT builds a critical evaluation database to document future projects such as grant proposals or administrative reports. Of more practical value is a finely tuned unit for that content area. Eventually, the result is a huge, readily retrievable database of lessons and units for all grade levels at the site. The subjective results of a successful library media program may be seen every single day in the increase in a schoolwide model for collaborative instruction. If it is generally true that "people make the program," then for library media, "The program empowers the people who teach it and the people who are taught." This program is absolutely essential to educational reform.

Fig. 12-3. Unit Evaluation Sheet

Teacher: ______________________________ Grade: ______ Period: ______

Unit: ____ Date: ________

What worked well:

What didn't work:

Section 4

Enrichment and Extension

Chapter 13

Technology and the Creative Final Project

Chapter 14

Connections

Chapter 13

Technology and the Creative Final Project

"During break, I overheard some girls talking about their multimedia projects—instead of boys."

—History Day

Fig. 13-1. Creative Presentation Ideas

Writing	Projects	Presentations	Technology
Advertisement: • Brochure • Newspaper • Oral Book-making Chart Crossword puzzle Diary: • Log • Journal Editorial Essay Graph Index Letter Newspaper story Music lyrics Poetry: • Couplets • Cinquains • Diamanté • Haiku • Limericks Proverb Quiz Résumé Review Writing domains: • Story • Report of Information • Evaluation • Description • Persuasion • Narration	Banner Bulletin Board Bumper sticker Cartoon Collage Diorama Display Drawing Flannel board Game License plate slogan Map Mobile Model Mural Photography Poster	Banquet Cassette tape recording Commentary Debate Demonstration Dialogue Drama / Play Experiment Fair Interview Lecture Lesson Mime Mock trial Panel discussion Pantomime Puppetry Radio program Role playing Round Table Simulation Skit TV program	CD-ROM image Chat room, e.g.: with authors Claris slide show Computer art Desktop publishing Digital camera images E-mail pen pals HyperStudio stack Internet images Laser disk clips and frames Multimedia presentation Overhead transparency PowerPoint presentation QuickCam clips or frames Scanner images T-shirts Video production Web page construction

Beyond Writing

As the name implies, the Research Process focuses on the *process* it takes to produce a research product. However, do you find that your educational situation is still mostly product oriented? The accountability factor is ever-present. Therefore, it is important to address the issue of final products to validate the practical application and extension of the Research Process.

Discussion of a final product naturally seems to fall at the conclusion of research. In reality, the Creative Presentation Ideas sheet seen in *Figure 13-1* is absolutely the first thing teachers need to consider at the beginning of collaborative planning. This is the first question that should be asked:

What do you want to accomplish with this research project?

Will the project supplement and enrich the content-area unit in progress, teach research skills and information management, address a specific technology need, cover a writing domain, or provide an attractive display of student work for Open House? The idea sheet helps shift the educational paradigm to more interesting, student-centered activities.

Content-Area Standard

Are many of the teachers at your middle school still requiring a written paper as the product, or is your school establishing educational reforms that require more hands-on lessons and creative efforts? I believe it is inherent in the library media program to aim toward creative innovations in the final product as the corollary to the information literacy focus on process.

Information Literacy

Seeing the excitement as a teacher realizes the possibilities of a radio talk show script, a banner, or a laser disk video clip integrated into an oral report makes being a library media teacher one of the most rewarding jobs in education. The synergy from the initial collaborative planning creates an extra energy that spills over into the research lessons. Students, in turn, get excited about what they will be producing, and information acquisition takes on a whole new meaning.

Important Idea

"This is the first thing that student has completed all year! She is so proud of her work!"

—ELL teacher

Technology Enriches Writing

If writing a report is, in fact, the desired choice for presenting information, it is important that students know how to extend a written report into a rich, visually instructional experience. The insertion of images into all parts of a report (*Figure 13-2*), from cover to title page to content, creates a more interesting, appealing, and informative project. Remember to review copyright and fair use laws. Following are some of the ways in which images can be retrieved and inserted into word-processed or desktop-published student reports:

Technology Proficiency

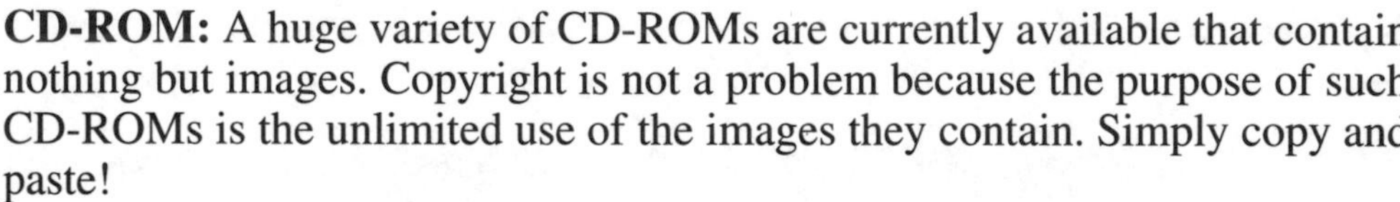

CD-ROM: A huge variety of CD-ROMs are currently available that contain nothing but images. Copyright is not a problem because the purpose of such CD-ROMs is the unlimited use of the images they contain. Simply copy and paste!

Laser disk: The advantage here is the capability of insertion of either still frames or video clips into multimedia presentation programs. Cost does not have to be a factor because many district and county central libraries house marvelous laser disk collections begging to be borrowed.

Internet: Have you typed "free clip art" into an Internet search engine? You will come up with a mind-boggling panorama of choices. Because it is incredibly easy to copy and paste Internet images, copyright privileges are often clearly explained on web sites. Fair use may apply for student reports.

Digital camera: The newest cameras offer the convenience of easy use with the sophistication of advanced features, combining the capabilities of both still and video imagery. There are no copyright problems here because the students will eagerly snap away at project realia, experiment results, and themselves!

ELL/Special Modifications

Computer software: As with CD-ROMs, computer software is available for images. Some software programs contain libraries for the express purpose of providing images for unlimited use. Draw programs, or the "draw" mode of an application suite, enable students to create hand-drawn images for insertion into reports. Although exciting for all students, this feature is especially interesting and educationally rewarding to special needs students. An example of a drawing created by an ELL student learning about America appears in *Figure 13-3*.

Scanner: This is perhaps the easiest, most accessible way for students to insert images found in books into their reports. Again, be sure to teach students about copyright and fair use. *Figure 13-4* is an example of a pathfinder placed beside the scanner in the library media center, which empowers students to work independently on technology enrichment.

Fig. 13-2. Technology-Enriched Report

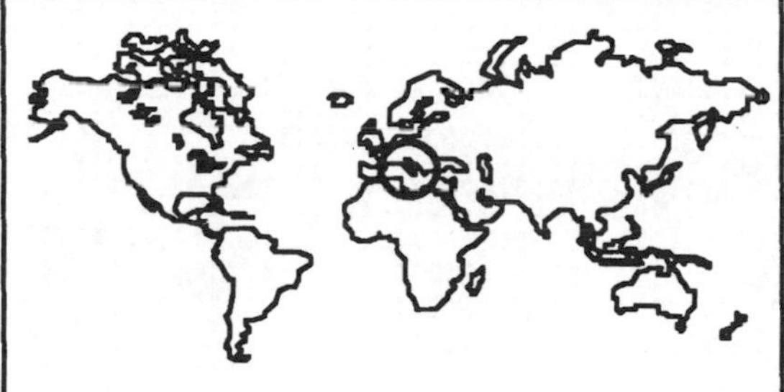

Renaissance Fact Box

Meaning: French for "rebirth"
Time period: 14th to mid-17th centuries
Place: Began in Italy
Inventions: Printing press, gunpowder
Notable: Revived thinking of Greeks

Image inserted from:

Digital camera
Internet
CD-ROM
Software clip art library
Scanner

Michelangelo

In this report you will learn about the artist Michelangelo. First you will learn about his early life and his personal life. Next you will learn about his art-work, specifically three important pieces of art that we consider to be masterpieces. Finally, we will see how the life and works of Michelangelo were affected by, or had an effect on, the period of art called the Renaissance.

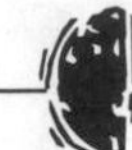

Fig. 13-3. Hand-Drawn Computer Map in Report

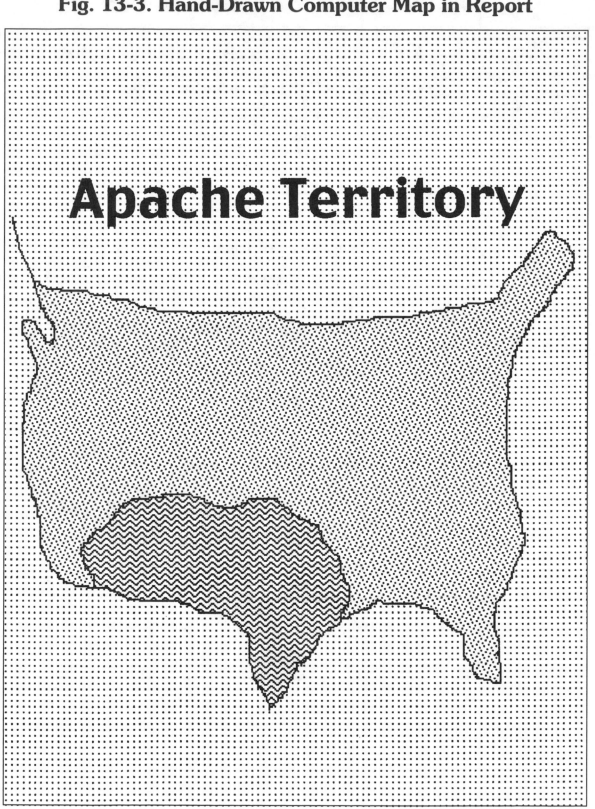

Apache Territory

Fig. 13-4. Scanner Pathfinder

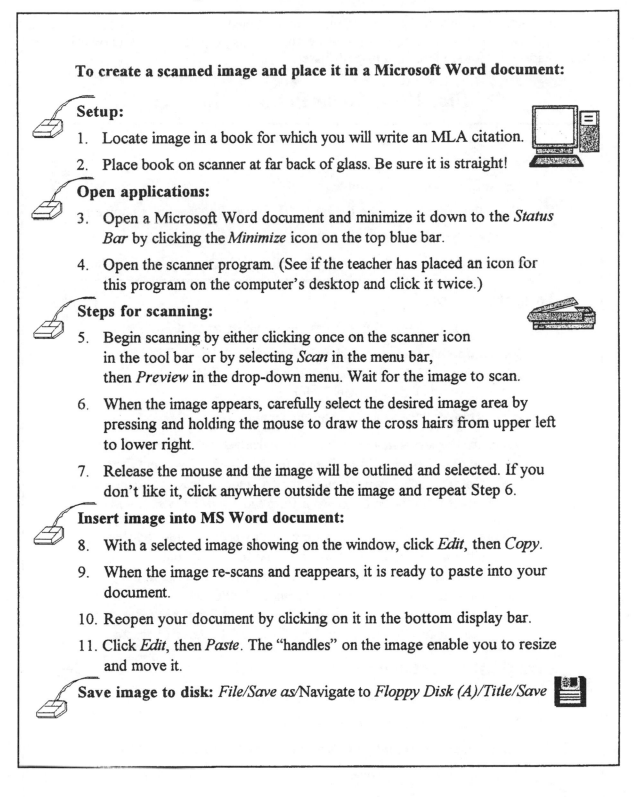

To create a scanned image and place it in a Microsoft Word document:

Setup:

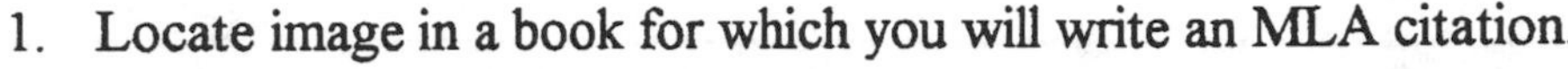

1. Locate image in a book for which you will write an MLA citation.
2. Place book on scanner at far back of glass. Be sure it is straight!

Open applications:

3. Open a Microsoft Word document and minimize it down to the *Status Bar* by clicking the *Minimize* icon on the top blue bar.
4. Open the scanner program. (See if the teacher has placed an icon for this program on the computer's desktop and click it twice.)

Steps for scanning:

5. Begin scanning by either clicking once on the scanner icon in the tool bar or by selecting *Scan* in the menu bar, then *Preview* in the drop-down menu. Wait for the image to scan.
6. When the image appears, carefully select the desired image area by pressing and holding the mouse to draw the cross hairs from upper left to lower right.
7. Release the mouse and the image will be outlined and selected. If you don't like it, click anywhere outside the image and repeat Step 6.

Insert image into MS Word document:

8. With a selected image showing on the window, click *Edit*, then *Copy*.
9. When the image re-scans and reappears, it is ready to paste into your document.
10. Reopen your document by clicking on it in the bottom display bar.
11. Click *Edit*, then *Paste*. The "handles" on the image enable you to resize and move it.

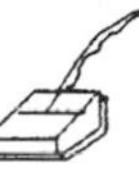

Save image to disk: *File/Save as/*Navigate to *Floppy Disk (A)/Title/Save*

Exciting Writing!

The ultimate writing experience, technologically speaking, is to use the notes gathered through the Research Process experience to write multimedia projects such as a PowerPoint presentation, made easy for students in this pathfinder.

Fig. 13-5. PowerPoint Pathfinder

Setup:

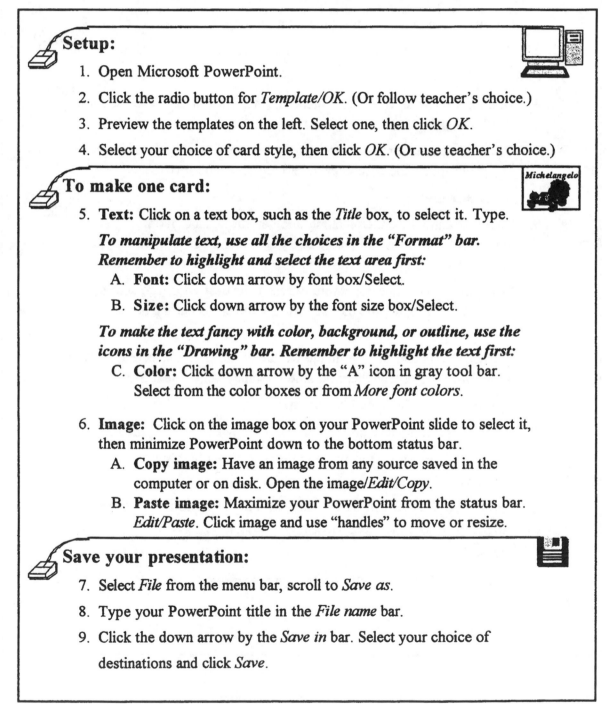

1. Open Microsoft PowerPoint.
2. Click the radio button for *Template/OK*. (Or follow teacher's choice.)
3. Preview the templates on the left. Select one, then click *OK*.
4. Select your choice of card style, then click *OK*. (Or use teacher's choice.)

To make one card:

5. **Text:** Click on a text box, such as the *Title* box, to select it. Type.

   To manipulate text, use all the choices in the "Format" bar. Remember to highlight and select the text area first:

   A. **Font:** Click down arrow by font box/Select.

   B. **Size:** Click down arrow by the font size box/Select.

   To make the text fancy with color, background, or outline, use the icons in the "Drawing" bar. Remember to highlight the text first:

   C. **Color:** Click down arrow by the "A" icon in gray tool bar. Select from the color boxes or from *More font colors*.

6. **Image:** Click on the image box on your PowerPoint slide to select it, then minimize PowerPoint down to the bottom status bar.

   A. **Copy image:** Have an image from any source saved in the computer or on disk. Open the image/*Edit/Copy*.

   B. **Paste image:** Maximize your PowerPoint from the status bar. *Edit/Paste*. Click image and use "handles" to move or resize.

Save your presentation:

7. Select *File* from the menu bar, scroll to *Save as*.
8. Type your PowerPoint title in the *File name* bar.
9. Click the down arrow by the *Save in* bar. Select your choice of destinations and click *Save*.

Chapter 14

Connections

"Less is more. Something as simple as the Research Process captures the complexities of educational reform."

—Author

Fig. 14-1. Information Literacy Standards for Student Learning

INFORMATION LITERACY

Standard 1: The student who is information literate accesses information efficiently and effectively.

Standard 2: The student who is information literate evaluates information critically and competently.

Standard 3: The student who is information literate uses information accurately and creatively.

INDEPENDENT LEARNING

Standard 4: The student who is an independent learner is information literate and pursues information related to personal interests.

Standard 5: The student who is an independent learner is information literate and appreciates literature and other creative expressions of information.

Standard 6: The student who is an independent learner is information literate and strives for excellence in information seeking and knowledge generation.

SOCIAL RESPONSIBILITY

Standard 7: The student who contributes positively to the learning community and to society is information literate and recognizes the importance of information to a democratic society.

Standard 8: The student who contributes positively to the learning community and to society is information literate and practices ethical behavior in regard to information and information technology.

Standard 9: The student who contributes positively to the learning community and to society is information literate and participates effectively in groups to pursue and generate information.

Ties to Standards, Literacy, and Information Literacy

Information Literacy

There are other teacher specialists on campus who work with the entire faculty, but the role of the library media teacher is unique. Like other special teachers, LMTs have their own curriculum and teaching strategies. Quite different is the importance of the collaborative process between LMTs and classroom teachers, which creates a unique venue for the integration of curriculum standards, literacy, and information literacy into daily lessons using information sources, literature, and technology.

ELL/Special Modifications

Other special areas such as speech, Title I, and resource specialist/special education support regular instruction by equipping students with special strategies for mainstream learning but may not be as completely dependent on collaboration. By contrast, the information literacy curriculum of the library media program is never taught in isolation. Do not confuse the pathfinders and direction sheets that appear throughout this book with an information literacy curriculum. They are not the same! Pathfinders are merely tools to accomplish the information management strategies, the lifelong learning skills inherent in information literacy.

Content-Area Standards Related to Research

Content-Area Standard

The practical research lessons in this book have demonstrated that one of the primary roles of an effective library media teacher is to teach information literacy through collaboratively planned lessons and units based on content-area standards. This is a powerful mandate for all schools to financially support this pivotal school site instructional position. An effective library media program does nothing less than keep a school site focused on standards, thereby modeling accountability strategies needed for periodic accreditation or the site review process.

Essential questions for the library media teacher to measure effective integration of curriculum standards with information literacy include the following:

- Are copies of state or district curriculum standards readily available in the library media center?
- Does the library media teacher have a good working knowledge of all standards-based units appropriate to the grade levels at the school?
- Are teacher requests for collaborative units and lessons measured against curriculum standards?
- Is the library media teacher a site and district leader in developing, promoting, and integrating curriculum standards?
- Does the LMT advocate standards-based lessons at faculty meetings, at staff development presentations, through newsletters, etc.?
- Is the purchase of LMC resources based on curriculum standards?

- Does a visually appealing library media center include displays promoting information, artifacts, and resources targeting standards-based themes and topics?
- Does the LMT/LMC sponsor promotions, events, or activities that highlight literature and technology that support standards-based themes and topics?
- Does a school site or LMC web page include a hyperlink to current district, state, and national curriculum standards?

Quintessential Literacy

Literacy

Remember the Title I reading teacher who asked, "Have all the teachers seen how this [research lesson] addresses literacy"? The Research Process embodies all aspects of literacy—reading, writing, speaking, and listening—and it easily provides opportunities for adapting each research step to accommodate high or low literacy needs.

- **Topic** is selected or adapted based on the availability of appropriately readable information.
- **Subtopic** information must be comprehensible.
- **Sources** are matched to reading ability, language, age, and grade.
- **Reading/thinking/selecting** for notetaking necessitates that the student (1) has decoded (read) information, (2) has comprehended (thought about) what was read, and (3) has evaluated and selected what is important to record as a note.
- **Notetaking** is the recording (writing) of information in a changed form, the criterion for whether learning has occurred. It is adjusted by amount and type (note cards or note sheets) to meet the needs of teacher, students, and time.
- **Sorting and numbering** notes requires students to reread their own material using critical thinking and evaluating strategies.

Literacy

How does literacy "happen" for students in the Research Process?

- **Reading:** The critical factor of information ownership occurs in the logical steps of accessing and reading information from a variety of sources, then evaluating and organizing information into notes.
- **Writing:** Notes are creatively constructed, through writing, into a unique paper or project.
- **Listening and speaking:** Prewriting and composing offer opportunities for students to listen to each other speak their notes to compose a rough draft. Oral reports of final papers offer further speaking and listening opportunities.

Information Literacy Standards Affect Student Learning

Goals for improvement in educational achievement can be attained through collaborative efforts between the library media teacher and classroom teachers to incorporate information literacy instructional strategies in all content areas. How can this be done in a practical way? Based on the 1998 version of information literacy standards (*Information Power*), the following discussion is an exercise in developing ideas to demonstrate how easy it is to adapt a wide variety of content-area lessons and activities to information literacy objectives.

Information Literacy Standards for Student Learning

Category I: Information Literacy

The student who is information literate:

Standard 1: Accesses information efficiently and effectively, as described by the following indicators:

1. Recognizes the need for information;

Social science idea: Locate information for a Civil War topic that utilizes primary source information gathered from the Internet, for example, Matthew Brady photographs.

2. Recognizes that accurate and comprehensive information is the basis for intelligent decision making;

Science/health idea: Use the Internet, newspapers, and magazines to explore a current disease to determine the effect on personal life choices.

3. Formulates questions based on information needs;

Language arts/current events idea: Develop questions to interview a contemporary world leader based on recent world events.

4. Identifies a variety of potential sources of information;

Science idea: Gather facts about cells from three technology formats such as CD-ROM, Internet, and laser disk.

5. Develops and uses successful strategies for locating information.

Social science idea: Use Boolean and keyword searching strategies in a favorite Internet search engine for a History Day topic.

Standard 2: Evaluates information critically and competently, as described by the following indicators:

1. Determines accuracy, relevance, and comprehensiveness;

Math idea: Compare online stock reports with those in a major newspaper to evaluate and predict a particular corporation's earnings.

2. Distinguishes among fact, point of view, and opinion;

Science/health idea: Compare online sources about a certain cancer against reference book information and a magazine article.

3. Identifies inaccurate and misleading information;

Music idea: Evaluate current music web sites for hype versus factual review.

4. Selects information appropriate to the problem or question at hand.

Current events idea: Research the historical background of a world current event to evaluate a nation's course of action.

Standard 3: Uses information accurately and creatively, as described by the following indicators:

1. Organizes information for practical application;

Science idea: Create a chart to reflect experiment data, then make a prediction based on the outcome.

2. Integrates new information into one's own knowledge;

Math idea: Understand why a particular formula or theorem works by exploring the mathematician who invented it and the context of his or her work.

3. Applies information in critical thinking and problem solving;

Math/economics idea: Compare percentages charged by different credit cards to select the best one (to apply for) and the worst one (to avoid).

4. Produces and communicates information and ideas in appropriate formats.

Science idea: Create a science fair project using a database and graph to plot experiment outcome data, a word processor to type the research paper, and a desktop publisher to create or include a supporting graphic image with labels.

Category II: Independent Learning

The student who is an independent learner is information literate and:

Standard 4: Pursues information related to personal interest, as described by the following indicators:

1. Seeks information related to various dimensions of personal well-being, such as career interests, community involvement, health matters, and recreational pursuits;

AVID idea: Use a topic-specific CD-ROM about careers to research personal career choices.

2. Designs, develops, and evaluates information products and solutions related to personal interests.

Any content area: Create an electronic portfolio through a choice of either HyperStudio or PowerPoint, depending on what work samples are included.

Standard 5: Appreciates literature and other creative expressions of information, as described by the following indicators:

1. Is a competent and self-motivated reader;

Language arts/special education idea: Use an electronic card catalog to search for pleasure reading selections at a school site or local public libraries.

2. Derives meaning from information presented creatively in a variety of formats;

Art idea: Peer evaluate multimedia advertisements. Required technology formats include digital cameras, laser disk or video clips, Internet downloads, and multimedia software.

3. Develops creative products in a variety of formats.

Social science idea: Present a moment in history in both an oral and written format incorporating a technology interface.

Standard 6: Strives for excellence in information seeking and knowledge generation, as described by the following indicators:

1. Assesses the quality of the process and products of personal information seeking;

Computer class idea: Evaluate a variety of general information electronic encyclopedias to make a recommendation for a class project.

2. Devises strategies for revising, improving, and updating self-generated knowledge.

Physical education idea: Create and update a web site about personal skill development in a sport.

Category III: Social Responsibility

The student who contributes positively to the learning community and to society is information literate and:

Standard 7: Recognizes the importance of information to a democratic society, as described by the following indicators:

1. Seeks information from diverse sources, contexts, disciplines, and cultures;

Social science idea: Use the Internet to conduct a comparison of human rights in countries around the world.

2. Respects the principle of equitable access to information.

Health/special education idea: Collaborate with a learning or physically disabled student to do a topic search using both print and nonprint resources.

Standard 8: Practices ethical behavior in regard to information and information technology, as described by the following indicators:

1. Respects the principles of intellectual freedom;

All research classes: Do not criticize topic selections of classmates.

2. Respects intellectual property rights;

All research classes: Credit bibliography sources scrupulously.

3. Uses information technology responsibly.

All students sign a technology Acceptable Use Agreement to use school equipment to access information responsibly.

Standard 9: Participates effectively in groups to pursue and generate information, as described by the following indicators:

1. Shares knowledge and information with others;

Social studies idea: Have class groups present skits about different battles of the Revolutionary War based on research using a variety of formats of information.

2. Respects others' ideas and backgrounds and acknowledges their contributions;

Foreign language idea: Select a partner whose cultural heritage will be researched, and present the information, using a variety of print and nonprint resources.

3. Collaborates with others, both in person and through technologies, to identify information problems and to seek their solutions;

Physical education idea: Have student groups research a national sports team, using a variety of sources of statistics to recommend team or individual player improvements.

4. Collaborates with others, both in person and through technologies, to design, develop, and evaluate information products and solutions.

Computer class idea: Have two class teams compete to create an innovative and informative Internet web site about their school.

Magic Bullet

The purpose of this book is to demonstrate, in a practical way, that the Research Process embodies integrated information management to build lifelong learning skills. The Research Process truly is a magic bullet for now and for the future of education. It integrates into one neat package almost every aspect of educational reform for which educators are and will be held accountable. It integrates both literacy and information literacy strategies and skills with content-area standards in meaningful lessons using technology proficiencies for both teachers and students. Use of process writing is an added bonus. This sounds like a huge mouthful, but in the end:

Q: How DO you eat an elephant?

A: One bite at a time!

Sources

"American Psychological Association." Accessed 14 Jul. 2000 <http://www.apa.org/about/>.

Beck, James H. "Michelangelo." Microsoft Encarta '99 Encyclopedia. 1999 ed.

Gibaldi, Joseph. *MLA Handbook for Writers of Research Papers*, fourth edition. New York: The Modern Language Association of America, 1995.

Harris, Nathaniel. *Renaissance Art*. New York: Thomson Learning, 1994.

"Michelangelo Buonarroti." Accessed 14 Jul. 2000 <http://www.michelangelo.com/buonarroti.html>.

"MLA Examples." Accessed 14 Jul. 2000 <http://ollie.dcccd.edu/library/Module4/M4-V/examples.htm>.

"Modern Language Association (MLA) Guide to Style." Accessed 14 Jul. 2000 <http://www.wilpaterson.edu/wpcpages/library/mla.htm>.

"Information Power, The Nine Information Literacy Standards for Student Learning." Accessed 14 Jul. 2000 <http://www.ala.org/aasl/ip_nine.html>.

Partridge, Loren. *Michelangelo: The Sistine Chapel Ceiling, Rome*. New York: George Braziller, Inc. 1996.

Summers, David. "Michelangelo." *The World Book Encyclopedia*. 1999 ed.

References

American Association of School Librarians and Association for Educational Communications and Technology for the American Library Association. *Information Power, Guidelines for School Library Media Programs*. Washington, DC: American Library Association. 1988.

Anderson, Mary Alice, ed. *Teaching Information Literacy Using Electronic Resources for Grades 6–12*. Worthington, OH: Linworth Publishing, Inc., 1996.

Beckett, Sister Wendy. *Sister Wendy's Story of Painting*. New York: Dorling Kindersley, 1994.

"The Big6™ Skills Information Problem-Solving Approach." Accessed 14 Jul. 2000 <http://big6.com>.

"Big6 Web Guide." Accessed 14 Jul. 2000 <http://www.clovisusd.k12.ca.us/alta/big6/b6chart.htm>.

"Bloom's Taxonomy's Model Questions and Key Words." Accessed 14 Jul.2000 <http://www.utexas.edu/student/lsc/handouts/1414.html>.

California School Library Association. *From Library Skills to Information Literacy: A Handbook for the 21st Century*, 2d ed. San Jose, CA: Hi Willow Research and Publishing, 1997.

"Computer Skills for Information Problem-Solving: Learning and Teaching Technology in Context." Accessed 14 Jul. 2000 <http://cricir.syr.edu/ithome/digests/computerskills.html>.

Eisenberg, Michael B., and Robert E. Berkowitz. "The Big Six & Electronic Resources: A Natural Fit." *The Book Report* (September/October 1997): 15, 22.

Farwell, Sybil. "Successful Models for Collaborative Planning." *Knowledge Quest* (January/February 1998): 24-30.

Gibaldi, Joseph. *MLA Handbook for Writers of Research Papers*, 4th ed. New York: The Modern Language Association of America, 1995.

"The Global Schoolhouse." Accessed 14 Jul. 2000 <http://www.gsh.org/NSTA_SSandC>.

Grover, Robert, and Jacqueline McMahon Lakin, "Learning Across the Curriculum." *CSLA Journal* 21, no. 2, (Spring 1998): 8-10.

"A Guide for Writing Research Papers based on Styles Recommended by The American Psychological Association." Accessed 14 Jul. 2000 <http://webster.commnet.edu/apa/apa_index.htm>.

Helping With Homework: A Parent's Guide to Information Problem-Solving. Syracuse, NY: Eric Clearinghouse on Information & Technology, 1996.

"The Librarians Guide to Cyberspace for Parents & Kids." Accessed 14 Jul. 2000 <http://www.ala.org/pio/cyber/cando.html>.

"Library Spot." Accessed 14 Jul. 2000 <http://www.libraryspot.com>.

Loertscher, David V. *Reinvent Your School's Library In the Age of Technology, A Guide for Principals and Superintendents*. San Jose, CA: Hi Willow Research and Publishing, 1997.

"Multimedia Rubric." Accessed 14 Jul. 2000 <http://users.massed.net/~augie/multi.html>.

Professional Growth Series. *Library Research Skills, Grades 7-12*, 2d ed. Worthington, OH: Linworth Publishing, Inc., 1995.

"Rubric for Information Processing Standards." Accessed 14 Jul. 2000 <http://home.maine.rr.com/memorial/library/rubric.html>.

Shepherd, Robert D. *Writing Research Papers*. Evanston, IL: McDougal Littell, Inc., 1994.

"Standards-Based Instruction." Accessed 14 Jul 2000 <http://www.rmcdenver.com/useguide/lessons/index.htm?>.

"The Steps to the Research Cycle." Accessed 14 Jul. 2000 <http://www.bham.webnet.edu/mod8cyl.htm>.

Stuurmans, Harry. *Nine Steps to a Quality Research Paper*. Worthington, OH: Linworth Publishing, Inc., 1994.

Sullivan, Helen and Linda Sernoff. *Research Reports, A Guide for Middle and High School Students*. Brookfield, CT: The Millbrook Press, 1996.

"Technology and Educational Reform." Accessed 14 Jul. 2000 <http://www.ed.gov/pubs/EdReformStudies/EdTech/>.

"Using the Internet for Research, K-12 Educational Resources on the Internet/WWW." Accessed 14 Jul. 2000 <http://www.blueroom.com/internet/IR-EDUCATION/IR-K12.htm>.

Index